DECOLONIZING FEMINISMS
Piya Chatterjee, Series Editor

Power
Interrupted

ANTIRACIST
AND FEMINIST
ACTIVISM
INSIDE THE
UNITED NATIONS

Sylvanna M. Falcón

UNIVERSITY OF WASHINGTON PRESS
Seattle and London

Power Interrupted was supported by grants from the Division of Social Sciences, the Latin American and Latino Studies Department, and the Chicano Latino Research Center at the University of California, Santa Cruz.

Material from chapter 2 was first published in *Critical Sociology* (2015): 1–12, DOI: 10.1177/0896920514565484, and is reprinted with permission from SAGE Publications. Material from chapter 2 first appeared in *Societies without Borders* 4, no. 3 (2009): 295–316, and is reprinted with permission from Brill Publishing. Material from chapter 4 first appeared in *Journal of Women's History* 24, no. 4 (2012): 99–120, and is reprinted with permission from Johns Hopkins University Press, copyright © 2012.

UNIVERSITY OF WASHINGTON PRESS
www.washington.edu/uwpress

Cataloging information is on file with the Library of Congress
ISBN 978-0-295-99525-0

The paper used in this publication is acid-free and meets the minimum requirements of American National Standard for Information Sciences—Permanence of Paper for Printed Library Materials, ANSI Z39.48–1984. ∞

To Aracely, the love of my life,
To Matt, for his love, support, and many years of happiness,
To my parents, Edgardo and Silvia, for giving me a blessed life, and
To the women in this book who fight for justice,
even when the odds seem against them . . .

Para Aracely, el amor de mi vida,
Para Matt, por su amor, apoyo, y muchos años de alegría,
A mis padres, Edgardo y Silvia, por darme una vida bendecida, y
Para las mujeres en este libro que luchan por la justicia,
aun cuando las probabilidades parecen en contra de ellas . . .

CONTENTS

ACKNOWLEDGMENTS

When I was an undergraduate at Santa Clara University, I confided in a small group of close friends that I wanted to be a writer. I wanted to write a book that had a political purpose. Given the supportive nature of my dear college friends, they purchased a book for me titled *Writers Dreaming: 26 Writers Talk about Their Dreams and the Creative Process* (1994) as a Christmas gift my senior year so that I could be inspired to make this goal a reality some day. I have never forgotten this kind gesture, and, nearly twenty years later, my goal has finally been realized.

Writing a book is difficult and, at times, even painful, but thanks to the support of the wonderful family, friends, and colleagues I would like to acknowledge here, I came out on the other end. I sincerely apologize if I have forgotten anyone who has been on this journey with me. I must first begin with my life partner and husband, Matthew Lehman. To him, I owe much. He prepared home-cooked meals for months on end without a single complaint, kept our house in order during what felt like never-ending workdays, and managed my moodiness when I struggled with my writing or with the stress of the job. I cannot put into words what his love and support mean to me; he has been by my side since our youth, and there is no one in the world I would rather take life's journeys with than him. Our daughter, Aracely, has brought us so much joy. I am so honored to be her mom. She is my dream come true, and I thank her for being such an awesome and loving daughter. With this book now complete, I have to keep my promise to her about writing a book (just for her) that involves her deep love of cats.

I would like to also thank other members of my immediate family for their support. In particular I would like to recognize my parents, Edgardo and Silvia Falcón. My parents migrated to this country from Peru in May 1966 and, like all immigrants, had high hopes and big dreams for the future. With only four hundred dollars in their wallets (which ran out after one month, so my aunt sent them forty dollars to help the following month), no family in the United States, and lacking English fluency, they left all that was familiar to them to see if they could find more opportunities in the United States at a time when the country was in the throes of racial segregation and conflict. But my dad had a medical degree at a time when the United States was actively recruiting doctors for rural parts of the country, even if they came from the "Third World." My parents first arrived in the US heartland—Wichita, Kansas—and eventually made their way to California in 1977. After several years of sheer determination and some good fortune as well, they were able to establish a financially secure life in the United States, of which my two brothers and I were the beneficiaries. I thank them for their sacrifices and hard work, and for giving me a very blessed life.

Next I have to acknowledge my remarkable feminist writing group—Dana Collins, Molly Talcott, and Sharmila Lodhia. I appreciate their profound love and support, as well as their honest and generous feedback on my writing. They have read versions of this book multiple times and offered me the words of encouragement I needed to complete the project. They are truly inspiring women.

I would also like to thank my wonderful academic advisors—Avery Gordon, Denise Segura, and Beth Schneider from the University of California, Santa Barbara, and Chandra Talpade Mohanty from Syracuse University. All were encouraging throughout the completion of my research and in my eventual transition to an academic position at the University of California, Santa Cruz (UCSC). I never lost sight of the fact that I was lucky enough to go through graduate school having these women as my mentors. More importantly, their generous mentorship did not cease when I graduated. I am deeply grateful to Avery for providing me with invaluable academic advice whenever I asked for it, even when she was in Europe. Denise and Beth have always been thoughtful of including me when it comes to new professional opportunities and have provided good advice, delightful conversations, and much laughter when I see them at conferences. Chandra has been nothing short of amazing in her warmth, generosity, and counsel when I have sought it. I thank them all profoundly.

I would like to acknowledge my department colleagues from Latin American and Latino Studies, who have provided me with a rich and provocative intellectual home. My warmest appreciation and thanks to Rosa-Linda Fregoso for being my mentor and collaborator, as well as Patricia Zavella for graciously welcoming me to the department in fall 2010. I would also like to thank other UCSC colleagues who have helped in my transition to campus, especially Dean Mathiowetz, Kimberly Lau, Deb Gould, Herman Gray, Kent Eaton, Miriam Greenberg, Steve McKay, Shelly Grabe, Marcia Ochoa, Felicity Amaya Schaeffer, Alessandra Álvares, Marianna Santana, and Dana Rohlf. Working at UCSC has been a pleasure because of the wonderful people mentioned here.

Other dear friends and supporters include the following, in no particular order of affection: Leisy Abrego, Carlos Alamo Pastrana, Hillary Haldane, Karl Bryant, Margaret Huang, Krishanti Dharmaraj, Khanum Shaikh, Shannon Gleeson, David Hernández, Sekou Franklin, Lorena Garcia, Michelle Jacob, Jennifer Nash, Bandana Purkayastha, Liz Philipose, Ejim Dike, Lisa Crooms, Tiffany Willoughby-Herard, Jeanne Scheper, and the brilliant community of scholars affiliated with the Future of Minority Studies program. Leisy Abrego has been a reliable and trusted friend; she provides the ideal balance of being a compassionate listener and offering just the right words of encouragement when things become difficult. Even though Carlos Alamo Pastrana lives on the opposite coast, he remains a loyal friend who always has my back. Bandana Purkayastha became my mentor as part of the Woodrow Wilson postdoctoral fellowship when I was in the midst of extensive manuscript revisions. She offered feedback at every stage of manuscript revisions, and I am truly grateful for her friendship and support.

The postdoctoral fellowships from the University of California Office of the President and the Woodrow Wilson National Foundation have been invaluable to my career. Special thanks to Sheila O'Rourke and Kimberly Adkinson from the UC President's Postdoctoral Fellowship Program, and to Caryl McFarlane and Ina Noble from the Woodrow Wilson National Foundation. I would also like to acknowledge my former research assistant, Ruth Kim, and my copyeditor, Rebecca Frazier, for their assistance with the manuscript. Lastly, I am profoundly grateful to Larin McLaughlin and Piya Chatterjee for believing in the project and in me. They pushed me to make the project better, and I thank them for engaging my work with such integrity. The entire team at the University of Washington Press who helped make my dream a reality also merit appreciation and recognition.

This research received generous grant support from a multitude of sources from the University of California: the Chicano Latino Research Center (UCSC), the Committee on Research Faculty Grant (UCSC), the UC Humanities Research Institute Grant, the UC Center for New Racial Studies, the UC-MEXUS Dissertation Research Grant, the UC Pacific Rim Research Mini Grant, the Humanities and Social Science Research Grant (UCSB), and the Graduate Research Mentorship Fellowship (UCSB) all provided support. The American Association of University Women Dissertation Writing Fellowship, the UC Office of the President, the Woodrow Wilson National Foundation, and the Hellman Fellows Program also supported the research and writing of this book at different stages of its development.

ABBREVIATIONS

ANC	African National Congress
CEDAW	Committee on the Elimination of Discrimination against Women
CERD	Committee on the Elimination of Racial Discrimination
DDPA	Durban Declaration and Programme of Action
DESA	Department of Economic and Social Affairs, United Nations
DRC	Durban Review Conference (2009)
ECOSOC	Economic and Social Council, United Nations
GA	General Assembly, United Nations
ICERD	International Convention on the Elimination of All Forms of Racial Discrimination
NAACP	National Association for the Advancement of Colored People
NAM	Non-Aligned Movement
NCNW	National Council on Negro Women
NGO	Non-Governmental Organization
OHCHR	Office of the High Commissioner of Human Rights, United Nations
POA	Programme or Plan of Action
PrepCom	Preparatory Committee meeting
SWAPO	South West Africa People's Organization
UDHR	Universal Declaration of Human Rights
UN	United Nations
UNCIO	United Nations Conference on International Organization

UWC	United Women's Conference (1945)
WCAR	World Conference against Racism, Racial Discrimination, Xenophobia and Related Intolerance
WEOG	Western European and Others Group

POWER INTERRUPTED

Introduction

The Challenging Road to the Durban Conference

COMPLETELY JET-LAGGED AND EXHAUSTED AFTER HAVING RE-
cently returned from the 2001 Non-Governmental Organization (NGO)
Forum Against Racism in Durban, South Africa, I turned on the television news in my Goleta, California, apartment and froze in disbelief. The
exhaustion somehow disappeared, and horror and shock suddenly con-
sumed me. The date was September 11, 2001. CNN was showing footage
of two airplanes crashing into the World Trade Center towers in New
York City on a repeat reel. The scenes of chaos and destruction on my
television screen will forever be a part of my memory, and I experienced
a range of reactions to what I was witnessing—horror, heartbreak, con-
fusion, anger. How could this happen? As we all tried to make sense of
9/11, I was also thinking about the 2001 United Nations (UN) World Conference Against Racism (WCAR) that had ended three days before the
attacks. The WCAR and its corresponding NGO Forum had become the
ideal targets of a powerful smear campaign, with critics suggesting a link
between the activism at the Durban proceedings and the 9/11 terrorist
attacks. By insinuating that the Durban gathering had fomented intolerance and hatred, the critics had managed to undermine and diminish
the difficult work of the thousands of activists—the majority of whom
were women—who had traveled to Durban to debate the meaning of racism and to discuss its origins and the contexts in which multiple racisms
thrive.

    Power Interrupted offers a critical historical analysis of the UN and
explores antiracist feminist efforts—specifically those corresponding to

the activism of feminists of color from the United States and Canada, and feminists from Mexico and Peru—to advocate for a more comprehensive approach to understanding racism at the UN level. Although the prior WCARs, held in 1978 and 1983, had largely regarded understandings of racism as being "gender-neutral,"[1] the 2001 Durban conference had prompted a discussion about the simultaneous convergence of racial and gender dynamics, known as "intersectionality" by feminist scholars.[2] The NGO Forum Against Racism, in particular, gave activists and advocates a space in which thousands of people from throughout the world could intensely debate and discuss the ongoing global challenges of racial discrimination. The goal of antiracist feminists was to expand the discussion of racism at the UN level by introducing new issues and perspectives, particularly because the UN had not explicitly addressed the issue of racism on a global level since the 1983 WCAR. As activists engaged in this work, they also discovered the strength of collaborative, transnational political organizing efforts.[3]

My research relies on the conceptual insights offered by transnational feminism and intersectionality to make feminist sense of the antiracism agenda at the UN level as well as the corresponding advocacy associated with the Durban conference proceedings. I use a combination of in-depth interviews, participant observation, and extensive document and archival data to situate contemporary antiracist feminist organizing from the Americas alongside a critical historical reading of the UN, including its agenda against racism. How do the social conditions of women globally become portrayed within this agenda? To what extent does this image dispute the notion of a universal woman—a deracialized everywoman who experiences discrimination in the same manner? How do "women's experiences" not become solely informed by those entities invested in depicting women as monolithic or as disconnected from the effects of geopolitical power? The answers to these questions reveal profound struggles over representation, power, and voice.

Leading up to the 2001 WCAR, a shift occurred at the UN level toward an understanding of women's social conditions based on the intersectionality of race and gender, and activists who dedicated themselves to disrupting a deracialized and decontextualized perspective bolstered these shifts. Intersectional and transnational approaches recognize that women are shaped by multiple marginalities, including those that result from material conditions that reflect global economies.[4] The struggle for this type of recognition at the UN is further complicated by geopolitical dynamics in which certain countries of the world are disproportionately empowered at the UN and tend to stifle the voices of those who are less powerfully positioned. This study of antiracist feminist activism investigates how a new understanding of women's social conditions based on the intersectionality of race and gender began to be explicitly reflected in the UN agenda against racism by 2001. It begins by addressing the sociohistorical institutional context and dynamics of the UN that shaped an agenda against racism, an agenda that dates back more than six decades and identifies all three WCARs and the 2001 NGO Forum as its key events.

I contend here that, because of three key factors, the UN agenda focused on racism offered a more *strategic context* for the activists I interviewed than the forums focused on women. First, former colonial powers and economically powerful countries had less credibility in this conversation given their history, to say the least. Second, the UN agenda against racism had better synergy with the radical politics of antiracist feminists grappling with the simultaneous or overlapping effects of imperialism, gender-based violence, colonialism, and so on. And third, a number of important milestones had been reached by the mid-1990s, including the downfall of South African apartheid and Namibia's independence.

The UN agenda against racism had primarily focused on combating the issue of apartheid, and for decades the UN had devoted considerable resources toward its dismantling. Apartheid was seen as a particularly egregious form of racial superiority and oppression, and therefore, beginning in the 1970s, the UN General Assembly (GA) had advocated for the complete isolation of the racist regimes in southern Africa. The GA drew a "distinction between the racial discrimination imposed by law and institutions in South Africa and other racial discrimination elsewhere in the world, where it was usually opposed by the law of the land."[5] The GA viewed liberation movements such as the African National Congress (ANC) in South Africa and the South West Africa People's Organization (SWAPO) in Namibia as the legitimate representatives of their people.

By the 1990s, the collapse of South African apartheid and the independence of Namibia became a reality, and made possible an opportunity to critically intervene in the UN agenda against racism. The politics of antiracist feminists would be ideally positioned to affect this existing discourse, which had largely remained static given the heavy focus on southern and western Africa. These monumental sociopolitical shifts in antiracism struggles created an opening in the UN agenda against racism for new frameworks for understanding racism; a similar opening has not come about with the UN agenda on women.

The resolutions adopted by the GA reflected a peripheral engagement with the intersection of gender and racial discrimination in the late 1970s and early 1980s that became strengthened and improved by the mid-1990s; the early resolutions primarily recognized the role of women in ongoing antiracist struggles, rather than advance knowledge and discourse about women's distinct experiences with racial injustice based on their subaltern subjectivities and positionalities. However, multiple UN documents began to incorporate the framework of intersectionality shortly preceding the 2001 WCAR.

DIVERGENT REACTIONS TO WORLD CONFERENCES IN BEIJING AND DURBAN

The September 11 attacks in the United States unleashed a storm of racist reactions that further emboldened the anti-Durban campaigns in the United States. The late Tom Lantos of California, a member of the US House of Representatives for nearly three decades, was a particularly harsh and outspoken critic. He urged the US government to "reflect upon the lessons of the WCAR" to "consider the most effective way of implementing a strategy to confront and defeat the forces of intolerance, hatred, and terror," which, for Lantos, had been in full force at the Durban conference.[6] Lantos and numerous other critics referred to the 2001 WCAR as a "racist conference" rather than a conference against racism. Lantos stated that the "UN World Conference on Racism provided the world with a glimpse into the abyss of international hate, discrimination, and indeed, racism. The terrorist attacks on September 11 demonstrated the evil such hate can spawn. If we are to prevail in our war against terrorism, we must take to heart the lessons of Durban."[7] This statement and others like it reveal how profoundly maligned the Durban conference had become by 2001, complicating the unfinished work of dismantling racism, patriarchy, and imperialism globally that had been renewed by the conference. These statements also threatened to silence—and even vilify—those activists committed to their eradication.

Lantos and others argued that their opposition to the 2001 WCAR— and everything the conference represented—had to do with the "singling out" of Israel. The Palestinian-Israeli conflict received nearly all of the conference coverage offered by the US media.[8] It is certain that, dating back to about the 1970s, the UN's overall agenda against racism has largely supported the Palestinian struggle for self-determination, which is aligned with global public opinion.[9] However, framing the 2001 WCAR debates as solely focused on Israel contributed to an erasure of the wide range of issues debated as part of the Durban conference. Participants of the 2001 WCAR and its corresponding NGO Forum discussed, often heatedly, subjects such as imperialism, the slave trade, caste systems, indigenous sovereignty, reparations, state violence, the plight of immigrants and refugees, war and militarism, and gender-based violence, to name a mere few of the topics. The hostility directed at the 2001 WCAR was disturbingly reminiscent of the US government's strong opposition to the two earlier WCARs in 1978 and 1983. It also resembled the behavior of the United States during the writing of the Universal Declaration of Human Rights (UDHR) in the late 1940s, when the US delegation, led by Eleanor Roosevelt, vehemently obstructed the racial justice efforts of African Americans.[10]

Feminist responses to September 11 underscore that the longstanding and unresolved ruptures between predominately white feminist groups and feminists of color remain unresolved. Groups such as the Feminist Majority Foundation supported plans for a US military response in Afghanistan. They launched a "campaign *for* Afghan women and girls"—not "*with*" Afghan women and girls—to stop "gender apartheid."[11] Absent from the campaign materials was any recognition of the historical and political factors that had empowered the Taliban in the first place, including any mention of US complicity in the region. The position of Feminist Majority Foundation and of other women's groups supporting US military involvement revealed a paternalistic and colonial logic that has long been a source of frustration and tension for feminists who identify as women of color or as US Third World feminists (and even radical white feminists). Especially troubling, the Feminist Majority Foundation credits its efforts as having had a "tangible impact" in improving the lives of

Afghan women and girls, rendering invisible the work of Afghan women themselves, such as activists affiliated with the Revolutionary Association of the Women of Afghanistan.[12] Support of the status quo can silence women of color, and by calling for a military intervention, groups such as the Feminist Majority Foundation now alarmingly viewed the US military as being instrumental to ensuring women's rights in the world.[13]

In contrast, women of color activists in the United States were largely against US military intervention and were strongly critical of feminist positions like the one adopted by the Feminist Majority Foundation. For example, INCITE! Women of Color Against Violence, which describes itself as "a national activist organization of radical feminists of color advancing a movement to end violence against women of color and our communities," created vibrant antiwar posters in response to the US-led Afghani invasion.[14] Another oppositional stance was taken by a group of feminist academics who released an antiwar statement titled "Transnational Feminist Practices Against War" urging feminists "to refuse the call to war in the name of vanquishing a so-called 'traditional patriarchal fundamentalism,'" acknowledging the complicity of other governments in the maintenance of "gender apartheid" in Afghanistan, and stressing that "a transnational feminist response views the impact of war and internal repression in a larger context of global histories of displacement, forced migrations, and expulsions."[15]

The division between those US feminists who supported military intervention in Afghanistan and those who opposed militarism in all its forms reflected profound racial fault lines that arguably parallel feminist dynamics at the UN level. Put another way, the UN agenda on women has been dominated by feminist politics steeped in Western-centric ideologies that represent interests different from those of the feminists from the antiracism forums. Most white feminists from the United States neglected to support the 2001 WCAR but gave strong support to the 1995 UN Conference on Women in Beijing.[16] My research aims to make visible a different set of women who are wholly committed to challenging neocolonial powers. To shift the analytical lens toward UN spaces focused on antiracism alters the feminist narrative about UN-based activism.

An analysis of the investment and divestment—in terms of both financial and political capital—by the US government in the 2001 WCAR and the 1995 Beijing conference highlights that the Durban conference mattered less than the Beijing conference. For example, the US government gave a financial contribution of $6 million for the Beijing conference, but contributed only $250,000 for the Durban conference.[17] Hillary Clinton, then First Lady of the United States, made a grand speech at the 1995 World Conference on Women. No one even close to her stature attended the 2001 WCAR to represent the US government.[18] At the Beijing conference, the US government's propaganda about "the triumph of US women's rights" resonated globally, regardless of its legitimacy. With the support of numerous (white) feminists, including Hillary Clinton, the US government touted US women as having "freedoms" unavailable to their unfortunate "Third World sisters." However, at the Durban conference, although the US government could tenuously claim "progress" in the area of civil rights, it had no such footing on the international front, given the legacy of colonialism and imperialism.[19] In contrast to its participation in the Beijing conference, the intent of the US government's participation in the Durban conference was to undermine it (see chapter 3).

The 2001 WCAR was fraught with conflict from the beginning, due, in part, to the exercise of US power during the proceedings. Yet the Durban conference offered an opportunity for a new set of social actors—that is, those not necessarily found in powerful advocacy positions at the UN World Conferences on Women or other UN women's committees or commissions—to engage in activism at the UN that was both feminist and antiracist in its formation. This point is not meant to diminish the significance of the Beijing conference, especially with regard to certain practices of transnational feminism. But, as sociologist Manisha Desai states, the world conferences on women and its corresponding NGO Forums "were contentious events with women from the South, not all of whom identified as feminists, challenging Northern women's conceptions of women's issues based solely on gender and sexuality."[20] What I contend here is that by the late 1990s the UN's antiracism agenda provided a vital opportunity for "women's issues" to move beyond a narrow perspective on gender and sexuality as disconnected from racial dynamics and processes in time for the 2001 WCAR.

The 1993 World Conference on Human Rights in Vienna, Austria, was also an important political moment for feminists in the genealogy of world conferences because one of the significant world conference outcomes was the explicit recognition that women experience human rights violations in a particular way because of their positionality. The issue of violence against women became conceptualized as a human rights violation and disrupted the public/private paradigm. The political strategies used to associate violence against women with human rights violations included the organization of a massive petition (called the "Petition to Promote and Protect Women's Human Rights") and the Global Tribunal on Violations of Women's Rights at the world conference. The purpose of the petition, which had been translated into twenty-three languages, was to call on government delegates to "'comprehensively address women's human rights at every level of its proceedings' and to recognize 'gender violence, a universal phenomenon which takes many forms across culture, race, and class . . . as a violation of human rights requiring immediate action.'"[21] The petition contained nearly 500,000 signatures, including thumbprints, from participants from 124 countries.[22] The Global Tribunal proved to be a significant event, in which women from around the world told their stories. Organizing the Global Tribunal took months of advance preparation and set a precedent for similar types of feminist-oriented public hearings at future world conferences, including at the Beijing and Durban world conferences.[23]

LINKING ANTIRACISM AND FEMINISM

I had the fortunate opportunity to travel to Durban with an international delegation of twenty women, predominantly US women of color feminist activists, to participate in the NGO Forum Against Racism.[24] Participating in the NGO Forum was an exhilarating experience: most of us survived on just a few hours of sleep so as to take full advantage of the unique opportunity the forum offered to debate, strategize, organize, and network. I was also a participant at the NGO gathering for the World Conference on Women in Beijing in 1995. Having a basis of comparison, I wanted to understand how feminist engagements at Durban would be similar to or differ from the proceedings at Beijing.

Most activists attend NGO Forums to participate in plenaries, organize workshops and strategy sessions, and engage in public actions and protests.[25] Even though the days are often long and exhausting—meeting other activists, learning about the issues, and experiencing the energy of a Forum can be thrilling—it is difficult for one to leave an NGO Forum the same person one was going in. At the conclusion of an NGO Forum, some activists attend the official UN world conference with government delegations (e.g. the UN World Conference Against Racism, the UN World Conference on Human Rights, the UN World Conference on Women), to lobby government representatives about the text of the official conference documents, known as the Declaration and the Programme of Action.[26] A number of preparatory intergovernmental meetings, known as Preparatory Committees or PrepComs, occur before the intergovernmental conference to debate and finalize the official world conference documents. It is not uncommon for NGO activists to lobby government delegates who are not from their own country in their search for supportive delegates who are willing to listen to them and possibly advocate their positions in the remaining days of debate.

The intergovernmental conference (in this case, the WCAR attended by government delegations) is the opposite of the NGO Forum in that it is a formal setting in which activists must work through government delegations; they cannot act on their own behalf.[27] Ideally a synergy develops between the NGO Forum and the intergovernmental conference, but this is not always the case. Logistics and politics can both play a role when actions taken at the NGO Forum and the intergovernmental conference are not mutually supportive. For instance, the NGO Forum for the 1995 World Conference on Women took place in Hairou, about an hour away from the intergovernmental meeting in Beijing, which complicated activists' efforts to lobby government delegates. For the 2001 WCAR, both the NGO Forum and the intergovernmental meeting took place in Durban, but UN officials rejected the documents adopted at the NGO Forum for the WCAR, the official intergovernmental conference (see chapter 3). In addition, NGO representatives had limited access to the government venue, severely restricting their ability to engage collectively in advocacy.

One of the most galvanizing moments of the NGO Forum in Durban was during the closing ceremony, on September 1, 2001, as then Cuban president Fidel Castro prepared to give the concluding address. My friends and I had arrived early to find seats in the stadium, and we were lucky to find spots in the last two rows. We watched with anticipation as a motorcade entered the stadium. Castro emerged from the second car with his fist in the air, and thousands of people went wild, chanting, cheering, clapping, and waving small Cuban flags. Clearly relishing the excitement, Castro faced the crowd, his stance defiant, as always. Eventually he made his way to the main stage, where four other men joined him.

As the crowd started to quiet in anticipation, a woman yelled, "Where are the women?!" Spontaneously, woman after woman stood and joined her: "Where are the women?! Where are the women?! Where are the women?!" The chant traveled across the stadium, eventually reaching us. Moved by the power of this collective questioning, our voices mingled with those of the thousands of other women in protest: "Where are the women?! Where are the women?! Where are the women?!" The chant lasted for what felt like several minutes. All the while, the men on stage, especially Castro, looked confused. Castro eventually shrugged and pointed to the female English-language translator onstage. Although it took several minutes for us to quiet down, the closing ceremony eventually began. But in those commanding minutes, women had challenged the notion that an all-male panel should—or even *could*—make the final remarks about racism at a global gathering. Women had disrupted, if only for a few minutes, a male-centric agenda against racism. These women had demonstrated a politics of antiracist feminism that I felt compelled to study. The research for this book sprang from this powerful experience.

CHALLENGING GLOBAL SISTERHOOD,
UNEVEN POWER RELATIONS

The emergent antiracist feminist activism surrounding the Durban conference produced key intellectual and political positions that were different from those that had dominated women's early advocacy efforts at the UN, particularly those stemming from the 1980s and 1990s. As feminist activists sought to shape international standards in the 1990s, emphasizing differences based on race, culture, or sexuality—or even acknowledging intragender dynamics—was neither the prevailing discourse nor the political objective. The UN units focused on women, such as the UN Commission on the Status of Women and the Committee on the Elimination of Discrimination against Women (CEDAW), gained traction largely by promoting an image of a deracialized universal woman. These units advance a global feminist discourse that is, as feminist scholar Elora

Chowdhury contends, "historically connected to earlier western feminist arguments surrounding a global sisterhood. . . . [It is a] hegemonic form of feminism [that] erases internal fractures and critiques of multiply located feminisms."[28] This type of feminism (what I consider the prevailing understanding of "UN-based" feminism) guided the UN World Conferences on Women and fostered the creation of transnational advocacy networks that remained largely wedded to the notion of a universal woman and to the idea that women would come together for a single overarching issue, such as violence against women.[29] Yet openings existed in other areas of the UN for pursuing an agenda different from the one developed in the units dedicated exclusively to women; UN spaces focused on racism, especially after the mid-1990s, turned out to be an opportune avenue in which to engage in intersectionality.[30]

Chowdhury writes about a political economy of feminisms in the US academy that "validate structurally and institutionally a politics that embraces pluralism, soft relativism, [and] diversity management through harmonious coexistence over productive engagement with conflict, inequality, and asymmetrical power relations."[31] Applying this insight to the UN—which is, after all, "like the academy," as one US interviewee noted—suggests that the political economy of feminisms at the UN elevates select political expressions of feminism there that are less radical, since the end goal is "harmonious coexistence" rather than meaningful structural changes or the redistribution of power and resources. Further, the UN is built upon a fusion of politics, economics, and values that reflect broader societal and global dynamics and realities, which in turn shape the compatible and tense feminist relationships that form in this space. Therefore, a political economy framework considers how historical, social, and economic conditions have shaped the UN's policies on antiracism.[32]

The "women's rights" agendas prevalent within the UN units exclusively focused on women disproportionately reflect the influence of the United States and the "global North." Feminists from these geographic locations attained and retained a high level of access and influence at the UN in the 1980s and 1990s. They were able to foster key relationships and, as time progressed, they became not only professionalized in that environment but also invested in that professionalism. Further, they adhered to a practice of feminism that could be endorsed by governments of countries such as the United States[33] because the women's rights agenda did not implicate US foreign policies, for example, in exacerbating global gender-based discrimination to nearly the same extent to which US foreign policies have been faulted for intensifying global racism.

Activists engaged in the UN forums on racism have for the most part adopted positions that differ substantively from those of the mainstream feminist activists engaged in the UN forums on women. The UN agenda on racism is more radical than its agenda on women, in that it is centered on overcoming imperialism, apartheid, and colonialism and on directly implicating the actions of the governments of the global North. These types of agenda matters—anti-imperialism, antiapartheid, and decolonialism—aligned with their ongoing antiracist feminist organizing efforts back home.

Governments in Latin America and in other global South and Third World nations, despite being disadvantaged in terms of economic capital, have exercised their social and cultural capital through the UN in a way that has allowed them to shape efforts, sometimes radically, against global racism. As a result, significant attention by the UN has been given to decolonization efforts, antiapartheid freedom struggles, and, now, a burgeoning movement for reparations.[34] The more economically powerful world governments, such as those of Canada, the United States, and France, find that because of the antiracism agenda pursued by global South and Third World nations, they primarily *resist* an antiracism agenda emerging from the UN rather than entirely controlling it.[35]

Intersectionality and Transnational Feminist Logics
for Examining Shifts in UN Discourse

At the heart of understanding this type of women's organizing lies the theoretical logics of intersectionality and transnational feminism. Scholarship on intersectionality and transnational feminism examines the complexities of power in relationship to patriarchy, racism, and other axes of domination and subordination. Hence, these approaches provide a useful framework for understanding the processes, dynamics, and contexts of antiracist feminist organizing at the UN level. The productive outcome of the feminist advocacy I explore in this research remains an expanded approach to racism in the contemporary period at the UN level that is cognizant of the tensions around conflicting human rights discourses between North America and Latin America,[36] and of the structural limitations of working within a megabureaucratic institution such as the UN.

Situating intersectionality and transnational feminism as theoretical approaches that work in concert is critical for understanding how antiracist feminists began to challenge the notion of a universal woman at the UN. By thinking about intersectionality in a transnational context, scholars can consider what is absent from, or even problematic with, current discourses about global racism.[37] Scholars of transnationalism can similarly interrogate how the theoretical model of intersectionality can clarify power dynamics by recognizing the specificities of comparative national contexts.

Intersectionality and the Universal Woman

Intersectionality theory arguably has its origins in US black and Chicana-Latina feminist thought, and has become integral to critical race theory, legal studies, social sciences, cultural studies, and women's studies, to name a few areas of application. Leslie McCall describes it as "the most important theoretical contribution" in women's studies scholarship.[38] Intersectionality theory has moved beyond the confines of the academy, as is evidenced by its circulation in activist communities and its emergence at the UN. It is a vital theoretical perspective that has emerged out of both activist and academic circles.

Kimberlé Williams Crenshaw, who participated in an expert seminar in Croatia in preparation for the 2001 WCAR,[39] has defined intersectionality as "a conceptualization of the problem that attempts to capture both the structural and dynamic consequences of the interaction between two or more axes of subordination. It specifically addresses the manner in which racism, patriarchy, class oppression and other discriminatory systems create background inequalities that structure the relative positions of women, races, ethnicities, classes, and the like."[40] Legal scholar Lisa Crooms argues from a slightly different perspective, noting that intersectionality affects positionality within social hierarchies wherein aspects of identity are relational rather than essential and where "identity is fluid rather than static, yielding few, if any, 'pure victims of oppression.'"[41]

Taken together, Crenshaw and Crooms offer complementary views about intersectionality, with Crenshaw using intersectionality to better understand subordination, and Crooms considering how intersectionality reveals the shifting nature of oppression.

Other feminist scholars have emphasized the level of interconnection that emerges with intersectionality but raise important concerns regarding its theoretical ambiguity. For instance, feminist sociologist Patricia Hill Collins recognizes intersectionality through her "matrix of domination" model, which refers to how oppressions are interdependent and interlocking,[42] and Gloria Anzaldúa's concept of *mestiza* consciousness links intersectionality to pluralistic worlds and social location.[43] However, feminist scholar Jennifer Nash contends that one of the difficulties with intersectionality theory is its ambiguity.[44] Is intersectionality meant only for women of color? Is it meant only to understand oppressions and subordination, or can it be used to understand privilege, power, and masculinity? Is intersectionality about identities, structures, or processes?

Sociologists Hae Yeon Choo and Myra Marx Ferree offer a useful typology of three distinct, yet complementary, theoretical approaches to intersectionality, which they describe as group-centered, process-centered, and system-centered. Group-centered intersectionality ensures that the voice of marginally subordinated people or groups is prioritized. It is a powerful method that places the subjects who are often being spoken about in a peripheral manner, if at all, at the center of analysis.[45] Process-centered intersectionality considers the role of power while acknowledging that "primary attention" must be given to "context and comparison . . . as revealing structural processes" that are essential for organizing power.[46] This approach uses intersectionality to understand that the "main effects" of labor markets or immigration, for example, are less about "giving voice" to marginalized groups than about understanding interconnected relationships. The system-centered approach stresses the fact that because intersectionality shapes the entire social system, it "pushes analysis away from associating specific inequalities with unique institutions, instead looking for processes that are fully interactive, historically co-determining, and complex."[47] Choo and Ferree favor this third approach, in which intersectionality is a "complex system" that can disrupt assumptions—such as that the economy is primarily about social class or that family is primarily about gender.[48]

According to feminist sociologist Christine Bose, a version of Choo and Ferree's system-centered approach is useful for examining "variation in the forms of gender inequalities across many nations."[49] Bose looks at "geographic [and] sociopolitical patterns," specifically, "transnational, regional, cross-cutting thematic, and unique national conditions," to understand how particular feminist concerns come to the forefront in any given national context. This argument is particularly useful for the analysis presented in this book because the intersection of geographic and sociopolitical axes shaped the political positions adopted by the activists I interviewed.[50] Their goals were influenced by the overlap of national and local contexts and were also informed by the national and regional coalitions that formed in preparation for the conference.

Intersectionality within the transnational sphere raises other critical factors to consider, as feminist sociologist Bandana Purkayastha has pointed out:[51] "A focus on transnational intersectionality should alert us to the position of those who are unable to afford access to technology to build virtual communities, to participate in a medium because they are not proficient in English, which has become the dominant language in virtual spaces, or to build transnational social lives because of active government surveillance and control of their lives or because they are too poor and isolated to access transnational tangible and virtual spaces."[52] As Purkayastha cautions, scholars can often be narrow-minded in the ways in which we conceptualize and identify the visible actions and processes considered transnational. Furthermore, as a result of the rapid migration of social life to virtual spaces, tangible geographic spaces no longer wholly contain social worlds, configurations of power, or structural processes. Intersectionality and transnationalism can work in both spheres—geopolitical and virtual—to challenge multilayered structures in which domination and marginalization coexist. Those with less power can work through the interstices of the structures of the powerful so that their often marginalized voices can come forward; they can also work across the borders or divisions of nation-states to challenge the structures that marginalize them.

A synthesis of the first model (giving "voice" to those who have been on the margins of UN discussions about racism) and the second (moving beyond an additive "oppression" approach toward an interactive model that considers relational power) is, as I show in this book, most evident at the

UN level.[53] The introduction of intersectionality is still very much in the early stages there, but one must be realistic in that certain spaces of the UN seem largely impervious to change. For example, it is hard to imagine the UN Security Council adopting an intersectionality approach meant to challenge the oppressive power of its permanent members (China, France, the Russian Federation, the United Kingdom, and the United States).

For the purposes of this research, I define intersectionality as the recognition that men and women do not experience racism in the same way, whether at the individual or at the structural level. Intersectionality, as used in this research, is about directly addressing the particular experiences of women who have been long overlooked in discussions about identifying remedies for racial injustice at the UN level. Further, multidirectional exertions of power coexist in international settings, and the identity categories of race, gender, and class are shaped by distinct national histories and regional contexts. Thus, while intersectionality may have one meaning in Canada and the United States and another in Mexico and Peru, multiple understandings or definitions of intersectionality can coexist in a significant way. The use of intersectionality must be contextualized then as a way to navigate the topography of particularism and universalism simultaneously.[54]

The translation of intersectionality for eventual UN-level adoption, which is for making policy or setting legal precedents, may not accurately reflect the innovative uses to which activists apply this theoretical approach. However, the UN's interpretation of intersectionality has expanded how the UN understands and defines racism institutionally, and this shift has ultimately provided antiracist feminist activists in the post-1990s transnational feminism period with a new point of departure. The link that activists have made between antiracism and feminism signals a fresh political engagement that leaves behind the UN-based feminism of the 1990s; it is an example of intersectionality because activists address both racism and patriarchy simultaneously and in multiple configurations.

Transnational Feminism and Geopolitical Power

Transnational feminist theory has developed along a trajectory that is quite similar to that of intersectionality theory in that it has been lauded for propelling feminist theory beyond a global model that privileges nation-states and is also viewed as little more than a buzzword undercutting the reality of domestic-based racism or other social inequalities.[55] The goal of transnational feminism is to move "beyond constructed oppositions without ignoring the histories that have informed these conflicts."[56]

To dislocate entrenched ideas that distinguish a "liberated West" from an "oppressive non-West," transnational feminist theory relies on the concept of relational positionality,[57] which, as sociologist Daiva K. Stasiulis points out, identifies how systems of power and domination can intersect to "position individuals and collectivities in shifting and often contradictory locations within geopolitical spaces, historical narratives, and movement politics."[58] As Chandra Mohanty argues, a reliance on binary oppositions can lead to a misinterpretation of the relations of power. Mohanty notes that "multiple, fluid structures of domination . . . intersect to locate women differently at particular historical conjunctures."[59]

By focusing on relational positionality, the practice of transnational feminism avoids obscuring local specificities or, in cultural studies scholar Ella Shohat's words, "paper[ing] over global asymmetries."[60] Relational frameworks retain the importance of local specificities without minimizing the degree to which global constructs such as capitalism and racism are linked to "economic, political, and ideological processes."[61] Because transnationalism is shaped by the relationships in global civil society that connect advocacy groups, networks, and social movements,[62] transnational feminism considers the ways in which movements and social actors denaturalize the nation-state by engaging in activism not only beyond national borders but also, at the same time, within local contexts.[63] For transnational feminist scholars, it is imperative to retain an analytical lens that does not suggest that women in Third World contexts experience identical systematic domination,[64] even in the service of unifying an antiracist feminist agenda.

The networks that these feminists form to advance political organizing strategies and to foster multilateral participation can cross borders without neglecting the ways in which geography informs advocacy issues. However, critics of transnational feminist networks point out that despite their cross-border perspective, the home base for too many of these networks is the United States.[65] Nonetheless, transnational feminist networks have been extremely valuable when they produce what political scientists Margaret Keck and Kathryn Sikkink refer to as a "boomerang pattern," which occurs when domestic-based NGOs "bring pressure on their states from outside" by transcending national systems of accountability and challenging international structures and systems.[66]

UN world conferences promote the "transnationalization" of people's struggles, guaranteeing that discussions of advocacy issues are not confined within their national borders (with the exception of the host country).[67] As sociologist Janet Conway states, "As social movements transnationalize, they enact new spatialities which necessarily demand re-imagining and renegotiating political relations among new ensembles of places, sites, and scales of practice. It is not just capital and states but social movements that actively produce space, place, and scale through their practices and discourses."[68] When transnational alliances form, agendas that were once conceived as being local must be recast in ways that lend themselves to broader grassroots organizing strategies. This can be accomplished only through an understanding of "the links in discourses, representations, and relative claims of oppression and rights" that tie together the experiences of different peoples or collectivities.[69] By conceptualizing how racism operates at a transnational level, feminists can also address local struggles as relational to other contexts.

The UN is often viewed as an international space because of its nation-centric structure. Feminists have endeavored to remake this international space by strategically engaging in advocacy and lobbying efforts that push beyond domestic insularity. They establish transnational alliances and, in turn, enter the space of the UN as an imagined collective. However, the UN world conference settings in which the international and the transnational merge also provide evidence of how power relations and the hierarchy of countries within the UN shape the exchanges that cross national boundaries.[70] In sum, the purpose of transnational feminist theory is to move feminist theory beyond the limitations of international or global feminisms, which remain wedded to the nation-state and the acceptance of the "West" as the center of power.[71] A focus on relational positionality—on the links that connect peoples and collectivities—and on internationalist solidarity are ways to resist the notion of a common patriarchy. By challenging and breaking away from the image of a universal woman, voices not often heard at the UN have been able to surpass the voices that have previously dominated the conversation about women's struggles.

My use of transnational feminism as theory also overlaps with my use of it as politics, as a framework, and as an analytic. Hence, I adopt Mohanty's view of transnational feminism embracing a feminism across borders but not borderless, meaning that feminist politics and solidarity do not have to be confined by borders (of nation, class, race, ethnicity, or sexuality) yet should be mindful of the reality that borders can in some cases have real power.[72] Similar to women's studies scholars Inderpal Grewal's and Caren Kaplan's transnational feminist concept of "scattered hegemonies," in which systems and structures of white supremacy, of imperialism, of capitalism, and so forth exist and dominate the world in a dispersed manner,[73] transnational feminism as it pertains to the antiracist activism covered in this research grapples with the interaction of a macrophenomena (global racism) and local agency. For the purposes of this research, I refer to transnational feminism as an anti-subordination logic that is mutually constructive or overlapping with intersectionality.[74]

STUDY DESIGN: FOCUSING ON THE AMERICAS

The research discussed in this book focuses on the activism of antiracist feminists from the Americas, specifically Canada, Mexico, Peru, and the United States. In each of these countries I spoke with activists who were working on issues affecting indigenous communities, African descendants, lesbians, and other communities of color, such as immigrants and refugees. I chose the Americas for several reasons. The First and Third Worlds interact in the Americas, with the United States playing a particularly dominant role in the region. The racial politics in each of these national contexts is vastly divergent, yet they convene—or collide—at UN world conferences. And an analytical focus on the Americas allows comparative analyses of matters of race and gender that are region-specific.

Canada and the United States played particularly influential roles in the Durban proceedings, both in the region and globally. Canada's government was the second after that of South Africa to vote in support of holding the 2001 WCAR; it may have hoped to tout its multiculturalism policies as positive ones to replicate globally. The Canadian government also paid for several activists to attend the world conference, including most of the feminists I interviewed.[75] This financial support suggests that, at least on some level, the Canadian government encourages the global participation of its citizens. Not having to fret about expenses—one of the most consequential of the factors that prevent activists from participating in world conferences—enabled Canadian activists to focus their energies on forming national coalitions, strategizing for the Durban proceedings, and organizing against racism in ways that previously had not been possible.

Feminist activists from Canada and the United States were overrepresented at the 2001 WCAR, and, not surprisingly, the largest proportion of participants at the NGO Forum was from the United States. My research reflects this fact: there were simply more activists from Canada and the United States to interview than from Mexico or Peru. For many US activists of color, the encounters with activists from outside the United States led to significant shifts in consciousness that would likely not have occurred if they had not gone to the conference and been confronted with the force of an anti-US imperialism movement.

Even though the research sample skews toward US-based antiracist feminist activists, the story of the UN's agenda against racism is about a global South movement. Many decades of UN efforts against racism resonated with concerns emanating from the global South against imperialism, apartheid, and colonialism. Moreover, it is the antiracist feminist interventions from Latin America by African descendants, lesbians, immigrants, refugees, and indigenous women that speak to the radical potential of what the UN's agenda against racism can become. The interviews with feminist activists from Mexico and Peru contribute to a rich genealogy of human rights that has been too often overlooked or lumped in with a Western discourse and movement.[76]

Mexico is uniquely positioned in that it is considered part of both North America and Latin America. In both instances, its positionality is distinct: in the North American triad, it has the least power; in Latin America, however, it is considered a powerful, and occasionally imperial, actor. It is usually depicted as a country with an indigenous past (similar to Peru), but increasing scholarship about and activism regarding the "third root," referring to the African ancestry of many of its citizens, has emerged in recent years.[77] Mexico's antiracist movement is relatively young, and the occasion of the Durban conference spurred new dialogues about racism within the country.

Peru's antiracist movement has gained visibility and traction since the early 2000s, with the Peruvian government even issuing an apology for racism to the Afro-Peruvian population in 2009, the only Latin American government to have done so.[78] Moreover, the government recently sanctioned a prominent media outlet, Latin Frequency (Frecuencia Latina), for its racist programming and initiated a judicial investigation into the vitriolic racist and sexist attacks against Monica Carrillo, an Afro-Peruvian feminist leader. Carrillo spearheaded the campaign to sanction Latin Frequency.[79] Peru's society is profoundly racist, and the gestures of acknowledging and apologizing for racism in the country are unprecedented, even if largely symbolic at this stage.[80]

REFLECTIONS ON POSITIONALITY, METHODOLOGY, AND TERMINOLOGY

"But you are an American," an interviewee from Peru named Angelica said when I asked how the September 11 attacks in the United States had affected her post–Durban conference experience. I smiled, perhaps awkwardly, and assured her that I would not be offended. She did not view me primarily as the daughter of Peruvian immigrants and as a feminist who is critical of the US government's actions in Latin America and other parts of the world, which is how I view myself. Rather, she saw me as a *Norte Americana* who might be sensitive to critiques about "my government" and offended by her views about people from the United States. In this moment, and in many others during the research process, social location took on added significance because of the power dynamics that affect the research process when investigating subject matters in which the US government has played a role.

I reside in a space of liminality between the United States and Peru because I have managed to retain transnational family connections and because of my activism. Since I am bilingual and bicultural, and because I do not conduct my research as a dispassionate outsider, I am privy to conversations that may not be open to detached or monolingual scholars. This liminality offers me an opportunity to negotiate the meaning of my social location in a way that would be different were I to engage in research without strategies of accountability and without an explicit commitment to social justice. Further, activist research can be instrumental in challenging the systematic benefits associated with being socially located in the United States.

Activist research and research about activism are not the same, but I have attempted to merge the two in the research design. Activist research reflects my own involvement in advocacy efforts at the UN and my consciousness of the privileges I embody because of my US citizenship.[81] I have tremendous respect for the energies and efforts I have witnessed from activists at the UN. UN advocacy is by no means easy work, and requires a great deal of strategic thinking, patience, and difficult compromises, especially because of the radical politics many activists embrace.

But even though I identify as an activist and a US-trained scholar, by studying social movements up close, I also grapple with the issue of representation. Specifically, who am I to represent these voices and these women? Sociologist Nikki Jones, who has movingly written about African American girls and inner-city violence, observes, "In almost any sort of ethnographic endeavour, the field researcher occupies a strange position. She belongs and doesn't belong at the same time, and necessarily so."[82] Jones describes the "shared intimacy of the field research experience" that she encountered as an observant participant: a researcher who reveals her identity in the field but may choose to limit her interactions.[83] Because of my role as an observant participant at the NGO Forum, I shared with other activists the deep sense of frustration that arose at the conclusion of the 2001 WCAR. Yet it would be unfortunate—and too simplistic—to portray the entire experience of the 2001 WCAR as problematic. As in real life, most situations have positive, negative, and mixed outcomes or experiences. This world conference was no exception. There were some important positive outcomes, as my interviewees attested, that have been rendered invisible due to the controversies related to the gathering. If there is any hope for genuine progress, then discussions about the prevalence of global racism *should* be conflict-ridden, difficult, and frustrating. The contentiousness is not the problem—the problem is when the discord becomes the primary lens through which the world conference's outcomes are viewed.

Further, because of a perceived shared privileged status, my position as an academic might suggest a natural rapport with the activists who were engaged at the UN. Yet the long-standing tensions between activist and academic communities are real, in particular when scholars appear detached and determined to extract as much information as possible about activists' experiences without a clear commitment to an advocacy issue or to a social justice cause. I negotiated these tensions throughout the research process, sometimes more successfully than others, in my attempt to be what Desai refers to as a "supportive interlocutor" with social movements.[84]

The story of the progression of an intersectionality framework within the UN's antiracism agenda is part historical and part contemporary. The context in which antiracist feminist activism was able to thrive at the UN and in which intersectionality was able to take hold there is best understood by accessing a range of qualitative data. To reconstruct a history as well as to analyze a contemporary moment, my methodology relies on archival research, participant observation, extensive UN documents, and a range of in-depth interviews.

My research draws from seventy-five activist interviews that I conducted with NGO Forum and 2001 WCAR participants from four countries: the United States, Canada, Mexico, and Peru. The interviews were conducted in New York City, San Francisco, Toronto, Ottawa, Mexico City, and Lima. The interviewees were diverse in terms of class, race, sexuality, and nationality. Some had expertise in negotiating the dynamics of UN spaces; others had no experience working at the UN level at all. I determined who to interview based on a combination of available records on the UN website about NGOs registered to attend the 2001 WCAR and snowball sampling from interviewees' referrals. In addition to engaging as an active participant at the 2001 NGO Forum Against Racism in Durban, I also engaged in participant observation at NGO and UN meetings related to the outcomes of the 2001 WCAR, including the 2009 Durban Review Conference at UN headquarters in Geneva and the Durban + 10 meeting in New York City in 2011.

I also conducted an additional six semi-structured interviews with US NGO representatives from five organizations (four of these organizations were not in attendance at the 2001 WCAR) that participated in the US government's treaty review hearing on its compliance with the International Convention on the Elimination of All Forms of Racial Discrimination (ICERD) in 2008 in Geneva.[85] I also analyzed several documents, including the official US government report, NGO reports, and documents released from the Committee on the Elimination of Racial Discrimination (CERD) about the hearing. I observed the treaty compliance review hearings as well. I transcribed the interviews and the discussion at the treaty compliance review hearing between the US government delegation and CERD members from a combination of personal and US Human Rights Network recordings on their website. At the hearing, CERD committee members, one after another, repeatedly referenced the lack of US support for the Durban conference as being highly unfortunate and deeply misguided.

In addition, I interviewed five UN officials and their staff, including Mary Robinson of Ireland, former UN High Commissioner for Human Rights and president of Ireland; and Doudou Diène of Senegal, former UN special rapporteur on contemporary forms of racism, racial discrimination, xenophobia, and related intolerance. These interviews were particularly fortuitous in that the opportunities to interview UN representatives at this level are extremely rare. More importantly, interviewing both of these UN officials brings critical institutional insights about their perspective on the possible role the UN can take in combating racism. As UN officials whose primary goals were facilitating a global forum in which productive discussions could unfold for both activists and government delegates (and not in advancing the political interests of a particular nation), they were able to provide me with some useful information about the behind-the-scenes challenges of preparing for the Durban conference.

I also conducted document research on the first UN conference in 1945—the United Nations Conference on International Organization (UNCIO)—at the University of California, Berkeley, and on the lengthy history of the UN's agenda against racism at the UN's depository libraries and on the UN website. I conducted archival research at Stanford University, the National Black Women's History archives, and the Library of Congress in Washington, DC; the Virginia Gildersleeve archives at Barnard College and Columbia University; and the National Archives at the University of Maryland. I also tracked media coverage of the UN's work against racism since the 1970s using LexisNexis Academic, focusing specifically on the three WCARs of 1978, 1983, and 2001.

I combed through thousands of pages of UN records to piece together the historical arc of the institutionalization of the UN, its efforts to dismantle racism, and the political manoeuvres of the important social actors that engaged in politics at that level. In my efforts to offer a historically contextualized analysis for the purposes of this research, I mapped the origins of the UN itself and its antiracism history to accentuate what made the UN's antiracism agenda an important and logical site for antiracist feminist activists to intervene by 2001. To tell the critical history of how the discourse of racism at the UN had expanded over the years, as I reviewed and coded these documents and records during my analysis, I relied on in-depth interviews and participant observation to offer the contemporary segment of this story. By juxtaposing these different sets of qualitative data, the antiracist feminist activism that emerges by the early 2000s is situated in relation to its significance. To shape an effective advocacy agenda in the present, one has to understand how the UN works and its historical precedents.

In my discussion about expanding the discourse of racism at the UN level, contested terms such as "global North," "global South," "First World," and "Third World" are used. Even though these may be imperfect descriptors, paying attention to who uses these terms and in which contexts is instructive for analyzing activism inside the UN.[86] As an institution, the UN is slow to change, and such geographic divisions are engrained in its bureaucratic language and structure. In addition, these terms still evoke an engagement with power that is largely driven by geopolitical boundaries that divide global North from global South and First World from Third World. Such dichotomies result in the "three-worlds metageography," according to women's studies scholar Jennifer Suchland, in which former state-socialist, or "Second World," countries have no visibility and no voice.[87] However, given the regional focus of this research on the Americas, this limited but still useful geopolitical terminology facilitates distinguishing between the different national contexts of this research.

Other terminology used throughout the book also merits brief discussion. As discussed here, the UN agenda against racism involves decolonization, antiapartheid, and anti-imperialism struggles. Though these movements may be informed by distinct genealogies and origins, many activists discuss them at the UN level in a way that does not remain wedded to their differences; rather, they address these movements as being interrelated, and their choice of vocabulary verifies this point. Similarly,

I am less concerned about how activists understand these struggles as distinct, and more compelled to understand their political objectives within the UN's antiracism fora. As such, my use of language such as "decolonialism," "anti-imperialism," "antiapartheid," and so forth is interchangeable throughout this book because it all comes under the purview of the UN's agenda against racism in all of its manifestations.

INVESTIGATING RACISMS: THE CIRCUITOUS MILIEU

The UN has provided numerous opportunities for discussing racism during the drafting of General Assembly resolutions, as part of the work of CERD in monitoring treaty compliance, and, most critically, as the focus of the WCARs. In these instances, groups from countries with little economic power—including countries in Latin America—were able to shape the UN's agenda against racism in the face of considerable contention. Thus, the UN agenda against racism is considered a "Third World" agenda (one coming from the global South) that is focused on colonialism, genocide, apartheid, imperialism, and other similar issues. This book takes into consideration this context and asks, just like the women at the NGO Forum Against Racism, "Where are the women?"

Decades of UN-led efforts to combat racism offer a foundation for understanding the historical significance and meaning of the 2001 WCAR. The precedence of the Durban gathering prompted me to reflect on how we—participants of this world conference—had arrived to this divisive moment on the global stage. It provoked me to ask a series of questions: How does power operate in this narrative when discussions about global racism ultimately produce a situation in which colonial and imperial powers are directly confronted? What effect, if any, do the so-called imperial origins of the UN (and even human rights) have on these debates about racism, including a feminist perspective of racism advanced through an articulation of intersectionality? In what ways do imperial powers respond to the agency exerted by colonized peoples and other people of color? And how has an increase in the presence of antiracist women activists and advocates at the UN level, especially since the 1990s, facilitated an expanded understanding of racism in the 2000s and beyond? None of these questions can be explored in a temporal manner because the historical backdrop for the 2001 WCAR is difficult to convey in a chronological timeline. Therefore, I have organized the book by first exploring the origins of the institutional context, as well as the politics, of UN membership for government bodies and NGOs because these two factors—the formation of the institution and its participating social actors or UN members—influence the environment and manner in which contemporary activists are able work at the UN today. Next, I consider the variant deployments of human rights discourses by these different UN members within a proposed constellations model to contend that the antiracist feminist agency occurring in relation to the Durban conference embodies a transnational feminist practice. Taken together, the origins of the UN, along with the politics of UN membership, provide the basis with which to contextualize the genealogy of the WCARs, unearth the challenges facing feminist activists determined to broaden the discourse of racism, and trace the progression of intersectionality in the antiracism forums of the UN. The organization of the book resembles the circuitous milieu that led to the Durban conference.

Like many transnational feminist and intersectionality scholars who seek to dismantle the power evident in academic renditions by reclaiming histories, my work begins with an analysis of historical events that help elucidate current trends of feminist antiracist activism. Activists' engagement at the UN level is unlike other activist forums because it takes place within the confines of an institution with a deeply fraught history. I begin with the first UN conference in 1945 held in San Francisco, California. Chapter 1 revisits three contentious debates from UNCIO to argue for the emergence of both a paradox and a counterpublic. As evident in the debates discussed in the chapter, the UN is a paradox in that it claims to be an institution promoting peace but encourages exclusion and violence. In addition, the tenor of these debates accentuates the deep-seated paternalism embodied by the "great powers" of the 1945 conference. The first debate was over the establishment of veto power for the five permanent members of the Security Council; the second concerned negotiations over the creation of the Trusteeship Council; and the third was triggered by Latin American proposals to legally ensure equal representation and participation for women at the UN. The "counterpublic," which refers to an oppositional space, involves "new" citizen-subjects, specifically from Latin America, who worked together around the core theme of building a democratic UN. Their coming together is the basis for the struggle over representation, power, and voice. Chapter 1 also discusses a little-known women's conference held in San Francisco at the same time about women's future role in the UN to show that the organizers of this conference replicated the elitism that dominated UNCIO.

Chapter 2 unpacks the politics of membership in the UN by exploring the concept of "UN citizenship." UN citizenship, which is dependent on economic, social, and cultural capital, determines the relationships that govern UN inclusion and exclusion for governments and NGOs alike. Obtaining UN membership does not translate into equal representation. Yet UN membership has increased significantly since 1945, triggering important epistemological shifts in the understanding of human rights. The second half of the chapter explores the different meanings or understandings of human rights as they relate to this research by suggesting that three constellations of human rights exist here: dominant understandings influenced by the Western legal apparatus, counterpublic approaches shaped by transnational feminist concepts, and social praxis, which speaks to the practice of human rights in daily life. Dominant understandings rest on modernist ontologies, the counterpublic realm hinges on relational ontologies, and social praxis signifies the struggle between the two ontologies waged at the level of politics and UN advocacy. The purpose here is to offer a richer portrait of the human rights landscape by elaborating on the social praxis constellation, which is the site in which to locate the antiracist feminist agency inspired by the Durban conference. The introduction and eventual integration of intersectionality at the UN level is informed by the negotiation of modernist and relational ontologies occurring in this third constellation. As discussed in this chapter, two prime examples of activist engagement within the social praxis constellation are US-based feminist advocacy efforts during a 2008 CERD review hearing that build on the antiracist feminist efforts started at the 2001 WCAR, and the intense twenty-year negotiations involving the UN Declaration on the Rights of Indigenous Peoples.

The next two chapters focus on the genealogy of the WCARs and on the intensive conference preparation by antiracist feminist activists for the 2001 WCAR. Chapter 3 situates the Durban conference in conversation with the preceding WCARs in 1978 and 1983; it also analyzes the meaning of intersectionality and gender in the 2001 WCAR documents. This chapter evaluates the 2009 Durban Review Conference, which was the official follow-up conference to the 2001 WCAR, to address how the practice of antiracist feminism has become increasingly complex in the aftermath of the Durban conference. Chapter 4 focuses on the nearly two-year preparatory period for the Durban conference. During this time feminists developed transnational connections, both symbolic and real, that aided their advocacy efforts for an approach to intersectionality that considered the specificities of context and resulted in an expanded discourse about racism.

Power Interrupted concludes with a discussion about how the global feminism prevalent in the 1980s and 1990s evolved into a practice of transnational feminism in the 2000s. In moving beyond the confines of the UN forums on women to the venues that focused explicitly on ending global racism, a different type of feminism emerges because it developed in UN spaces created to address racism rather than narrowly defined women's issues. As such, intersectionality—together with a consideration of geopolitical spaces, historical narratives, and political situations—becomes essential to transform the discourses of racism, antiracism, and human rights. The concluding chapter explores what I refer to as the "new universalism of intersectionality" that materialized in this evolving phase of feminist engagement at the UN, and summarizes the views about the importance of the UN from the antiracist feminists who played a role in its development.

1

Race, Gender, and Geopolitics
in the Establishment of the UN

The men like to hear themselves very much.

—BERTHA LUTZ, UNCIO DELEGATE FROM BRAZIL, 1945

WORLD WAR II WROUGHT UNPRECEDENTED DEVASTATION: CITIES were bombed, urban centers destroyed, soldiers and civilians imprisoned or enslaved, and millions killed.[1] Before the war had officially ended, world leaders started creating a new multilateral institution that would, ideally, prevent future global wars, maintain international peace and security, and promote human rights.[2] Beginning in April 1945, government delegations from forty-nine countries gathered for the United Nations Conference on International Organization (UNCIO) in San Francisco, California, to design the charter for the institution we know today as the United Nations.[3]

The UN that emerged from these deliberations was colonial and patriarchal in its structure and intent, shaped by proposals formulated at the Dumbarton Oaks and Yalta conferences of October 1944 and February 1945, respectively.[4] The four "great powers"—the United States, the United Kingdom, the Soviet Union, and China—were the only countries to attend these conferences, and their delegations' recommendations gave economically powerful countries structural advantages. US Secretary of State (under Eisenhower) John Foster Dulles, who participated in the Dumbarton Oaks and Yalta conferences, stated that the proposals "had the defects which usually occur when a few big powers get together to decide how to run the world," and noted that powerful countries "generally, and naturally, conclude that the best of all possible worlds is a world which they will run."[5]

The ratification of the UN Charter was contentious, as delegates from less economically advantaged nation-states struggled to establish representation, power, and voice for their countries against the authority of the more powerful nation-states. Three key UNCIO debates discussed in this chapter—regarding the veto power in the Security Council, the creation of the Trusteeship Council for colonies, and the representation of women at the UN—illustrate how the majority of delegates were unwilling to passively accept the proposals for the UN as configured by the United States, the United Kingdom, the Soviet Union, and China. The early efforts of these delegates to mold the institution into a more democratic ideal speak to their pursuit of justice on the one hand, and a desire to disrupt power consolidated at the top on the other. In other words, the origins of the United Nations involve multilevel resistance to a colonial impulse that is well documented in UNCIO records.

The coexistence of modernity and coloniality shaped the debates that sprang from the deep-seated paternalism of the "great powers" that was evident throughout the conference proceedings. The debates also led to the formation of a counterpublic—"an oppositional space in which networks, organizations, and individuals who share certain values or identities engage with one another around a core theme."[6] In the context of the 1945 conference, "new" citizen-subjects who had been left out of the conversations at Dumbarton Oaks and Yalta comprised the counterpublic determined to build a more democratic UN together.

The representation of women at the UN was also the subject of a related conference that took place in San Francisco on May 19, 1945. Known as the United Women's Conference: Women's Share in Implementing the Peace (UWC), its purpose was to talk specifically about the role of women in the peace-making process. Those conference proceedings provide additional insight into the efforts undertaken by women of the Americas to increase their stake in the UN; it is also the beginning of a rich and complicated genealogy of feminist advocacy at the UN level. Furthermore, UWC records reveal that an active engagement with racial injustice was yet to develop.

An analysis of each of the three key UNCIO debates suggests that the UN is a racialized and gendered institution. Since men racialized as white and elite controlled the creation of this multilateral organization, any efforts to democratize it have directly challenged their patriarchal, colonial, and ethnocentric expressions of power. Committed and ardent representatives from the global South and from Third World nations have banded together to challenge this power, demonstrating what the UN *could* represent for women, colonized peoples, and people of color.

THE GEOPOLITICAL CONTEXT

A central goal of the United States and of other economically powerful nations during UNCIO was to retain control over their capital and resources and their empowered position on the global stage.[7] This objective is an example of what Peruvian sociologist Anibal Quijano refers to as the "coloniality of power." Quijano describes this model of power as having two axes: "the codification of the differences between conquerors and conquered in the idea of 'race,'" and the establishment of "a new structure of control of labor and its resources and products."[8]

At the center of this model of power are the "unfinished projects of modernity and coloniality."[9] Humanities scholar Walter Mignolo states, "What appears as paradox is the node . . . between the rhetoric of modernity announcing salvation, happiness, progress, development, etc., and the necessary logic of coloniality—appropriation of natural resources, exploitation of labor, legal control of undesirables, military enforcements of the law in order to ensure 'salvation' through the imposition [of] the interests and world view inherent to capitalist economy."[10] The exercise of the coloniality of power assumes that colonized peoples and people of color need to be governed, and this, in turn, dismisses their humanity. Even if "human" is a universally accepted category applied to every person at birth, this status is tenuous for many, and it can be lost precisely because of the projects of modernity-coloniality. As Mignolo notes, the concept of "human" as conceived in the 1948 Universal Declaration of Human Rights excludes "quite [a] large portion of the global population."[11]

The operation of power is never linear or merely hierarchical. Power is controlled not only through top-down measures of institutional domination but also through resistance to such displays of domination. This multidirectionality is best understood through a process that feminist political scientist Cynthia Enloe describes as "reading power backwards and forwards."[12] In this reading of power, the story of the formation of the UN becomes a stirring account of the intervention of constituencies outside of the "great powers" that made essential contributions to the UN Charter. Reading power backward and forward brings to light the critical contributions of the Latin American delegations that argued passionately against the power of veto in the UN Security Council; the concerted attempts of US civil society organizations to transform the agenda by linking human rights to global political struggles; and the work of a small group of feminists from Latin America who secured the legal rights of women to be represented and to participate at the UN.

Global realities of the time influenced deliberations at the UNCIO. Segregation in the United States was deeply engrained, and apartheid would be imposed in South Africa in 1948.[13] A vast number of countries of the world were under European colonial rule, which was justified as a conduit for bringing "civilization" and "modernity" to the native populations of the colonies. The majority of the world's women were without basic rights; many were ineligible to vote and could not own property.[14] Indigenous communities across the world experienced ongoing devastation and displacement, and the fate of the colonial peoples of the world was uncertain. These origins served as the backdrop for UN negotiations and contributed to the multiple levels of geopolitical division at the UNCIO, both within as well as among the delegations.[15]

In the United States, Southern Democrats held enormous power in the US Senate. Determined to maintain Jim Crow laws established in the previous century, they became increasingly concerned that the new international institution would empower the cause of African Americans and bring additional support to campaigns against segregation, disenfranchisement, and lynching.[16] The US delegation had to ensure that the UN would both enshrine the United States' global position of power and appease racist senators, whose votes were needed to approve the charter. The only way to mollify the senators was through the insertion of Article 2 (7) in the UN Charter, which protected domestic jurisdictions from interference by an international governing body, and local politicians from rebuke.[17] The charter eventually included a modest acknowledgment of human rights "without discrimination against race, sex, condition, or creed."[18] The fact that the United States hosted the UNCIO at a time when the rights of women and people of color had little meaning in the US is one of the flaws and contradictions that are at the heart of the United Nations.

It also bears mentioning briefly the frequency with which references to God were made in the opening and closing sessions of the UNCIO. President Harry Truman and some of the members of the US delegation injected an unmistakable Christian tone into the opening and closing sessions. In Truman's opening remarks, for instance, he stated, "We beseech Almighty God to guide us in the building of a permanent monument to those who give their lives that this moment might come. May He lead our steps in His own righteous path of peace."[19] Secretary of State Edward R. Stettinius Jr., chair of the US delegation, referred to the "righteous cause" in which the participants of the UNCIO were engaging, yet he was adamant that racial problems stemming from conflicts with African Americans and American Indians would have no opportunity to enter the conversations at the UNCIO.[20] In other words, even though some delegates apparently felt that they were fulfilling God's will, doing God's work did not seem to have anything to do with matters of racial or gender justice, and instead perpetuated those injustices. Furthermore, anyone who did not embody these same Christian values was deemed less human or nonhuman.[21]

In the early days of the UNCIO, government delegates debated the role that NGOs and other private citizens might play in the proceedings. Some delegations argued that the conference needed to maintain a gravitas and that opening the conference to nongovernment entities would diminish its importance. Although the conference was ultimately open only to government delegations, several nations, including the United States, Mexico, and Canada, added advisors, assistants, and consultants to their rosters.

The chairs of each of the delegations from the four sponsoring governments served as co-presidents of the UNCIO. The chairs rotated responsibility for facilitating the plenary sessions and the key committee meetings. The four governments were not a cohesive group, however: China was often disrespected by the other powers, particularly the United States; the United States was at odds with the Soviet Union over voting rights; and the United Kingdom was intent on retaining and strengthening its colonial empire against the wishes of the other governments.[22]

No people of color were in the US delegation, and Virginia Gildersleeve, dean of Barnard College, was the only woman to serve as an official delegate. Unable to secure a position for the National Association for the Advancement of Colored People (NAACP) in the delegation, the US State Department eventually asked the organization to serve as an official consultant.[23] W. E. B. Du Bois and Walter White represented the NAACP,[24] and Mary McLeod Bethune represented the interests of the National Council on Negro Women (NCNW), though she attended the UNCIO with her NAACP affiliation.[25] Ralph Bunche, the highest-ranking African American in the US State Department, also served as an official advisor. Representatives from five US women's organizations and dozens of other NGOs also engaged in the proceedings as consultants.[26]

UNCIO records reveal that the UN Charter was a deeply contested document for government delegations around the world and even for organizations serving as conference consultants, although the tensions that surrounded its ratification are not visible in the final product. In the United States, thirty-seven organizations did not support ratification, and they testified before Congress, submitted written statements, and sent telegrams to express their opposition.[27] Far more organizations supported it, however, and although the NAACP, the National Women's Christian Temperance Union, the Post War World Council, and the Socialist Party had reservations about the charter, they did not oppose its ratification. Opposition from those with less power stemmed from concerns about the consolidation of power at the top, which would structurally disadvantage smaller nations and colonized peoples.

Even in the midst of these debates, as the "model of global power" and the resulting formation of a new world order shifted from England to the United States,[28] the social and political interests of all of the "great powers" remained aligned. As Quijano has said, the interests of the small white minority in power were "explicitly antagonistic" to colonized peoples and people of color resulting from the context that "no area of common interest between whites and nonwhites and, consequently, no common national interests for all of them [exists]."[29] This antagonism undergirded the rationale used by the great powers as UNCIO participants debated the structure of the Security Council, the Trusteeship Council,[30] and women's role at the UN.

The United Nations Security Council comprises five permanent members: the United States, the United Kingdom, China, Russia (formerly the Soviet Union), and France.[31] Each has veto power, which gives each the ability to trump a majority decision by the other Member States. The Security Council is essentially undemocratic, and its structure, which was outlined in the Dumbarton Oaks and Yalta proposals, was—and remains—a controversial issue, in part because it "reflects power relations of 1945."[32] The permanent members have remained unchanged since that time, and many commentators argue that the Security Council does not represent current economic and geopolitical realities.[33]

In the deliberations over ratification, the debate about the structure of the Security Council was the most contentious. The four sponsoring governments had clearly anticipated that this would be the case at the UNCIO. The short letter of invitation to the representatives of other countries sent by the United States on behalf of itself and the other three sponsoring governments concluded with an explanation of and justification for the Security Council's voting procedures.[34] The smaller nations recognized that such veto power would permanently disempower them, and in one speech after another, delegates from the governments of Australia, Cuba, Brazil, Colombia, Uruguay, and many other nations declared in unflinching terms that the veto was a power grab that would favor the few nations at the top. Delegates from New Zealand referred to the proposed structure as an "evil voting system," and Lebanon called it just plain "evil."[35] Members of the Cuban delegation repeatedly expressed concern about the sponsoring governments' permanent member status, stating that "the realities of history show a group of great powers could undergo changes" and that the designation of permanent status compromised sovereignty.[36]

During the debate, the Australian delegate, Prime Minister Francis M. Forde, contended that if the veto power could not be eliminated, its use should be restricted. Each member of the Security Council has one vote, with nine affirmative votes required to approve decisions on procedural matters. Forde and others argued that if the term "procedural matters" were given "a wider and more liberal definition," the veto power of each permanent member would be correspondingly narrowed.[37] Another delegate from New Zealand, expressing utter frustration with the "inadequate position of small powers on the Council," pointed out that the veto would undermine "collective" security.[38] The New Zealand delegation proposed increasing the membership of the Security Council and linking the work of the council more directly to the General Assembly as a way to give the smaller nations a presence on the council, particularly in matters of war. The Mexican delegation immediately offered their support for New Zealand's proposals. Expanding the Security Council or tying it to the General Assembly was unacceptable to the US delegation because, it argued, even giving a "voice" to smaller nations on the council would weaken the council's mandate.[39]

During UNCIO negotiations, the US State Department prepared a list of the most frequently asked questions that department representatives had heard with regard to the Dumbarton Oaks proposals. The crux of these questions had to do with the possibility of the abuse or misuse of power by the four sponsoring governments. Examples of the questions include: "Is any great power going to be able to veto enforcement action against itself?" "How will national contingents be able to stop aggression by a great power?" "Would revolution or insurrection in a member state or in colonial territories constitute aggression?"[40] Ultimately, after weeks of debate, the subcommittee assigned with securing approval of the Security Council's voting structure received a twenty-three-item questionnaire from the other conference participants designed to fully clarify the voting procedures. The responses issued by the four sponsoring governments left much to be desired.[41] Forde pointed out that the responses were "not based on any consistent principle," meaning that they were inadequate or incomplete.[42] The inadequacy of the responses suggests that the sponsoring governments were unwilling to consider alternative structures. As Gildersleeve pointed out, "Once the five powers agreed upon something, it was almost impossible to change it."[43]

Challenges to the permanent members' coloniality of power came from multiple directions, including Latin America and the Pacific region.[44] In one of the last meetings of the UNCIO, the Brazilian delegate restated his principle opposition "to granting any 'veto' power to the permanent members of the Security Council"[45] and noted the support for this opposition from many of the conference participants: "The public opinion of many, if not most, of the nations represented here was opposed to the veto power and the best means of making the Yalta voting procedure acceptable would be to provide for free, frank, and full review of the Charter. Only with the provision for such review would the Charter be applauded by world opinion."[46] If an amendment to limit the veto was not possible at the time of the UNCIO, Brazil and numerous other delegations proposed the compromise of reviewing the charter in the future.

Latin American governments generally tried to maintain a cohesive regional bloc during UNCIO negotiations, and the delegation from Mexico proposed that its regional interests would best be represented if the Security Council's configuration granted one Latin American government permanent status on the Security Council.[47] The numerous amendments proposed by Latin America in regards to the Security Council were done in the spirit of representation, power, and voice. These efforts did not go unnoticed, as Forde declared,

> One of the great lessons, the permanent lessons of this Conference, to me, has been this: I thought at the beginning of the Conference, the speeches were made in this hall, the [sic] some of the Latin American countries were perhaps over-insistent upon one point. That is the point that small nations, the smallest nations, had a sense of dignity and self-respect, which was really the basis of their international life. . . . The greatest lesson that I have learned from this Conference is the insistence on the rights of every nation, on its right to put its views forward with courage and vigor. I now accept fully from my heart the speeches made at the earlier sessions of this Conference, especially the magnificent speech made, I think, on the second day of the Conference by the very distinguished Foreign Minister of Colombia.[48]

The voting delegate from Colombia ended up voting against the Yalta formula, which determined the voting structure of the Security Council, for two reasons, principle and political. The delegate said, "The proposed voting procedure would put the question of peace or war in the hands of any one of the five powers. This was contrary to the principle by which a simple or stated majority should decide issues in the international organization." In terms of the political reason, the delegate argued that the great powers "acted in good faith, [though] they had made a mistake." He continued, "Unanimity could not be obtained by blocking genuine discussion and ample investigation by the Security Council. The veto meant in effect that the interests of four great powers would be subjected to the will of one. The result would always be an agreement not to act."[49]

In addition to opposing the structure of the Security Council, the Latin American delegations proposed other names for the UN, such as the Permanent Union of Nations (offered by the Mexican delegation), in order to find a name "that does not imply discrimination against any state."[50] Gildersleeve served on the committee that chose the name and was taken aback at the objections from the Latin American countries:

> I had one other important task on Committee I/1. That was to get the name of the United Nations definitely settled. The United States, of course, wanted the official delegation to be "The United Nations," and it was my job to get Committee I/1 to make this definite recommenda-tion. I did not anticipate much difficulty and so was painfully surprised when the discussion revealed considerable difference of opinion. Most of the Latin nations objected strongly to a plural form. They wanted some collective noun like "league" or "union" or "association." I began to be afraid that the vote would go against us, and I wondered what my delegation would do to me for failing them on this critical point.[51]

Gildersleeve's points suggest that the US delegation was unprepared for the resistance that was mounted against its interests. More importantly, she indicates that the Latin American approach to the formation of a multilateral institution differed substantially from that of the United States in that the Latin American delegations, as a collective bloc, was concerned about the perceived discrimination that would affect smaller nations, even when it came to the institution's name.

Arguments against the veto power continued until the final few days of the UNCIO and received nearly daily coverage in the newspapers. Gildersleeve knew that the US Senate "would never agree that a vote of other nations should oblige this country, against its will, to use its armed forces or sacrifice some part of its territory or in other ways give up control over its own affairs."[52] Reading power backward and forward, as Enloe suggests, shows that the debate over the veto was about more than the veto itself. It was concerned not only with democracy but also with the respect and dignity of all peoples. The five permanent members of the Security Council repeatedly stated that Latin American and other reluctant delegations of smaller nations "must trust in the good faith and good intentions of the great powers" to make the right decisions on behalf of the UN.[53] The veto became so controversial that the only strategy left for the sponsoring governments was essentially to threaten the protesting delegations: if they were not willing to accept the veto, there would be no United Nations. This risky tactic proved successful: after several weeks of meetings, government delegations concluded that they could not sabotage the formation of a multilateral organization over the veto issue. The five great powers assured their permanent status and retained their veto power.[54]

The Latin American delegations were not going to passively accept the demands of the sponsoring governments. The reading of power backward and forward recognizes these early displays of resistance by Latin American delegations as producing a situation in which the "coloniality of power" was being directly challenged. The powerful governments, in turn, were willing to engage in collective punishment if they did not get their way. Today, nearly seventy years later, because the majority of government delegations are still dissatisfied with the veto, the structure of the Security Council remains the Achilles' heel of the UN.[55]

THE TRUSTEESHIP COUNCIL AND THE MAINTENANCE OF COLONIAL RULE

Although colonialism was a critical issue in the mid-1940s, especially given the burgeoning decolonization movements,[56] the Dumbarton Oaks proposals did not influence the formation of the Trusteeship Council during UNCIO proceedings because the United States was not initially interested in a public discussion about it. This can be attributed to a number of factors. The United States publically supported self-determination for former colonies, and, at the same time, was not willing to have an international organization determine the fate of its strategic interests in the Pacific. Other powerful governments, however, including France and the United Kingdom, had an interest in protecting their colonial territories. The status of colonial territories had to be addressed in some capacity because it was an international issue, so a new UNCIO committee comprised of the colonial powers formed to discuss trusteeship. It was unusual not to have a template from the Dumbarton Oaks proposals, as noted by a French delegate: "We felt somewhat like Cinderella, so far as we had no shoes with which to walk."[57] Even though trusteeship had not been included in the Dumbarton Oaks proposals per se, some advance planning had occurred on the part of the British delegation and the US State Department before the UNCIO.[58]

From the beginning, the trusteeship system was not, at its core, about independence from colonialism. The rationale for the system, according to the great powers, was that "peoples not yet able to stand by themselves under the strenuous conditions of the modern world" inhabited the colonial territories.[59] The new committee proposed that because these colonial governments managed the funds established for their former colonies, they should retain authority over these territories.[60]

The proposed trusteeship system focused on the islands in the Pacific, and colonialism in Africa was entirely neglected. Du Bois, who was frustrated with this narrow view, declared that the committee was ignoring the predicament of the majority of colonized peoples in Africa, whose suffering was caused by capitalistic interest in "cheap . . . labor and forced servitude."[61] US interests accounted for only 3 percent of all colonial territories,[62] and since the intent of the Trusteeship Council was to guarantee that the colonial powers retained their hold over their territories, the United States had no stake in expanding the discussion of colonial territories to Africa. The United States' "global designs," as Mignolo has called them, were eventually realized when former colonies in Asia and Africa "moved under the arm of Uncle Sam."[63] The establishment of the Trusteeship Council bolstered the coloniality of power by naturalizing the idea of race and by introducing a new structure of control.[64] The US military establishment played a particularly visible role,[65] as Gildersleeve noted in her memoir: "When we were discussing questions which bore directly on national security, we always had admirals and generals present, galaxies of them at times! I remember one occasion in Washington when we took up the thorny matter of trusteeship and the Pacific islands, and had across the table from us the Secretaries of War and the Navy as well as admirals at one end of the room and Army generals at the other."[66] Rather than questioning the military presence, Gildersleeve accepted it and seemed to have relished it. The US military and the US delegation collaborated because the government was determined to extend social control over labor and resources.[67] The Pacific region was instrumental to the global designs referenced by Mignolo, and the former African colonies were essential to the capitalist interests mentioned by Du Bois.

Records of the negotiations, not surprisingly, reveal a deep paternalism on the part of the colonial powers toward the territories, which did not have any representatives on the committee, as evidenced by the racialized language used during the deliberations, where reference was made to "uncivilized," "savage," "backward," and "primitive" peoples. Jan Christiaan Smuts, a delegate from the Union of South Africa, and its former prime minister, referred to colonial peoples as "backward in development" and "not advanced enough to look after themselves."[68] Smuts, of British heritage and the primary writer of the preamble to the UN Charter, was an outspoken segregationist, who when asked by a journalist "if he considered black persons human beings in the definition of the United Nations Charter he had drafted as chairman," replied with a resounding "no."[69]

The UK delegate, Robert Gascony-Cecil (also known as Lord Cranborne), expressed the most blatant paternalism during his speech, describing the colonies as ranging from the "most primitive" to "highly civilized":

> Many of these territories are small, poor, and defenseless and could not stand on their own feet. Many of them are extremely backward. Many need a helping hand to build roads and communications, to set up modern health systems, to introduce scientific methods of agriculture, and to encourage the spread of education, which is fundamental to all progress. *Take away the helping hand and such territories would rapidly relapse into barbarism.* What we can give them is liberty and free institutions. We can gradually train them in the management of their own affairs, so that, *should independence ultimately come*, they will be ready for it.[70]

The view reflected in Cranborne's statements point out that independence from colonial rule was not a foregone conclusion. Cranborne's views were not unique in this regard. By using the "rhetoric of modernity" and the "necessary logic of coloniality" as identified by Mignolo, Cranborne, Smuts, and others perpetuated a racialized discourse of paternalism. Their goal was to hinder colonial independence whenever, for instance, the political structures adopted by colonized peoples differed from those imposed by colonial powers. Anything colonized peoples might attempt to implement to further their rights was portrayed as a sign of remaining "backward" or "primitive."

Cranborne's speech contained what was perhaps an admission of the true reason for suppressing independence: the colonial powers' reliance on the colonies' natural resources—one of the axes of Quijano's coloniality of power. Cranborne stated, "But I can tell you that, in the earlier stages of this war when my country was grimly fighting a vastly stronger foe, only the existence of our African colonial empire, the essential materials which we could draw from it, and the reinforcement route to the Middle East across the heart of Africa, saved us from defeat."[71] The modernity-coloniality projects are unmistakable here. In addition to pointing to the link between colonial logic and the appropriation of natural resources, these speakers suggest that modernity—that is, progress and development—could be achieved only by colonial territories through colonialism's "helping hand." The outcome of this debate was, on the surface, the creation of the Trusteeship Council; however, its more debilitating outcome was the further entrenchment of the coloniality of power as the norm.

In the final day of negotiation, the Iraqi delegate, Mohammed Fadhel al-Jamali, the country's minister of foreign affairs, expressed great disappointment in the establishment of the trusteeship system. Concerned that the rights of territories and the wishes of colonial peoples had been entirely neglected, al-Jamali stated that territories were completely "at the mercy of the trustee power."[72] Peter Fraser, prime minister of New Zealand, who served as chair of the commission, forcefully refuted al-Jamali's assertions, stating, "We have not trampled upon the rights of any nation or any peoples."[73]

The discourse of racialized paternalism cannot be disentangled from the territories' strategic military utility. One of the parameters proposed for inclusion in the trusteeship system was "to abstain from the military training of natives for other than police purposes and defense purposes."[74] Yet the approved proposal contains the following statement: "The administering authority shall be empowered to make use of volunteer forces, facilities, and assistance from the trust territory in carrying out the obligations undertaken by the administering authority to the Security Council in this regard and for local defense and the maintenance of law and order within the trust territory."[75] In other words, colonized peoples could be used as additional military forces against their own people at the complete discretion of the colonial authorities. Military utility was also necessary for the expansion of capitalism, and this added another layer to the logic of coloniality. Diplomacy, economic pressure, and military strength are all necessary in the opening of foreign markets, and all three were discussed in the deliberations about the Trusteeship Council.

The trusteeship debate also provided an opportunity for African Americans and colonized peoples throughout the world to show international solidarity. The NAACP was steadfast in its support of colonized peoples, because it saw colonialism as linked to its own struggles against racism in the United States. The NAACP sponsored its own conferences in April and May of 1945 to discuss colonialism. Du Bois was concerned with the US delegation's weak position in regard to colonial peoples, specifically in terms of the lack of representation of colonial peoples in a multilateral institution meant only for state governments.[76] Du Bois, who considered colonialism a racial project and colonial peoples as racialized (or "nonwhites"), proposed an amendment to the government delegations that addressed both racial equality and colonial independence. He, as the representative of the NAACP, repeatedly linked Third World decolonization with racism in the United States, intertwining the liberation of colonial peoples with the equal rights of African Americans.[77]

Colonized peoples had no presence or voice at the UNCIO. However, Du Bois, Mary McLeod Bethune (president of the NCNW), and other black leaders from the NAACP kept raising the issue of liberation for colonized peoples in connection with broader African American struggles.[78] For example, during two separate events about the San Francisco conference—a public speech and a press conference, respectively—Bethune said that the fate of the colonies was "vitally tied up with that of all racial minorities the world over"[79] and that "the Negro [has become] aligned with all the colored peoples of the world."[80]

Unfortunately, the trusteeship system and formation of the Trusteeship Council solidified the economic and military control of the permanent members over colonized peoples. The system was a methodological way for former colonial powers to retain their power—economically as well as militarily—for the foreseeable future, paralleling the retention of power by these nation-states in the Security Council. Similar paternalistic justifications were employed in both debates: the colonial powers declared that colonized peoples were neither ready for the responsibility to govern themselves nor prepared to be fully engaged participants in world affairs.

A reading of power as suggested by Enloe shows that the efforts of certain government delegates and African American consultants were critical in ensuring that the issue of colonial territories would not be resolved easily or without dissent. In fact, the United States did not want the topic discussed at all. According to Eslanda Robeson, wife of singer, actor, and activist Paul Robeson, and someone who followed the negotiations in San Francisco closely, the issue of trusteeship was of the utmost importance. She said, "This is an issue which the powers now here for the conference hoped would not come up; they trusted we would not be well informed enough to bring the issue up forcefully and it is now causing some concern with the delegates who had not been instructed how to meet it."[81] Time after time, delegates and consultants stated on the record that the trusteeship issue was not being resolved in a manner that was even remotely fair to colonial territories. These displays of resistance were harbingers of the decolonization movements that began to erupt shortly after ratification of the UN Charter.

NEGOTIATING THE REPRESENTATION AND PARTICIPATION OF WOMEN

The paternalism evident in the debates over trusteeship and over the veto in the Security Council also led to the near exclusion of women on government delegations at the UNCIO. Of the 160 signatories to the UN Charter, only four were women, and two of those four came from Latin America.[82] They were Virginia Gildersleeve from the United States, Bertha Lutz from Brazil, Minerva Bernardino from the Dominican Republic, and Wu Yi-Fang of China. Even though Gildersleeve was an advocate for women's education, she did not endorse the amendments from Latin America that advanced "gender equality" at the UN, as she found them to be unnecessary. Upon learning of her selection to the US delegation, the *Washington Post* reported that Gildersleeve was "no feminist thinker."[83] In contrast, Lutz and Bernardino identified as feminists. Lutz was a prominent leader in the Brazilian suffrage movement, and Bernardino was the president of the Inter-American Commission of Women.[84] The views and actions of these three women delegates symbolize the broad political differences between US and Latin American interests. It was the Latin American women who called for more radical reforms, and it is due to their efforts that the charter contains explicit language that addresses the equal participation of women at the UN today.

Overlapping with UNCIO proceedings, women convened to discuss their role in securing peace as well as their role in the UN at the UWC held on May 19, 1945, in San Francisco. Together, the UNCIO debate about women's participation and the proceedings of the UWC mark the beginning of a lengthy and complicated feminist genealogy of UN advocacy that continues to the present day.[85] The proposals made by Latin American delegations at the UNCIO and the speeches made by the UWC participants reflect ongoing tensions regarding race, gender, and class.

The UNCIO Debate on Women's Participation

During the UNCIO, Latin American delegations issued several proposals for amendments to the UN Charter. As shown in table 1.01, Brazil, Mexico, and the Dominican Republic offered joint proposals, and Uruguay offered its own proposal, which also received the support of Brazil and Mexico. The tenor of these amendments was explicitly about ensuring that women would have equal access to the UN in terms of representation and participation. The objective of the amendments was to strengthen the language of antidiscrimination based on sex and, occasionally, race. The various texts for the amendments retained consistent views about the equal presence of women within the UN. In the end, Uruguay's proposal received the most support, and its text served as a template for the final language of the UN Charter. For the Latin American feminist delegates, representation and participation were not just about employment opportunities at the UN but also about being able to participate, on an equal basis with men, in setting the organization's agenda.

The efforts of the Latin American feminists were not well received. Most male delegates from the powerful countries did not want to hear about women or the status of women and would have preferred that these feminists had just gone away. Gildersleeve acknowledged in her

TABLE 1.01   Latin American Amendments and Proposals to the UN Charter about Women, 1945

COUNTRY	DATE	PROPOSED TEXT	PROPOSED PLACEMENT IN UN CHARTER
Brazil-Mexico-Dominican Republic	5/5/1945	"To ensure respect for human rights and fundamental freedoms, without discrimination against race, sex, condition, or creed."	Chapter 1 (Purposes)
Brazil-Mexico-Dominican Republic	5/5/1945	"Representation and participation in the General International Organization shall be open to men and women under equal conditions."	Chapter 5
Brazil-Mexico-Dominican Republic	5/5/1945	". . . and promote respect for human rights and fundamental freedoms and foster the democratic principle of equality of status, opportunity, and responsibility for men and women."	Chapter 9 (Arrangements for International Economic and Social Cooperation)
Brazil-Mexico-Dominican Republic	5/5/1945	"There should be a Secretariat comprising a Secretary-General and such staff as may be required, all positions being open equally to men and women."	Chapter 10 (The Secretariat)
Uruguay	5/12/1945	"Representation and participation in the organs of the Organization shall be open both to men and women under the same conditions."	Chapter 4

Sources: United Nations Conference on International Organization, "Amendments to the Dumbarton Oaks Proposals Submitted by the Delegations of Brazil, the Dominican Republic, and the United States of Mexico," May 5, 1945; and "Summary Report of Eighth Meeting of Committee I/2," May 15, 1945 (for Uruguay proposal).

memoir that the "British and the American men hated being lectured on the virtues and rights of women," whereas other nations, which Gildersleeve referred to as "backward," were not as hostile toward the feminists' concerns.[86] Gildersleeve was not convinced that the UN Charter needed the openly feminist language proposed by the Latin American and Caribbean delegations; rather, she believed that women needed to prove themselves to their male colleagues. In her memoir, she often placed the burden on women to demonstrate that they were qualified, rather than challenge men's sexist beliefs or institutional patriarchy:

> One or two of the men [of other nations] spoke to me with admiration of the feminists, especially of Dr. [Bertha] Lutz. Perhaps in the backward countries, where women have no vote and few rights of any kind, spectacular feminism may still be necessary. My English friend Caroline Spurgeon, with whom I lived so long, used to tell me that I did not appreciate the need of militant feminism because I had not been trampled upon enough.[87] If I had lived my life in England in the old days, she told me, I would have been very different. I still believe, however, that at this stage in the advancement of women the best policy for them is not to talk much about the abstract principles of women's rights but to do good work in any job they get, better work if possible than their male colleagues.[88]

As shown in this passage, Gildersleeve's privileged position blinded her to seeing the concrete ways in which the rights of some women in the United States—those who were poor and working-class and of color—were constantly trampled. It also insulated her from the social realities of, and even contact with, people of color. She apparently did not seriously consider the remarks of Bethune, who, during a public speech about the UNCIO, stated that the United States "must do a great deal of house cleaning in her treatment of minority groups here at home."[89] Moreover, Gildersleeve acknowledged that she was disconnected from other women's movements when she said that women from the "backward countries" had no rights whatsoever—women in the presumably backward countries of Brazil, Uruguay, and the Dominican Republic already had, for example, the right to vote.

Once it was determined that the Uruguay amendment had received more endorsements for inclusion than the other proposals, the debate about whether such an amendment was necessary ensued. Uruguay argued that it "would recognize the contributions of women to peace, and that the historical evolution of women's rights clearly proved the great value attached to inscribing the principle of equality of treatment for women in laws and other public documents."[90] Those who were opposed claimed, first, that the amendment could encourage international interference in domestic affairs (the US delegation asserted at every opportunity during the conference proceedings that the UN must not interfere at the domestic level). Second, those who were opposed maintained that the amendment was unnecessary, since the UN Charter implicitly advocated nondiscrimination. This argument was not persuasive, since human rights were not even mentioned in the Dumbarton Oaks proposals. Further, because of the pressure from NGOs, human rights had become an issue at the UNCIO. Eventually delegates from Australia, Brazil, Belgium, Canada, the Netherlands, Norway, the United States, and Uruguay formed a subcommittee to draft the official language for a new paragraph. The adopted paragraph, which appears as an article in the UN Charter, reads as follows: "The Organization shall place no restrictions on the representation and participation of men and women on an equal basis in its principal organs and subsidiary organs."[91]

Shortly after participating government delegates signed the UN Charter, the Brazilian delegation continued its feminist agenda by submitting a declaration on June 7, 1945, that urged the creation of a commission to study the political, civil, and economic status of women and the limited opportunities available to women, with a particular focus on sex-based discrimination. Brazilian delegate Lutz, one of the four women who signed the UN Charter, sought a "radical" transformation of the status of women. She pointed out that the commission was urgent because "nowhere in the world do women have complete equality with men."[92] Lutz also pointed out that it was in the "aggressor nations" of Japan, Italy, and Germany that "the rights of women were particularly limited"; perhaps she sensed that singling out these nations would pique the interest of other delegations invested in opposing the Axis powers.

One of the bolder aspects of the Brazilian declaration was that only women would staff the commission.[93] Bernardino of the Dominican Republic, another women who signed the UN Charter, endorsed Lutz's remarks by mentioning that the Inter-American Commission of Women (of which Bernardino was the president) "had been working along the lines called for in the Brazilian declaration."[94] The Mexican delegate also offered support for the Brazilian declaration and suggested an amendment (which Brazil accepted) about how any future commissions on women should cooperate with other official commissions throughout the world.

Gildersleeve and Wu of China (another of the four women signatories) disagreed with Lutz and Bernardino. Gildersleeve's opposition was partly related to her own efforts to form a commission on human rights; her statements suggest that she thought her commission would make a separate women's commission unnecessary.[95] She argued that the human rights commission "would be effective in bringing about the eventual disappearance of such [sex-based] disadvantage." She further stated that the position of US women "was well established and equal opportunities for women had often been demonstrated in action."[96] Gildersleeve did not acknowledge the structural, institutional, and individual barriers that women of different racial and class backgrounds experienced in the United States. Wu was not as opposed to the Brazilian declaration as Gildersleeve; she preferred the creation of a "special committee" to study the status of women. A special committee, however, would not be as visible or as permanent as a commission, and, because of its temporality, would not have the same access to resources.[97]

Far more delegations were in support of the Brazilian declaration than against it. In fact, thirty-three national delegations supported Lutz's efforts—well over the majority. Although the women's commission was not approved at the UNCIO, it did become a reality in June 1946, when the UN established the Commission on the Status of Women. The mandate of the Commission on the Status of Women, which reports to the Economic and Social Council (ECOSOC), reflects the tenets of the Brazilian declaration insofar as it focuses on promoting "women's rights in the political, economic, civil, social and educational fields."[98]

UNCIO debates about the role of women should be situated alongside the occasion of UWC, which offers another lens for viewing power as it relates to the potential role of women at the UN. Here the discussion about women's involvement at the UN ranged from the boldly feminist to the outright benign. However, the complete exclusion of African American women as speakers and panelists at UWC points to the dominant racial and class hierarchies of the conference's organizing committee, and within the (US) women's movement as well. Only by reading power backward and forward can we identify how hierarchical power dynamics may in fact be reified and replicated as they exist in dominant spaces.

The United Women's Conference

The topics discussed at the United Women's Conference ranged from education, foreign policy, and postwar rebuilding efforts to issues of human rights and women's role in peacekeeping efforts. The speakers were prominent women with a range of affiliations, including the American Association of University Women (AAUW) and Mills College (a private women's college in Oakland, California), as well as consultants, advisors, and delegates of the UNCIO. The women who spoke at the UWC, including those from Latin America, were formally educated, privileged, and racialized as white women. The organizational sponsors for the UWC were from US women's groups such as the San Francisco Girl Scout Council, the AAUW, the National Council of Catholic Women, and the National Council on Negro Women. Aurelia Reinhardt, president emeritus of Mills College, singled out the National General Federation of Women's Clubs (GFWC) at the UWC as "the most inclusive one representing womanhood of our United States."[99] At the time, the GFWC and the AAUW were largely segregated organizations.[100] A tacit acceptance of the exclusion of women of color in the GFWC and at the conference was evident when Reinhardt commented, "Most of you women belong to my organization."[101] This statement is a stark reminder of who participated in the UWC: predominately US women who were privileged and white. Bethune's absence here was particularly striking, given that her organization sponsored the conference, and that she was an official consultant to the US delegation and the only black woman representative at the UNCIO.

Similar to the UNCIO's opening, the UWC opened with "A Woman's Prayer," which was repeated again later during the day. Besides setting a Christian overtone for the conference, the text of the prayer reinforces acceptable societal concerns for women: domesticity, home, children, and friendship. The prayer went as follows:

> I, a woman, do pledge myself before my God to share with all women in implementing peace.
>
> I shall not allow terror and greed, cruelty and oppression to invade my domestic tranquility.
>
> I shall encircle my hearth and my home with a warmth of human affection.

I shall strive to give my children and my children's children a world that is secure and free.

I shall teach them to love and lend aid to their fellow men as I shall do.

And, above all, I shall clasp the hand of my neighbor from sea to sea in lasting friendship.[102]

The religiously inspired verse, by Carol Norton, vice chair of the executive committee and a member of the AAUW, assumes a common connection among all women. It does not acknowledge racial, ethnic, geographical, religious, secular, or other divisions. In short, these acceptable societal concerns reflected the different realities among women in terms of race and gender. Consequently, the prayer implicitly acknowledged that national security, militarism, and foreign policy—all emphasized and discussed extensively at the UNCIO—remained male domains.

The incorporation of the prayer assumed, moreover, that all of the women participating were Christian. Mignolo notes that for Christians, religion is "the ultimate point of reference of civility and the correct life," meaning "the idea and the category of man" is based on the imaginary of a Christian life.[103] This privileging of Christianity at the UWC as well as at the UNCIO contributed to the volatility surrounding the issue of trusteeship, because anything that fell outside the rubric of Christian values, morals, and beliefs was viewed as suspect, inadequate, and, in some respects, dangerous to Christianity.

The opening prayer's emphasis on motherhood and nurturing suggests that a woman who deviated from these values would be deemed less of a woman or even a non-woman. In this scenario, womanhood can be lost or, in fact, never achieved, if norms stray away from those of white Christians. Moreover, the reference to "domestic tranquility" presumes that those reciting the prayer are not under threat. In other words, the audience for this prayer did not include women being racially persecuted.

Following the opening prayer, Reinhardt opened the day's proceedings by contending that the women gathered at the conference had come "less as feminists than as humanists."[104] In referring to the "intelligent meeting of the responsibilities and privileges that come because of womanhood," she suggested that being a woman entails unique responsibilities and privileges. Reinhardt, a longtime social advocate for women's education, was as concerned with women obtaining an education as she was with women meeting gendered expectations in the home.[105]

Josephine Schain, the chair for international relations for the National Federation of Business and Professional Women's Clubs, discussed food in terms of consumption, production, and distribution. She stressed the interdependent nature of the world and how the United States had a stake in ensuring that the global living standard is elevated. She noted that to prevent war, people's basic needs for food must be met, and that the United States "can help those people on to their feet."[106] Schain was alluding, of course, to how the politics of food is intertwined with the politics of commerce: "We are going to have to have an interest in the people who are going to buy our foods, who are going to keep our factories open, who are going to give these jobs to sixty million men." For Schain, women's share in implementing peace was related to how the free market could provide jobs for "sixty million men."[107] In making this assertion, Schain linked capitalism to masculinity, and, thus, masculinity to the coloniality of power.

Vera Michelis Dean, of the Foreign Policy Association, offered her analysis of women's contributions to the UN. Dean, whose speech also stressed nations' reliance on one another, referenced World War II and stated that "no nation, no matter how rich and powerful . . . has been able to win this war alone." Consequently, no one can "win the peace alone" either. With a tone that was markedly different from that of the preceding speakers, she cautioned against "developing a policy I would call one of 'security imperialism.' In this the United States is not alone. Every nation is now talking in terms of its own security."[108]

Dean's remarks also conveyed a concern, even a fear, that indigenous peoples and communities of color in the United States would use the UN to advance their liberatory causes. In her analysis of women's contributions to the UN, Dean associated "the Indian problem" (referring to the Iroquois Nation) with "international evil": "It is really sad to find how many people say, 'Well, what is the solution to the German problem? What is the solution of the Indian problem?,' as if all you had to do was write out a prescription and then bring it to the neighborhood drugstore and you will have a panacea for all international evils!"[109] Dean cautioned the audience not to expect too much from the formation of the UN, but at the same time was critical of the conduct of the United States at the

UNCIO, where US delegates treated compromise as "a capital sin in international affairs." Dean closed her speech by urging the audience to become invested in foreign policy, and she lauded the fact that public opinion in the United States had "urged our government to introduce the question of trusteeships into the discussion of the Charter."[110]

Helen Dwight Reid, chair for international relations at the AAUW, discussed how integrating civil society groups into the newly formed UN was a "unique experiment of direct representation."[111] Reid focused her comments primarily on the creation of the ECOSOC, and was the first speaker to acknowledge the forty-two US civil society organizations whose members served as consultants to the official government delegation.

When Gildersleeve spoke, she did not stray from her personal belief in hard work and the need to educate women that she had promoted as dean of Barnard College. She opened her talk by distancing herself from earlier feminist assertions about women's unique role in peacemaking efforts, stating, "I do not, however, agree with those who talk as if there were some magic, abstract formula which we could find that would enable us all, just because we are women, to bring about and to maintain and to improve the peace of the world." She reiterated this theme in her closing comments:

> I think women can help greatly to implement the peace and improve the future state of the world, but not just by sitting still and being women and loving peace. I think they have got to translate those ideas into practical, wise, trained, competent action. That is what I am trying to do here at the San Francisco Conference. I am not specifically a woman. I am a delegate. I serve my sex I think best and I serve my country best that I am representing by trying to be a good delegate and do my job as competently as possible; if I can, as competently as my colleagues on the United States delegation do.[112]

Gildersleeve's closing remarks reflect a perspective different from that of her memoir, in which she was critical of the behavior of her colleagues on the US delegation, especially of their disrespectful treatment of the government delegations from smaller nations, and she suggested that this behavior reflected a willful ignorance of international affairs.[113]

The afternoon and evening sessions featured speeches by Bertha Lutz and Minerva Bernardino. Both speeches strongly supported women (particularly when compared to those of the earlier speakers) and promoted Latin America as a region of progress and social change. They highlighted how their delegations from Brazil and the Dominican Republic, respectively, had promoted the cause of women at the UNCIO. Since throughout the UWC there had been repeated discursive distancing from identifying as feminists and from women's movements, these two speeches had a decidedly different tone and content from those of their contemporaries.

Lutz, who spoke after Gildersleeve, did not tiptoe around her experiences with sexism at the UNCIO. Offering what she called an impromptu speech, Lutz defined the "main difficulties in this Conference" as stemming from discrimination and bigotry. Noting the lengthy workdays at the UNCIO and her having to be mindful of her position as a woman in a room full of men, she stated, "It seems to me that the main difficulties in this Conference as elsewhere are some of those things that are fundamental in human nature: its interests, its prejudices, the conflict of interests, and the conflict of prejudices. And then there is, at the same time, a higher plane. There is a desire to surmount these prejudices and to rise above the interests and to come to a common accord."[114] Maintaining that she did not want to elaborate on how people overcome their prejudices, Lutz noted that those prejudices could lead to discrimination that would severely limit "opportunities given to women in [an] international organization and with the way in which [the] international organization is going to affect women."[115]

Lutz also expressed frustration with the men at the UNCIO. Though she commented on their amicability, she stressed that they "are really not a bit convinced that it is necessary to have women in an international organization, and most of them would much rather the women were out of it or, if they are in it, that they would keep quiet and let the men do the organizing entirely themselves." And, in a clear rebuke of Gildersleeve's earlier remarks, she stated, "I take the stand that when there are only eight women in a conference of eight hundred men, there is no reason why some of them should not be women delegates."[116]

Lutz described how the Latin American delegates, with the support of the Australian delegation, had worked together in the interest of women by proposing amendments to the UN Charter that would give women "a legal footing in the international organization." Without mentioning Gildersleeve by name, Lutz declared that US women needed to support the efforts of the Latin American delegations.[117] Lutz likely recognized that alienating Gildersleeve entirely would provide no strategic benefit, as Gildersleeve was the most powerful woman at the UWC and, as a result, at the UNCIO.

Bernardino expanded on Lutz's points regarding the persistent support of Latin American delegations in advancing efforts regarding women. In her short speech she recognized the seven Latin American countries that had already secured women's right to vote: Ecuador, Brazil, Uruguay, Cuba, the Dominican Republic, Guatemala, and Panama.[118] The content of her speech aligned with the tenets of her organization, the Inter-American Commission of Women, which focused almost exclusively on education and suffrage.

The women who organized and spoke at the UWC—including the women delegates to the UNCIO—were engaged in a type of feminist intervention. These women made history by creating a space that was an alternative to the nearly exclusively male domain of the UNCIO. The participants entertained ideas that sometimes transcended, but often reinforced, subjects that were considered appropriate for women. Yet, although the UWC covered issues pertaining to education, political rights, economics, foreign policy, and human rights, the conference documents reveal little in the way of active engagement with matters of racial injustice.[119] The participants—including Lutz and Bernardino, as well as Gildersleeve, to an extent—were primarily advocating for the rights of women who already enjoyed positions of privilege when compared to the majority of women of color in the United States and throughout the world.

The women of the UWC had access to a level of capital that gave them elevated status in the realms of education and politics. They were not only highly educated but also had the benefits of white privilege. Even if they had been aware that women were treated unequally, they did not consider this inequality in relationship to race or ethnicity. Rather they reference some type of common patriarchy. Reading power backward and forward reveals then that power did not reside solely with men and that, in fact, it shifted, depending on context and social location. In the nearly exclusively female space of the UWC, the women delegates to the UNCIO were admired and exalted, but these same women experienced an entirely different reception at the UNCIO. Whether consciously or not, the organizers of the UWC created racial, gender, and class hierarchies that were similar to those found at the UNCIO.

Most of the women at the UWC had a connection or commitment to women's education. Having advanced degrees meant that even if these women did not know each other personally, they knew or understood each other socially. Because they occupied the same social circles and had the same status, many expressed great affection for one another. Their shared status likely insulated them from becoming politicized with respect to the issues of women who were not part of their circle. Due to the homogeneity of the UWC audience, discussions of difference were limited, particularly in terms of race. This omission is striking given the time at which these conversations were taking place. Even representatives from Latin America failed to account for the experiences of race and racism, missing an opportunity to advance an inclusive feminist agenda. Bernardino, for instance, due to her service in the regime of dictator Rafael Trujillo, would have been well aware that her country's government openly supported a philosophy and discourse of *antihaitianismo*—in which any open acknowledgement or affirmation of African ancestry was brutally erased.[120] Trujillo ordered the massacre of thousands of Haitians in 1937 and had encouraged settlements to increase the number of whites in the 1940s.[121]

Reading power backward and forward reminds us of the importance of examining who was represented at the UWC, who spoke, and the content of their speeches. None of the speakers addressed racism or racial injustice in any direct way, and most kept the discussion about women's equality in terms of public life, such as holding public leadership positions. Even though the UWC disrupted business as usual in some regards by creating a gendered space for women to discuss international politics, the conference also reified racial and ethnic divisions.

This critique of the colonialist impulses of the white feminist elite at the UNCIO and at UWC is not meant to be dismissive of the efforts made by these women; rather, it helps situate these early interventions in the complicated trajectory of feminist human rights activism. Women's activism at the UN has never been without tensions, as the historical records assessed here attest. The UNCIO and the UWC each offered a setting for the display of feminist power on the international stage, but their outcomes were different. The addition of critical "gender equality" language in the UN Charter is a victory that should be attributed to the work of Latin American delegates such as Lutz and Bernardino. But, like the 2001 WCAR (which US mainstream white feminists did not support), the UWC was a missed opportunity for feminists. Bethune's attempts to acknowledge the human rights of colonized peoples or of other people of color did not receive any serious consideration at UWC.

CONCLUSION: UNDERSTANDING THE UN AS A GENDERED AND RACIALIZED INSTITUTION

The contentious debates that arose during the UNCIO over the structure of the Security Council, the formation of the Trusteeship Council, and the role of women in the UN offer an understanding of the UN as a gendered and racialized institution. Viewing the UN in this context, where masculinity and coloniality can be considered hegemonic components of its institutional structure, is only part of the story, however. The content of the three debates shows that the formation of the UN also involved concerted efforts to resist displays of power that evolved into a struggle over representation, power, and voice. At the heart of this struggle were the dynamics of gender and the dynamics of race.[122]

The dynamics of gender (as well as race) influenced heated debates during the UNCIO over power and transparency within the UN, and even contributed to geopolitical tensions between the conference's four sponsoring governments—the United States, the United Kingdom, China, and the Soviet Union—and other participating governments. Men negotiated primarily with other men, and the women who served as delegates and advisors were placed on committees to negotiate the traditionally feminized topics of education, human welfare, and even human rights. Women had no entry into the masculine territories of national security or militarism. Even the UWC did little to promote the substantive interests of women within the UN, particularly within areas perceived to be masculine.

The dynamics of race (and gender) at the UNCIO became apparent in the alliances formed by participating governments to debate the issues of the veto and trusteeship. Here race became intertwined with the regional interests and national security concerns of the "darker nations."[123] When some of the government delegates from Latin America worked together to raise grave concerns about the veto, they formed an important political bloc and presented a unified regional strategy based on their status as smaller nations (in terms of size and market economics). They claimed the moral high ground, making integrity a point of comparison to the problematic behavior of other governments. The great powers asserted their role in terms of paternalistic responsibility. Nevertheless, their objective, expressed through an explicit affirmation of the coloniality of power, was economic control via resource extraction and military control.

The racial and patriarchal logics that undergird the coloniality of power were employed during the formation of the UN in an attempt to silence the voices of the less powerful, making Mignolo's question— "Who speaks for the 'human' in human rights?"[124]—all the more urgent to consider. This question reflects the central concern of UNCIO representatives from Latin America and the Pacific region. At what point do colonized peoples, people of color, and women have an opportunity to speak for themselves, or to even speak at all? At what point do they have the opportunity to contribute to the decolonization of human rights? At the UNCIO, those occupying the highest levels of power felt entitled to do the speaking for everyone about everything. Many of those left out of the conversations in Dumbarton Oaks and Yalta actively resisted, however, constantly challenging the status quo imposed by the great powers. This counterpublic of new citizen-subjects attempted to dismantle the coloniality of power and shape what the UN would be, or could be. The shared oppositional space was a site of conflict but also became a site of hope for colonized peoples, people of color, and women as well.

An intersecting counterpublic also emerged at the UWC. It opposed the patriarchal notion that only men have something to say about multilateralism, yet its formation was also problematic because it reproduced, and even celebrated, barriers based on race, class, and gender among women. The UWC is an example of how counterpublics should not be viewed as idealized oppositional spaces. They can, in fact, reproduce the power dynamics that result in the continued marginalization of certain communities.

A reading of power backward and forward is essential to thoroughly understand the complex nature of the tensions that arose at the UNCIO.

The great powers felt so threatened by the resistance exerted by other governments that they proposed foregoing the establishment of the UN entirely if these delegates continued to press for modifications to the structure of the Security Council. In comparison, the Latin American regional bloc successfully pushed to incorporate language that established women's representation in and access to all arenas of the UN. Further, the debates about trusteeship allowed links between racism against African Americans and colonized peoples throughout the world to become apparent.

The nuanced view of power presented here exposes the flaws and contradictions that weaken the UN, even to this day, but it also reveals why the UN continues to be an important institution for constituencies worldwide, despite the problems of representation that have troubled the institution since its founding. Member States with little economic power and activists and representatives of accredited NGOs use the UN's conferences and forums to air their grievances and to advocate for the human rights of all global citizens. An analysis of the UNCIO gathering in 1945 underscores that even entities with little economic or military power are by no means powerless.

2

UN Citizenship and Constellations
of Human Rights

> It is precisely in the field of human rights that Western culture must
> learn from the South if the false universality that is attributed to
> human rights in the imperial context is to be converted into the new
> universality of cosmopolitanism in a cross-cultural dialogue.
>
> —BOAVENTURA DE SOUSA SANTOS,
> "TOWARD A MULTICULTURAL CONCEPTION
> OF HUMAN RIGHTS," 2002

THE UNITED NATIONS HAS GROWN SUBSTANTIALLY SINCE 1945.
The current number of Member States stands at 193, a considerable increase from the original 51.[1] In addition, other constituencies now claim
a space in the UN, specifically NGOs that advocate for a wide range of social, economic, political, and other issues. The ability of an NGO to navigate within the UN can vary, and this in turn shapes its power to be heard
and to influence policies and political actions. Human rights is just one of
the many dimensions of the UN's work and is arguably a minor endeavor
at the UN when compared to its other work. Feminist activists who advocate for human rights—a set of principles and values that establish standards for human dignity—as a discourse, model, or metaphor in their
justice-based organizing efforts are of particular interest here.[2]

Once governments and NGOs become UN members, they are entitled
to certain rights. Nation-states must be recommended by the UN Security Council and approved by the UN General Assembly (GA). Those entities admitted as members are eligible to serve on various councils and

commissions, to present prospective resolutions on the floor of the GA, to negotiate and lobby with other government representatives, and to nominate prospective candidates for various positions as UN officials. To become members of the UN, NGOs must complete a lengthy accreditation process.[3] The rights associated with UN accreditation include eligibility to observe UN proceedings (such as treaty review hearings by CEDAW and CERD) and to lobby government delegates during world conferences.[4] In both cases, members gain a type of citizenship, which I refer to here as "UN citizenship," that affords them access to the relationships and power structures that govern inclusion and exclusion at the UN.

As citizenship scholars so aptly remind us, obtaining citizenship in no way guarantees the ability to practice those rights or even to have equal access to them.[5] Access to economic, social, or cultural capital not only influences which entities become members but also shapes a member's ability to realize the rights and benefits of UN citizenship. Governments and NGOs with superior economic capital have historically played a disproportionately dominant role within the UN. Despite the prevailing importance of economic capital, some Member States (including those excluded from the Dumbarton Oaks and Yalta deliberations) and some NGOs have used their social and cultural capital to invoke their UN citizenship rights to advance their interests. Some groups disadvantaged in terms of economic capital have formed counterpublics, alternative and oppositional spaces contrary to the interests of more powerful world governments such as Canada, the United States, and France; as part of these counterpublics, some groups have managed to challenge and even shape some of the UN's agendas in certain circumstances.[6] For example, at the Durban conference, some NGOs, along with supportive government delegations from Africa, forced a discussion about classifying the transatlantic slave trade as a "crime against humanity." The United States and its allies were vehemently against this categorization because it could augment calls for reparations; they tried desperately to stop it, but were unsuccessful.[7]

Each constituency working at the UN level engages with human rights differently. Here, multiple understandings of human rights come together in spaces that I call "constellations." In each constellation different but related strands of thought intermingle, and no one strand is superior to another. There are three constellations of human rights at the UN reflected in this research: dominant understandings, which are related to the Western-influenced legal apparatus of laws, treaties, and courts; counterpublic approaches, which embrace transnational feminist concepts of antiracist epistemology and relationality; and social praxis, which corresponds to a negotiation between the first two constellations about how people on the ground practice and negotiate human rights in their advocacy efforts and daily life.[8] I believe there are other constellations of human rights operating within and outside of the UN beyond the three presented in this chapter; however, these three are the ones most evident in this research.

The dominant understandings contained in the first constellation rely on a universal human nature that is reflected in "the specific experiences, needs, and values of affluent white Western men."[9] This constellation represents the prevailing discourse on human rights at the UN. The counterpublic approaches of the second constellation reflect alternative feminist and antiracist epistemologies of human rights that form an ontology that is relational, in contrast to the absolutist positions associated with the dominant discourse. The struggle between these two constellations is waged within the political fora and social institutions, including the UN.[10] The third constellation assesses what cultural anthropologists Shannon Speed and Jane Collier refer to as the "social life of rights" and offers a richer picture of the human rights landscape. An examination of these three constellations reveals the changing nature of political and social engagement with the concept of human rights, and indicates that the meaning of what human rights could, or should, become relies on sociopolitical interests.[11] More importantly, the social praxis constellation is where the positioning of human rights has been particularly creative, productive, and dynamic.

UN CITIZENSHIP AND THE AGENDA AGAINST RACISM

Two central components form the basis of UN citizenship. The first concerns membership: the UN grants membership rights and the UN member, in turn, agrees to be a "good citizen" by fulfilling certain responsibilities. For example, Member States pay dues, and NGOs affiliated with the UN submit periodic reports documenting how they benefit the institution. The second component is more compelling, yet less researched: it concerns how governments and NGOs *practice* their UN citizenship. Hence, UN citizenship constitutes a social practice.[12]

The rights associated with UN citizenship encompass "a hybrid set of relationships" that are nurtured by social interaction. Interactions between and among similarly positioned UN citizens—such as among members of the UN Security Council with veto power—can be considered horizontal relationships. In contrast, relationships between powerful UN councils, such as those between the Security Council and the GA, can be considered vertical because nations on the Security Council have far greater power than other Member States in the GA,[13] reflecting the dichotomy of inclusion and exclusion that defines UN citizenship. Similar vertical and horizontal relationships shape interactions between and among accredited NGOs working inside the UN because a hierarchy of power can also exist with these organizations.

All of the vertical relationships at the UN are highly political and can be extremely contentious, particularly when related to the process of selecting representatives to serve on various UN councils. During the spring of 2001, for example, for the first time in the UN's history the United States did not receive enough votes to retain a seat on the UN Commission on Human Rights.[14] The three seats allotted to nations comprising the Western European and Others Group (WEOG)—to which the United States belongs—were given to the governments of France, Austria, and Sweden. The US government was furious, and the US media repeatedly pointed out that Sudan had representation on the commission, implying that Sudan had taken the United States' spot, when in fact it was Sweden that had replaced the United States.[15] There is also a vertical relationship between the Economic and Social Council (ECOSOC) and NGOs that is a result of the lengthy NGO accreditation process. NGOs must overcome a number of institutional obstacles to acquire UN accreditation, which structurally disadvantages, limits, and regulates the role of nongovernmental actors.

The horizontal and vertical relationships that are associated with UN citizenship are best understood by situating them in relation to capital. Pierre Bourdieu has argued that capital, which is unevenly distributed and accumulated, shapes the "structure and functioning of the social world."[16] Ultimately, the power of a UN member, whether a Member State or an NGO, is defined by its access to capital, and it is that power that can facilitate the advancement of human rights ideologies and discourses.[17]

For Member States, economic capital can foster political gain because governments can afford to send their representatives to engage in negotiations at UN headquarters in Geneva or New York City to protect their interests. In contrast, governments with less economic capital have to be selective and choose which UN meetings to attend; as a result, their participation in negotiations or other policy matters can be severely limited. In the case of the 2001 World Conference against Racism (WCAR), an unprecedented third Preparatory Committee (planning meetings that precede world conferences, known as PrepComs) occurred just a few weeks prior to the Durban conference. Attendance by Third World governments, especially those of Africa and Latin America, was low for this essential meeting. Consequently, during deliberations over the content of the Durban Declaration and Programme of Action (DDPA) (the official conference documents), the participating government delegates approved language that limited the rights of indigenous peoples. As political analyst Walden Bello notes, when the economically powerful nations are left in charge, "you're really going to have solutions that are very narrow" and ones that protect their political interests, which include curtailing progress made in some areas.[18]

Economic capital plays an important role in determining whether NGOs are able to acquire and retain UN accreditation. For established NGOs in particular, economic capital facilitates participation in UN proceedings in ways that are not entirely dissimilar to those experienced by economically secure Member States. The multimillion-dollar budget of an organization such as Amnesty International, which has offices throughout the world, is significantly larger than the budgets of the considerably smaller regional organizations with only a handful of staff (if any). Amnesty International can afford to send its representatives to lobby at UN meetings in Geneva or New York City if needed, and as a result, is able to build key relationships with UN members that can help advance its agendas.[19] Moreover, Amnesty International's very name carries a level of authority and visibility that an unknown NGO cannot match. Such authority and visibility is an example of what feminist sociologist Millie Thayer refers to as an "intangible political resource."[20]

Social capital refers to the potential benefits derived from existing social networks and relationships, whereas cultural capital refers to the intimate understandings of how an institution or structure works. An organizational representative relies on social and cultural capital for lobbying and advocacy purposes. For NGOs, social and cultural capital determines how successful their lobbying efforts at the UN will be.[21] When NGO representatives develop relationships with the right UN diplomats, government delegates, and NGO networks, their social and cultural capital increases. For example, during the US government's 2009 review hearing for the CERD treaty in Geneva (which I discuss in more detail below), I noticed staff from Human Rights Watch having drinks and sharing casual conversation with members of CERD at a local hotel bar. When I discussed the incident later with another NGO representative who had also seen this interaction, she said, "I think it is difficult, because you can't expect organizations not to use the advantages and relationships that they already have . . . that's ridiculous. But it's just not the same access."[22]

An NGO's lack of access, or social capital, also limits its cultural capital. NGO advocates familiar with UN procedures and protocols can increase their cultural capital because they understand how the system works and what it values. Small or newly formed NGOs often lack the cultural capital needed to make an impact. Ultimately, the cultural capital valued at the UN derives from privilege: advanced and prestigious educations, English fluency, foreign service careers and diplomatic training, certain upper-middle-class life experiences, and opportunities abroad.[23] This biographical background produces an "ideal type" of UN diplomat and NGO representative who can understand and feel comfortable with those who share the same profile.[24]

Although the possession of a great deal of economic capital is usually equated with great power, it may in fact not always be enough to prevail in the contests that play out at the UN. During the lead-up to the 2003 US-led invasion of Iraq, the US government, which is recognized as the most economically powerful member of the UN, was unable to use its considerable economic capital to convince the Security Council—in particular, France, which has veto power—to support its proposed resolution to send in military troops. The United States' consequent decision to illegally invade Iraq turned the world against it. Less than eighteen months after the 9/11 attacks, the US government had managed to politically isolate itself, especially once it became clear that Iraq did not have weapons of mass destruction, as former Secretary of State Colin Powell had so vehemently claimed at the UN. Thus effective diplomatic engagement with other Member States involves more than economic power, even at the Security Council level. It requires fostering social and cultural capital as well.

The cultivation of social and cultural capital takes a great deal of time and investment, both economically and politically. These efforts can lead to what UN expert Sally Morphet refers to as "patterns of cooperation" among Third World or global South countries at the UN. These patterns are "often overlooked or dismissed by states from the First World as of little consequence."[25] It is these relationships, however, that have been instrumental in advancing an antiracist agenda at the UN that is diametrically opposed to the interests of the economically powerful.

In considering the content and tone of a number of resolutions adopted by the GA from the 1970s through the 1990s, one can see the "patterns of cooperation" that emanated from the Third World. Resolutions are nonbinding recommendations that express the opinions of the GA; thus they constitute a reflection of the political interests of the Member States that have achieved access to the UN and are a matter of the global record. The resolution titles that contain words such as "racial discrimination," "apartheid," "imperialism," "colonialism," and "racism," and the resolutions that explicitly contain language in their text referencing racism, are the ones selected here to reconstruct the UN's "Third World" agenda against racism.

The primary foci of the 1970s resolutions that can be considered part of the UN's agenda against racism include doctrines of racial superiority, racist propaganda, and the displacement of African people by white settlers.[26] The GA has long maintained that, as an institution, the UN "has a special responsibility to oppressed peoples and their liberation movements" from South Africa, Namibia, Zimbabwe, and Palestine,[27] places that are physically distant from the West and the global North. As a result of foreign policies and military interventions, however, the West and the global North were politically invested in and connected to tensions in the African and Middle Eastern regions, and often exacerbated racial and ethnic conflicts there. The themes of these 1970s resolutions range from endorsing the independence of former colonies and peoples to condemning apartheid in southern Africa and supporting liberation fighters and movements. Many of these resolutions emphasize the right to self-determination and repeatedly condemn, in quite forceful language, the military, economic, and political involvement of foreign governments that have contributed to apartheid, segregation, and land displacement.[28]

The most controversial resolution adopted by the GA in the 1970s was Resolution 3379 (1975), which equated Zionism with racism. Governments from the Middle East, South Asia, and northern Africa sponsored the controversial resolution, also known as the "Zionism = racism" resolution. In total, seventy-two governments (none of which was from the West or the global North) voted in favor of the resolution; thirty-six voted against the resolution; and thirty-two cast abstention votes. The GA had linked South African apartheid to Zionism as early as 1973 with Resolution 3151, which dealt with "policies of apartheid of the Government of South Africa." This resolution had forcefully condemned the apartheid-Zionist relationship by referring to it as "the unholy alliance between Portuguese colonialism, South African racism, zionism, and Israeli imperialism," and it chastised Portugal, South Africa, and Israel for offering one another "political, military and financial aid" to sustain this relationship.[29] The resolution states that the GA was left with no option but to "*determin[e]* that zionism is a form of racism and racial discrimination." This resolution had haunted the 1978 world conference on racism, which the United States and Israel boycotted.[30] In 1991 the GA overturned Resolution 3379, but the "Zionism = racism" topic returned with a vengeance at the 2001 WCAR.[31]

In the 1980s the GA continued to approve a series of resolutions against colonialism, apartheid, and foreign support of apartheid states. The GA's endorsement of liberation movements resulted in the adoption of resolutions supporting freedom fighters against colonialism, such as GA Resolutions 37/1 (1982) and 37/68 (1982), and validating the legitimacy of their armed struggle against oppression. Additional resolutions adopted by the GA during this decade dealt with granting observer status to leaders of national liberation movements (37/104 in 1982; 39/76 in 1984), opposing the creation of a new racial constitution for South Africa (38/11 in 1983), the torture of children from South Africa and Namibia (42/124 in 1987; 43/134 in 1988), and the setback experienced by the UN subcommission on minorities due to a lack of funds in the mid-1980s (41/143 in 1986). New subjects covered in GA resolutions from the 1980s included condemnation of the death sentences of antiapartheid leaders and freedom fighters, and support for the Palestinian Intifada.

The 1980s resolutions against apartheid in South Africa, and southern Africa in general, are numerous, and they are stark reminders of the gravity of the situation for the black majority population there. The GA adopted positions against the death sentences imposed on South African freedom fighters and the torture of black South African children. GA appeals for clemency warned the South African government "the continued repression against and executions of opponents of *apartheid* are bound to have grave repercussions."[32] The GA resolutions on the torture of children in South Africa contained strong diplomatic language, such as "appalled," "outraged," "vigorously condemns," and "strongly condemns," with concerns ranging from the forced recruitment of children with the aim of turning them against their country to the existence of "rehabilitation camps" that "serve the racist regime's strategy of physically and mentally abusing black South African children."[33]

Other GA resolutions dealt with proposed structural changes in South Africa. In Resolution 38/11 (1983), for example, the GA fiercely opposed proposals for a new constitution that would "deprive the indigenous African majority of all fundamental rights, including the right to citizenship, and to transform South Africa into a country for 'whites only,' in keeping with the declared policies of *apartheid*." The GA, noting "the enforcement of the proposed 'constitution' will inevitably aggravate tension and conflict in South Africa and in southern Africa as a whole," urged the Security Council "to take all necessary measures . . . to avert the further aggravation of tension and conflict in South Africa and in southern Africa as a whole."[34] The Security Council endorsed a series of sanctions against the racist regime during this period. Other GA resolutions regarding South Africa, such as opposition to their application to the International Monetary Fund for credit and the use of mercenaries to sustain apartheid, contained strong and assertive language. The numerous resolutions concerned with South Africa and with imposing sanctions are evidence of the GA's commitment to dismantling apartheid.

The GA adopted resolutions in the 1990s ventured into some new areas. Resolutions on South Africa and Palestine, and on the implementation of a UN declaration in support of former colonies, were prevalent during this decade. The pressure on South Africa eventually became unsustainable, resulting in apartheid's demise. The South African government received an invitation to rejoin the GA in 1994, after having been unseated twenty years earlier. The GA also started to adopt new resolutions that explored the issues of women and literacy, ethnic cleansing and racial hatred, and migrant women. By the late 1990s, GA resolutions began to incorporate language such as "gender mainstreaming," which refers to the systematic integration of a gender analysis into all aspects of the UN's programs, as well as language such as the "gendered dimensions of racial discrimination" in the drafting of its resolutions about women. The GA resolutions continued to use the term "doubly vulnerable" that had appeared in the few resolutions from the 1970s and 1980s that talked about women. For instance, a GA resolution about migrant women (47/96, 1992) situated them as "doubly vulnerable" owing to their migrant status and their gender.[35]

The GA resolutions from the early 1990s that deal with South Africa contain a strong tone of outrage and anger at apartheid's continued existence. After the adoption of the "Declaration on Apartheid and Its Destructive Consequences in Southern Africa" in 1989, which guided the work of the Special Committee Against Apartheid (created in 1963), the GA resolutions on South Africa continued to strongly condemn the treatment of children in South Africa (particularly those who had been detained and severely abused while in detention), and the cooperative relationship between states unwilling to uphold the oil and arms embargoes and other sanctions against the racist regime.[36] The GA specifically aimed its displeasure in this regard at Israel. The GA also denounced the use of mercenaries in sustaining apartheid, and the execution, detentions, and torture of antiapartheid freedom fighters, as it had done in previous decades.

For the multiple GA resolutions titled "Policies of Apartheid of the Government of South Africa," the votes by Member States were often split, specifically with regard to the subsections condemning the political relationship between South Africa and Israel;[37] the affirmative votes, however, were sufficient to retain the disputed sections about apartheid. Following the release of antiapartheid leader Nelson Mandela in February 1990 and the celebratory occasion of the first democratic elections in South Africa in 1994, which resulted in Mandela's presidency, GA resolutions of the mid to late 1990s focused on lifting global sanctions on

South Africa, normalizing relations with the newly elected government, and praising the dismantling of the apartheid system.

Resolutions adopted by the GA from the 1970s through the 1990s detail the UN's commitment to the eradication of racial injustice. They also reveal that the UN considered race and gender to be on parallel, rather than intersecting, paths. The overarching themes of the GA resolutions adopted in the 1970s to address racism dealt with apartheid, colonialism, imperialism (including foreign support of these global problems), occupation, and Zionism. This rather expansive set of issues did not adequately grapple with the question of how any of these issues affected women in particular. Control over women's bodies is an essential element of maintaining colonial domination, but the infliction of violence on women's bodies was never fully considered in the 1970s (or even in the 1980s). GA resolutions from the 1970s tended to emphasize that women were part of the social movement to overcome racism but were not necessarily contributors who could, or should, change the boundaries of the social movement itself.

South African apartheid remained a top concern for the GA in the 1980s, as did the situation in Namibia. The GA, growing increasingly preoccupied with apartheid's resilience and with the South African government's moves to further entrench the system, called upon the Security Council to impose sanctions. Yet the GA resolutions did not address apartheid's horrendous impact on women in any substantive way. The GA completely ignored sexual and gender-based violence during the apartheid era, for instance. This indifference to women's realities was apparent when the GA encouraged the incorporation of racial matters in the UN Decade for Women but not the simultaneous integration of gender in either the First or the Second UN Decade to Combat Racism and Racial Discrimination.

A marked shift occurred in the context of GA resolutions during the 1990s, however, creating an opening to advance an expanded conceptualization of racial discrimination. By the mid-1990s, the end of apartheid in South Africa, the release of Nelson Mandela, and Namibian independence provided an ideal opportunity to broaden the conversation about racism. These monumental events were considered victories for the UN, and they created a context in which the discourse of racism could be revisited. By the 1990s, the GA acknowledged that additional forms of racism existed, an important departure from resolutions adopted in previous decades.

It bears mentioning that the "patterns of cooperation" instrumental in adopting these multiple GA resolutions about racism can be attributed to the formation of the Non-Aligned Movement (NAM). NAM, an international association of states that are not formally aligned with any major power bloc, is another example of the influence that collective pressure can generate. Formed in 1961 in resistance to the political machinations of the Cold War, the association's members currently represent about two-thirds of the UN's Member States. NAM's agenda, as defined at its first summit in Belgrade in August 1961, is "great power disarmament, elimination of colonialism, economic development, the right of all countries to self-determination, UN reform, [elimination of] apartheid, and Palestinian rights."[38] By the 1970s NAM had become the "engine" of activity at the GA, "especially in economic and development planning."[39] Initially composed of nations that were not aligned with "the Western or the Soviet-led military pacts," NAM's membership and strength increased due to the worldwide decolonization movements that began in the 1950s and continued through the 1970s.

As a result of the efforts of NAM countries, the GA endorsed the actions of liberation movements that were attempting to dismantle apartheid by expelling the South African government from its membership in 1974 and granting credentials to the African National Congress (ANC, which was viewed as a terrorist organization by the US government) and the Pan Africanist Congress as the legitimate representatives of the South African people.[40] The GA also granted observer status to other liberation movements, including the Palestinian Liberation Organization and the South West Africa People's Organization (SWAPO). More recently NAM has worked with the Group of 77 (G-77), the largest intergovernmental bloc of nations at the UN, in pursuit of "major foreign policy issues."[41] In 2006 former UN Secretary-General Kofi Annan acknowledged the "outstanding partnership" between NAM and the UN during his ten years as secretary-general: "I could not have done it without your support. What little I have achieved [as UN Secretary-General] is with the support I have received individually or collectively."[42]

Social capital and cultural capital together have played a decisive role in maintaining and shaping the UN agenda to eliminate racism.[43] This agenda is not just about the adoption of radical, or even progressive, positions, though these elements certainly are involved. It is also about end goals and the methods used to promote them. For the most part, the UN agenda against racism has encompassed the primary objectives of anti-apartheid and anticolonialism, which are championed by most nations. This signifies a challenge to the interests of the colonial powers—both former and present-day—whose capital has been derived in large part from the labor of slaves and the exploitation of colonial resources. The actions of these governments have revealed the depth of the systematic racism that they support, and this in turn weakens their social and cultural capital in debates about racism. When it comes to racism, however, the social and cultural capital of Third World governments allows these countries to position themselves as the legitimate voices of authority when it comes to antiracism. If the global North had more control over the positions adopted by the GA when it came to matters of racism in all of its forms, then the language proposed would have been far more benign because its economic and political interests would be at stake. For this reason, many voted against or abstained from voting in support of these GA resolutions about racism.

THE ACCREDITATION PROCESS FOR NGOS

NGOs must have UN accreditation to enter UN headquarters in New York City and Geneva and to participate in or observe UN world conferences and other meetings. ECOSOC determines accreditation, also known as "consultative status," for NGOs. As of September 1, 2011, 3,536 NGOs had consultative status with ECOSOC, a relatively small number in comparison to the number of NGOs that exist globally.[44] In 2007 the figure was 3,050, signaling an increase of nearly 500 accredited NGOs in the span of a few years. Most were from Europe, which was represented by 37 percent of the NGOs (see table 2.01). Although Asia had the greatest regional population, at 60 percent, it was represented by only 16 percent of the NGOs.[45]

ECOSOC manages fourteen specialized agencies, including the United Nations Children's Fund, and fourteen functional and regional commissions. It also issues policy recommendations to Member States.[46] Through ECOSOC, the UN offers impressive direct relief services, which account for more than 70 percent of the UN's human and financial re-

TABLE 2.01   Comparison of Accredited NGOs and Population, by Region, 2007

REGION	ACCREDITED NGOS (PERCENTAGE)	REGIONAL POPULATION* (PERCENTAGE)
Europe	37	11.07
North America	29	5.04
Asia	16	60.39
Africa	11	14.42
Latin America and the Caribbean	6	8.58
Oceania	1	0.51

* Percentages were obtained by dividing the total world population by the regional population.

Source: United Nations, Department of Economic and Social Affairs and United States Census Bureau, International Data Base.

sources.[47] ECOSOC also receives considerable media attention through its celebrity ambassadors such as Angelina Jolie, Nicole Kidman, Shakira, and Orlando Bloom, to name a few.

The NGO accreditation process is deeply political. NGOs, unlike governments, must reapply for accreditation every year, and accreditation can be rescinded. In contrast, once a government is a member of the UN, its "citizenship" cannot be revoked unless the General Assembly votes to do so based on a recommendation from the Security Council.[48] Moreover, unlike governments, NGOs must submit periodic reports on how their respective organizations benefit the UN, a requirement that reinforces the vertical citizenship structure of NGOs in relation to the Member States. The NGO must show that the work it does is of interest to the UN and that it supports, rather than challenges, the UN's mandate. NGOs that are deemed overly critical can be at a disadvantage. Whether they are providing a social service or data and statistics that may be unattainable by UN officials, NGOs are subordinate in the UN power structure and thus are always at risk of losing their accreditation.[49] However, this should not suggest that NGOs automatically lose their accreditation if they retain a level of critique; rather, the threat of losing accreditation is always looming.

Consultative status is divided into three categories: general, special, and roster. Large international NGOs, such as Amnesty International and Human Rights Watch, have general consultative status because their "area of work covers most of the issues on the agenda of ECOSOC and its subsidiary bodies." Special consultative status is usually for smaller NGOs that have a "special competence in, and are concerned specifically with, only a few of the fields of activity covered by the ECOSOC." Lastly, roster consultative status is for NGOs that have a "rather narrow and/or technical focus" and NGOs that have "formal status with other UN bodies or specialized agencies," such as the World Health Organization and the International Labour Organization.[50]

The Department of Economic and Social Affairs (DESA) manages the NGO accreditation process; DESA is part of the Secretariat, one of the principal organs of the UN system. Accreditation involves six steps, as shown in figure 2.01.[51] First an NGO registers online with DESA's NGO branch. Upon approval the NGO Branch requests the organization proceed with the application process. The application requires the completion online of a ten-page questionnaire and the submission of financial and other background information about the NGO in either English or French, though the documents are available in the other official UN languages for reference. English and French are "the UN Secretariat working languages." NGOs must submit their materials by June 1 of the year before the year in which they hope to acquire consultative status. After this date, applications are not considered until June 1 of the following year.[52] After June 1, the NGO Branch begins review of submitted applications to verify their completeness before forwarding them to the Committee on NGOs. The committee then schedules a session to review the NGO's application. Up to two NGO representatives can attend the session. Attendance is not required, but it is recommended. If an NGO's application is delayed or is considered inconclusive, continued review can be postponed until the following year. In cases of delay or postponement, the Committee on NGOs may encourage the NGO to send representatives to the next meeting to clarify outstanding questions and to avoid further delays. These DESA meetings about NGO accreditation occur at UN headquarters in New York City.

The Committee on NGOs, which consists of representatives from nineteen Member States, considers a number of factors. First, the work of the NGO must be deemed relevant to ECOSOC. Second, the NGO must have been officially registered for at least two years, and must have

FIGURE 2.01   The NGO Accreditation Process at the UN

An NGO registers online with DESA's NGO Branch.

|

Once accepted, DESA requests the NGOs continue with application process.

|

The NGO must complete online a ten-page questionnaire and submit
financial and other background information. All materials must be
completed in either English or French.

|

Materials must be submitted by June 1 or review
of applications is postponed until the following year.

|

Approved NGO applications are put on the agenda of the Committee
on NGOs, and the meeting date to review applications is set. The NGO
may send one or two representatives to the session in New York City.

| |

IF RECOMMENDED TO ECOSOC	IF DENIED
Once ECOSOC approves, the NGO receives official notification from the Secretariat about its consultative status.	The Committee on NGOs determines that the NGO's application is inconclusive, which further delays its accreditation until the following year.
The NGO must submit a report every four years on how its work benefits the UN.	NGO Committee may encourage the NGO to send representatives to the following year's review to prevent additional delays. The application goes through the review cycle again.

Source: UN Department of Economic and Social Affairs, NGO Branch.

a "democratic decision making mechanism." Third, most of the organization's funding should be derived from "contributions from national affiliates, individual members, or other non-governmental components."[53] The committee meets semiannually to decide which NGOs to recommend for consultative status. Once an NGO is approved by ECOSOC, the Secretariat sends a notification that specifies whether the NGO has been granted general, special, or roster status. In return, NGOs that receive general or special status agree to submit a report every four years on how their activities benefit the UN.[54]

Several steps of this NGO accreditation process correspond directly to the issue of capital. The organization must have Internet access to even be considered, and the application packet must be submitted in either English or French; this requirement affects a large number of NGOs from Latin America and Asia, as well as parts of Eastern Europe, the Middle East, northern Africa, and the Pacific Islands. Requirements regarding minimum existence and the decision-making process, privilege forms of organizational structure similar to a hierarchical global North model. Activists that operate as a collective—as organizations without an official president or as a group that functions without a formal structure created by bylaws, for instance—are not eligible for accreditation. In short, organizations, groups, or communities that operate in a manner unfamiliar to the global North model need not apply. Independent activists are also ineligible for accreditation; they must secure an affiliation with a formally accredited NGO to gain access to the UN.

The review process can be delayed if a representative of the organization is not present during the hearing in New York City, because a question or problem could arise with the application. Although a representative is not required to be present at the first review, the fact that such a presence is beneficial indicates that enormous economic capital is required, or at least expected, to engage in the accreditation process— New York City is not known for bargain hotels or inexpensive food. Yet smaller NGOs and even individuals have managed to circumvent this hurdle to some degree by allying themselves with accredited NGOs. For instance, I was a graduate student when I traveled to Durban and had no formal NGO affiliation; I had the opportunity to attend because of my prior relationship with WILD for Human Rights, which was based in San Francisco at the time. Organizations such as WILD for Human Rights, and many of the others in this research, formed delegations of scholars and activists who were not, at the time, working for that particular organization. Accredited NGOs allowed us to get around the capital-intensive accreditation process, which would have prevented our participation in the 2001 WCAR and in the corresponding NGO Forum. Finally, it can take well over one year to receive approval for accreditation, and up to or more than two years if applications are deferred; many organizational changes can take place in that span of time, including changes in staffing, funding, and resources—and even political direction.

Activist Julie Chen, whom I interviewed in 2003, identified a structural form of bias that makes accreditation difficult for certain human rights organizations: "There's a committee on NGOs for ECOSOC that . . . approves whether or not they can have accreditation. But for the last few years, human rights groups have been having a very hard time getting accreditation. It is getting much harder. So if you don't already have accreditation, you may not ever get it if you are a human rights group. And if you do have accreditation, you are being scrutinized very carefully. There have been several challenges to human rights groups because of their work."[55] The accreditation process for human rights groups becomes further complicated, according to Chen, when countries that are traditionally unfriendly to NGOs, such as Syria, Iran, Iraq, India, and Pakistan, sit on the committee. Chen further noted that when "our allies can't get in," reaccreditation can become contested: "So it's a very tricky, internal, bureaucratic, boring, but important step that is raising questions about how people are going to be able to access this institution. And that's relevant for grassroots organizations around the world. It's hard enough to even get the budget to be able to participate in these meetings, but if you also have to go through these hoops to get accreditation papers to be able to go, it's a whole other challenge." Chen's point about access highlights the levels of obstacles that NGOs must overcome—from interacting with ECOSOC members who dislike NGOs to securing travel funds for attending meetings or conferences—and illustrates the politicized nature of securing accreditation. Furthermore, even when accreditation is granted, access to all UN events is not always guaranteed. For example, in 2011 representatives of accredited NGOs were denied admission to the UN's Durban + 10 meeting in New York City, which took place during the sixty-sixth session of the GA.[56] The politics of the accreditation process are entirely beyond the control of NGOs, since it is up to the UN committee to determine each NGO's status. Nevertheless, organizations such as Amnesty International—given the breadth of its work, its reputation, and its expansive networks of international supporters—are unlikely to be entangled in the politics of the process since they have an established record of acquiring general consultative status. However, NGOs are just as likely as governments to be caught up in power hierarchies that reflect the amount of social capital possessed by individual organizations.

Margaret Keck and Kathryn Sikkink note, "Power is exercised within networks, and power often follows from resources, of which a preponderance exists within northern network nodes. . . . But because of the nature of the network form of organization, many actors (including powerful northern ones) are transformed through their participation in the network."[57] Keck and Sikkink address the resource imbalance that exists between the global North and the global South. Networks are beneficial in that they can transform our ideas and also clarify processes that otherwise would be murky. Yet those same networks facilitate an overrepresentation in the UN arena of organizations from the global North, and this reality contributes to the tense dynamics between organizations based in the global North and those in the global South.[58]

Although the UN promotes geographical representation on its committees and commissions, this principle does not apply to NGOs (see table 2.01). UN officials, such as former UN Secretary-General Kofi Annan, have spoken passionately about the integration of NGOs into the UN, yet those words have not been matched with action. No revisions to the NGO accreditation process have been proposed to facilitate the involvement of NGOs from underrepresented regions. The structure of the UN continues to support a culture of elitism.[59] The institutional barriers to NGO accreditation (such as the language requirement for application documents) prevent equal participation of organizations that lack sufficient social, cultural, and economic capital. This raises urgent concerns about the largely problematic NGO accreditation process. In short, the NGO accreditation process is meant to be exclusionary.

Despite these obstacles, many of the NGO representatives and activists who attended the 2001 WCAR were not part of the elite NGO spectrum. Some worked in a single room in an old building, others worked out of their homes, and still others had no formal meeting space. Some managed to get around the institutional and structural barriers imposed by the UN by working with women's groups in the United States that had accreditation, or by "borrowing" the accreditation of another NGO (such as in my case). These women were able to circumvent the UN's elitist culture that exists in contradiction to the egalitarian universalism that the UN claims to support.

How is the approach of activists representing communities relegated to the margins in human rights debates from the 1940s dissimilar or overlapping with the UN's appeal to human rights standards, specifically within the context of key documents such as the Universal Declaration of Human Rights (UDHR)? For Alberta Beatríz "Bety" Cariño Trujillo, an indigenous woman activist from Mexico assassinated by a state paramilitary group for her human rights activism in Oaxaca in 2010, the "daily business of human rights" is one that cannot be sidelined.[60] So how does Cariño's commitment to the "daily business of human rights," which is deeply rooted in the struggles of her people against a powerful and violent state, become as meaningful to the production of human rights discourse as the legal frameworks that shape international treaties? More importantly, in taking up the point raised by Boaventura de Sousa Santos that opens this chapter, what can be learned "from the South" about the limits placed on the discursive production and practice of human rights by the global North?[61]

When discourse is associated with an institution, as is the case with human rights and the UN, it becomes extremely powerful. By moving beyond a narrow political discourse about human rights based in a tradition of liberal humanism, modes of discursive *production* become as pivotal as modes of discursive *practice*. Today, the production of human rights discourse and its related practice is no longer limited to powerful government delegates or UN diplomats. Further, the multiple constituencies that engage with human rights today do so by referencing a different set of epistemologies and ontologies by which they produce and practice human rights.[62]

By conceptualizing human rights within a constellations model, the various strands of its discursive production can be disentangled. The purpose of this exercise is to decipher the spaces in which human rights have been innovative and, perhaps in some cases, linked. In each constellation, diverse but related strands of thought intermingle, and no one strand is superior to another. Three constellations of human rights operate at the UN level: dominant understandings, which are related to the Western-influenced legal apparatus of laws and the courts; counterpublic approaches, which embrace alternative epistemologies based on transnational feminist and antiracist politics; and social praxis, which reflects how social actors mediate between the first two constellations through their practice of human rights.[63]

Other constellations of human rights beyond this triad may very well be operating within and outside of the UN; however, based on my research with antiracist feminist activists throughout the Americas region, these three engagements are the most evident. Of particular interest to this research is the third constellation, social praxis, because of its grounded approach to the discursive production and practice of human rights that contributes to the shaping of the UN's discourse on racism and antiracism. The ways in which human rights become negotiated and strategically used in advocacy efforts in this space uncovers a critical bridging between legal and non-Western-dominated approaches to human rights advocacy.

UNPACKING THE TRIAD CONSTELLATION: ENGAGEMENTS AND DISCURSIVE PRODUCTION

The UN is a unique space in that it brings together a range of voices, from the radical to the conservative, from longtime diplomats to grassroots activists. Their understandings of human rights form the basis of their advocacy efforts and converge in this shared space. The approaches to human rights practiced by the many antiracist feminist activists I have interviewed represent a departure from the strict legal understandings of human rights that can prevail at the UN. The nonlegal approach to human rights represents an expanded view of what Walter D. Mignolo calls a "polycentric discourse on human and rights"[64]—or, more pointedly, not what de Sousa Santos terms a *"mestiza* conception of human rights"[65]—that demands consideration of these alternative feminist and antiracist epistemologies of human rights.[66] The three constellations of human rights described below offer a framework for analyzing how human rights are constructed and practiced in relation to the UN, and how, in turn, the UN's human rights agenda must also contend with and negotiate the application of nondominant production and practices of human rights engagement in the social praxis constellation.

Dominant Understandings

Dominant understandings of human rights correspond to laws and legal approaches. This schema is deemed dominant because of the institutions (i.e., court systems, the UN) that regulate and structure societies. Laws constructed to protect human rights, especially in the political and civil realm, gain power through the use of acute language that refers to "human rights violations" and identifies breaches as actions "against international law." This language presumes the gravitas of an offense and suggests that repercussions will follow. Egregious cases can make their way to the International Criminal Court,[67] or, in the case of the Americas region, to the Inter-American Court on Human Rights. The United States retains an observer status in both legal systems, since it has not officially joined them.[68]

After the adoption of the UN Charter in 1945, the UN drafted a series of core human rights treaties. Human rights treaties are considered international laws and establish standards and expectations. The UN has nine core human rights treaties, each of which is monitored by a human rights treaty committee of independent experts.[69] ICERD, completed in 1965, was the first treaty. CERD, established in 1970, monitors the implementation and compliance of ICERD. The CEDAW committee, established in 1982, monitors compliance of the CEDAW treaty (also known as the Women's Convention).[70] CERD and the CEDAW committee meet continuously and are thus critical sites for an investigation of the discourse of race-based and gender-based discrimination at the UN. By early 2014, 176 governments had ratified ICERD, and 187 had ratified the Women's Convention.[71] The United States was one of the first nations to support ICERD, signing the treaty in 1966, the same year that Canada, Mexico, and Peru became signatories. Even though the United States did not officially ratify the treaty until 1994, during the Clinton administration, its signature in 1966 signaled an important, although not necessarily positive, shift in US policy that began after World War II.[72]

The Office of High Commissioner for Human Rights (OHCHR) is the principal organ at the UN tasked with the promotion and monitoring of human rights. OHCHR describes human rights as follows: "Universal human rights are often expressed and guaranteed by law, in the forms of treaties, customary international law, general principles and other sources of international law. International human rights law lays down obligations of Governments to act in certain ways or to refrain from certain acts, in order to promote and protect human rights and fundamental freedoms of individuals or groups."[73] Given the UN's governmentality structure, the OHCHR identifies governments as having "the primary responsibility to protect human rights"; therefore the role of the OHCHR is to "provid[e] assistance to Governments, such as expertise and technical trainings in the areas of administration of justice, legislative reform, and electoral process, to help implement international human rights standards on the ground."[74] By stressing the legality of human rights, the OHCHR serves to reinforce a modernist ontology based on the dualism of illegal versus legal. By primarily associating human rights with the legal apparatus, laws, which rest on a modernist ontology, become informed by those entities and social actors that create and interpret laws. Moreover, the legal systems that form to uphold those laws are often imperfect and discriminatory, with the laws themselves being unevenly applied, observed, and enforced.

Given that these are dominant understandings of human rights, social actors in the other constellations have to be familiar with this methodology. They may opt to not engage in its mechanisms, or even adopt an oppositional stance to this constellation, *but even human rights production and practice in the counterpublic constellation are responding in some way to the dominant sphere.* The rigidity of modernist ontology as it pertains to human rights law is based on a binary construction of illegal versus legal, or, as Mignolo frames it, between "human" and "nonhuman."[75]

Counterpublic Approaches

When Mignolo asked who speaks for the "human" in human rights, he was referencing a context in which a majority of the world's people— slaves, women, indigenous peoples, and so forth—had been entirely excluded from the discursive production of human rights.[76] Hence, a counterpublic approach to human rights acknowledges not only its imperial origins but also the ways in which constituencies who were never viewed as having human rights in the 1940s during the drafting of the UDHR assert them today. Consider the bold actions of two indigenous (Mapuche) women from Chile during the Americas PrepCom for the 2001

WCAR in Santiago, Chile. During the opening session of the intergovernmental meeting, the two women "walked right up to the podium" where the president of Chile, Ricardo Lagos, was about to speak, and "denounce[d] his treatment of Indians in Chile." President Lagos was shocked by this political action and publicly reprimanded the women for their "undiplomatic" behavior after they were removed by security. But the representatives of NGOs in attendance applauded the courage of the women, who had attempted to make their demands heard on their own terms, and the activists walked out in solidarity, chanting, "We are a peoples!," "End racism!," and similar phrases.[77]

The counterpublic approach in this research highlights transnational feminist concepts of cross-border solidarity, relationality, and antisubordination. Part of what informs these transnational feminist concepts are relational ontologies. This oppositional perspective correlates with what Colombian anthropologist Arturo Escobar refers to as "the political activation of relational ontologies." He states, "At stake in many cultural-political mobilizations in Latin America at present, it is argued, is the political activation of relational ontologies, such as those of indigenous peoples and Afro-descendants. These relational ontologies can be differentiated from the dualist ontologies of liberal modernity in that they are not built on the divides between nature and culture, us and them, individual and community; the cultural, political, and ecological consequences of taking relationality seriously are significant; relationality refers to a different way of imagining life (socio-natural worlds)."[78] This "political activation of relational ontologies" emerges because indigenous communities and African descendants and other similarly marginalized peoples come to understand the socio-natural world contrarily to white Western men.[79]

Movements and efforts to decolonize human rights are engaged in a practice of reclaiming human rights within the counterpublic constellation. Based on this research, this reclaiming can occur within the confines of institutions.[80] As Mignolo points out, decolonizing human rights can be about "placing yourself in the space [of] imperial discourse . . . [to] argue for radical interventions" from the political perspective of marginalized communities.[81] However, the counterpublic approach to human rights does not seek institutional validation. Rather, its purpose is to discursively produce and practice human rights in ways that can be generative and dynamic. In this constellation, human rights are not only about legal norms but also about an envisioning of human rights that moves beyond the rubric of civil, political, social, economic, and cultural rights. To imagine human rights anew, then, requires the creation of new models of discursive production and practice. To decolonize human rights, activists must then "move away (de-link) from the imperial consequences" of the 1940s period. Therefore, it is in the counterpublic constellation that decolonizing human rights becomes a pivotal undertaking and movement.

Cariño's point about "the daily business of human rights" fundamentally speaks to advocating for human rights beyond a (white) Western-centric model. In doing so, the secular orientation of a modernist ontology is also challenged. Indigenous communities as well as African descendants in Latin America have been particularly active in this regard. For instance, indigenous communities in the Americas have made the assertion that land—*as a being*—also has rights.[82] African descendants in the region have also gained increased visibility since the 2001 WCAR, and in the process of preparing for the WCAR not only embraced the term "African descendant" but also demanded an engagement with human rights that acknowledged their history of enslavement. This recognition is significant because slavery received the classification of a "crime against humanity" for the first time at the 2001 WCAR.

The counterpublic constellation relies on relational ontologies because these approaches are about, as Maria Lugones states, "beings in relation rather than dichotomously split over and over in hierarchically and violently ordered fragments."[83] As such, the discursive production and practice of human rights is distinct from the other two constellations, especially as the first constellation (dominant understandings) relies on a clear division of legal and illegal, and the third constellation (social praxis) strives to negotiate and mediate between modernist and relational ontologies.

Efforts to decolonize human rights suggest that a "pluriversality of human rights," as cultural studies scholar Rosa-Linda Fregoso calls it, can coexist with universal human rights.[84] More importantly, the discursive production and practice of human rights in the counterpublic constellation is not wedded to the UN's legalistic methodology, nor does it seek to gain legitimacy or validation from the UN. In this counterpublic constellation, the discursive production and practice of human rights is largely irreconcilable with the dominant constellation; however, this tension is negotiated and contested within the social praxis constellation.

Social Praxis

The social praxis constellation sits between the first two constellations because it represents a process of mediation between the dominant understandings and counterpublic approaches, involving a distinct practice of human rights. Anthropologists Shannon Speed and Jane Collier refer to this type of practice as the "social life of rights" to signal the vibrancy with which a multitude of social actors engage in the production of human rights: "The intellectual efforts of those seeking to develop a framework for understanding the social life of rights would be better directed not towards foreclosing their ontological status, but instead by exploring their meaning and use. What is needed are more detailed studies of human rights according to the actions and intentions of social actors, within wider historical constraints of institutionalized power."[85] Focused on the violent situation in Chiapas, Mexico, Speed and Collier address how the UDHR "can have the opposite effect of rendering indigenous leaders vulnerable to state sanctions" rather than "protect[ing] individuals from arbitrary punishments by their governments."[86] In order to avoid "another form of colonialism," which occurs when human rights are used to "impose Western values on unwilling peoples," Speed and Collier contend that it is necessary to endorse the efforts of "indigenous groups in Chiapas [to] obtain the political autonomy they need to develop their own understandings of human rights" so that the "cooperative efforts among groups with different histories and values . . . prevail."[87]

The ability of human rights to empower and give voice to the world's racial minorities and colonial peoples depends on much more than the passage of laws and their enforcement by the courts. The social praxis is a constellation in which a form of political autonomy can thrive because social actors, from indigenous activists to African descendants, are seeking to remake human rights. In other words, their engagement with the discursive production and organization of human rights is about offering their interpretations and perspectives to broaden narrow constructions of human rights. After all, human rights do not exist, as anthropologist Richard Wilson points out, "outside of discourse, history, context, or agency."[88] Efforts to put theories of human rights into practice—not simply to attend conferences and draft documents—often manifest as social struggles over power, political voice, and resources.[89] This is essentially an ontological contest in which the objectives of transnational feminism are pitted against the Western legal apparatus. It is the "sum total of all struggles to define and realize universal human dignity and rights."[90] It contrasts the actions of human rights activists with those of non-activist stakeholders who conceptualize human rights exclusively in terms of laws and public policies. Furthermore, the project of human rights includes metaphorical engagement with discourse as well.

Sociologists William Armaline, Davita Glasberg, and Bandana Purkayastha refer to the process of developing an understanding of human rights that stretches beyond the legal framework as the "human rights enterprise": "Where sociology does not presuppose the relevance or inevitability of the state, human rights instruments and the formal human rights regime comprise only one small piece of the larger whole. The human rights enterprise represents this whole, where grassroots struggles outside of and potentially against the formal state arena are seen as equally relevant to interpreting, critiquing, and realizing human rights in practice."[91] Limiting human rights to treaties or other legal instruments results in the complete erasure of the other ways in which human rights may be interpreted and invoked. In thinking of human rights as an enterprise, the project of human rights must include informal engagements with discourse and social praxis.

NGOs that are granted accreditation gain access to the power structures and relationships associated with UN citizenship. Representatives are eligible, for example, to observe UN proceedings and to lobby government delegates during world conferences. Because access, even for UN members, is frequently constrained by social, cultural, and economic capital, deciphering where to focus an NGO's efforts—choosing a context for advocacy—is a key deciding strategy for influencing the UN's agendas. As de Sousa Santos points out, evaluating context allows parties to "distinguish progressive politics from regressive politics, empowerment from disempowerment, [and] emancipation from regulation,"[92] and these factors can determine how much influence an NGO will have.

The two examples discussed here involve CERD and the UN's Declaration on the Rights of Indigenous Peoples. First, the shifts in CERD's approach to eventually account for gender dynamics resulted in an expanded interpretation of the treaty's intent for the purposes of treaty compliance hearings with State Parties. In other words, debates about the gendered dimensions to racial discrimination were not part of the committee's conversation prior to 2000. This means that strategic advocacy efforts by feminist activists today can make ICERD, written in the 1960s, relevant to their particular issues. I use the 2008 US government treaty review hearing before CERD as a relevant case study for understanding how interpreting ICERD in an expanded way was useful for antiracist feminist activists. Second, the debates over the UN's Declaration on the Rights of Indigenous Peoples exemplify the deep gulf between modernist and relational ontologies.[93] The two decades of fraught negotiations involving indigenous leaders underscore how dissatisfying navigating the social praxis constellation can be for activists as well.

Moving beyond Notions of Gender Neutrality: How CERD Addressed Intersectionality in the 2008 Hearing of the US Government

As of 2014 CERD had issued thirty-five general recommendations (see table 2.02). Before 2000, CERD's recommendations had established a pattern that emphasized racial discrimination solely in the public sphere. This pattern was disrupted in 2000, when CERD adopted General Recommendation 25, which recognizes the gender dimensions to racial discrimination and the realities of discrimination and violence against women in the private sphere. Antiracist feminist activists hailed General Recommendation 25 as a breakthrough. But CERD's earlier recommendations reveal an implicit gender bias that shaped how the committee interpreted the meaning of racial discrimination until 2000. For decades, CERD reinforced the perspective that racial discrimination occurred solely in the public sector, which is where men largely experience violations of their human rights. Further, CERD members resisted an integration of gender, cautioning that it would be too complicated for the governments being reviewed to assess. In 1996 CERD member Luis Valencia Rodriguez stated, "Proposed amendments would complicate the reporting obligation for States parties, particularly if [Member States] had to refer to the gender implications of racial discrimination with respect to each of the articles of the Convention."[94]

TABLE 2.02 CERD's General Recommendations, 2013

NUMBER	YEAR	TITLE
1	1972	States Parties' Obligations (Art. 4)
2	1972	States Parties' Obligations (Art. 9)
3	1973	Apartheid
4	1973	Demographic Composition of the Population (Art. 9)
5	1977	Reporting by States Parties (Art. 7)
6	1982	Overdue Reports (Art. 9)
7	1985	Legislation to Eradicate Racial Discrimination (Art. 4)
8	1990	Identification with a Particular Racial or Ethnic Group
9	1990	Independence of Experts
10	1991	Technical Assistance
11	1993	Non-citizens
12	1993	Successor States
13	1993	Training of Law Enforcement Officials in the Protection of Human Rights
14	1993	Definition of Discrimination
15	1993	Organizing Violence Based on Ethnic Origin
16	1993	References to Situations Existing in other States
17	1993	Establishment of National Institutions to Facilitate Implementation of the Convention
18	1994	Establishment of an International Tribunal to Prosecute Crimes against Humanity
19	1995	Racial Segregation and Apartheid
20	1996	Non-discriminatory Implementation of Rights and Freedoms
21	1996	Right to Self-determination
22	1996	Article 5 and Refugees and Displaced Persons
23	1997	Indigenous Peoples
24	1999	Reporting of Persons Belonging to Different Races, National/Ethnic Groups, or Indigenous Peoples
25	2000	Gender-related Dimensions of Racial Discrimination
26	2000	Article 6 of the Convention
27	2000	Discrimination against Roma
28	2002	The Follow-up to the World Conference against Racism, Racial Discrimination, Xenophobia, and Related Intolerance

(continued)

TABLE 2.02 *(continued)*

29	2002	Article 1, Paragraph 1 of the Convention (Descent)
30	2004	Discrimination against Non-citizens
31	2005	Prevention of Racial Discrimination in the Administration and Functioning of the Criminal Justice System
32	2009	The Meaning and Scope of Special Measures in the International Convention on the Elimination of Racial Discrimination
33	2009	Follow-up to the Durban Review Conference
34	2011	Racial Discrimination against People of African Descent
35	2013	Combating Racist Hate Speech

Source: United Nations Office of the High Commissioner for Human Rights, CERD.

Unlike world conferences, which occur on occasion, CERD meetings occur semiannually. Treaty compliance hearings are a venue where articulations of racism are negotiated and can be the basis upon which general recommendations are conceived. Governments must submit reports on how they are complying with ICERD. NGOs also have an opportunity to submit their own reports about government compliance with a treaty, known as "shadow reports," which the UN committee can review. The US government has been reviewed three times—the first time just weeks before the 2001 WCAR, the second time in 2008, and the third time in August 2014. The second hearing, held in February 2008 at UN headquarters in Geneva, was remarkable in that for the first time the members of CERD specifically highlighted women's experiences with gendered violence and reproductive health issues as a matter of racial justice.

I observed the 2008 hearing along with over 120 other NGO representatives. After Fatima-Binta Victoria (Burkina Faso), the CERD chair, called the hearing into session, special rapporteur Linos-Alexander Sicilianos (Greece) summarized his committee's assessment of the US government's report on ICERD compliance. Sicilianos's opening presentation was wide-ranging in substance: he discussed the problematic ways in which the United States narrowly defines racial discrimination legally; the maltreatment of undocumented people and refugees, especially following the attacks on September 11, 2001; and the troubled US criminal justice system, in which racism is evidenced by police brutality against people of color, the overpopulation of people of color in prisons, and the overrepresentation of people of color on death row. Sicilianos also pointed out areas in which the US government's views differed from those of CERD, and the substantive discrepancies that existed between the US government's official report and the NGO shadow reports, which are counter-reports about the United States' record. Some of the questions asked by Sicilianos and other CERD members came directly from the language proposed to the committee by representatives of US NGOs.[95]

The 2008 US treaty review hearing offers insight into how the social praxis constellation operates. In preparing for the treaty review process, US activists identified human rights standards based on the treaty and then formulated advocacy principles upon which to build their assertions of racial injustice.[96] In other words, there is no mention of reproductive rights in ICERD, yet activists offered their interpretations of the articles in ICERD in which reproductive justice could be applied. Their efforts were compelling enough to CERD that they received attention during the hearing itself. Such a strategy necessitates a fluency in the language of human rights and the ability to negotiate and lobby with members of a UN committee.

Debates over "Fundamental Philosophical Issues": The UN's Declaration on the Rights of Indigenous Peoples

The contentious negotiations between government delegates and indigenous leaders over the adoption of the UN's Declaration on the Rights of Indigenous Peoples provides another example of the tensions that can emerge in the social praxis constellation. The two decade long debate exemplifies the deep divide between modernist and relational ontologies. Introducing the issue of land into a debate about human rights—in particular because of the role land plays in the lives of indigenous peoples and because they view land as being on par with the worth of people—is noteworthy, especially because land "goes beyond [the] traditional idea of human rights."[97] When some participants raised reservations about the appropriateness of including a provision about land in a Declaration on Indigenous Peoples, the government delegate of Bolivia pointed out that land and indigenous culture are intertwined.[98] Some negotiators thought that expanding the traditional description of human rights was a positive development, as Alfonso Martinez, one of the UN negotiators, noted; other government delegates vehemently disagreed.

In the end, although the UN Declaration on the Rights of Indigenous Peoples passed with much fanfare at the GA, the compromises that had to be made to achieve the near consensus suggest that reconciling modernist and relational views can be a challenging task.[99] Consider the breakdown of the vote: in September 2007, after twenty years of difficult deliberations, four countries (Australia, Canada, New Zealand, and the United States) voted against adopting the Declaration, 143 countries voted in favor of it, and 11 countries abstained. The Declaration's reception among indigenous leaders was mixed, with some hailing the Declaration as a long-overdue achievement and others considering it to be "a deeply flawed document" that they could not endorse.[100]

The compromises made favored Western-based understandings of land and the law. For example, Article 10 of the Declaration on the Rights of Indigenous Peoples addresses issues of forcible removal, stating, "No relocation shall take place without the free, prior and informed consent of the indigenous peoples concerned and after agreement on just and fair compensation and, where possible, with the option of return." In this article, the language is such that indigenous peoples can still be removed from their land, albeit not "forcibly," though the meaning of this word is entirely unclear. More importantly, the wording of this article in no way protects indigenous peoples in conflict with, for example, corporate desires to extract natural resources from indigenous lands. Other articles in the Declaration about land are similar in intent; they have the appearance of concern for the plight of indigenous peoples and for understanding or respecting the "distinctive spiritual relationships" (Article 25) with land, yet not at the expense of sacrificing Western beliefs about individual land ownership or corporate expansion. This Declaration is not a decolonial platform, even though any pertinent document about the rights of indigenous peoples would incorporate the project of decoloniality.

The disputes that surfaced in relation to the Declaration on the Rights of Indigenous Peoples were over "fundamental philosophical issues"[101] (think second constellation) that divided the government delegates who were tasked with preserving the power of their nation-states from the indigenous leaders who were seeking to uphold self-determination, autonomy, and the inherent dignity of indigenous peoples.[102] Arguments about the definition of terms such as "indigenous," the "right to self-determination," and "collective rights" versus "individual rights," and about whether to use the term "peoples" (plural) prolonged the lengthy negotiations.

The social praxis constellation is the space in which activists who opt to engage in UN advocacy strive to reconcile dominant understandings and counterpublic approaches. In their advocacy efforts, they take platforms, inspirations, values, ethics, and ideas from the counterpublic constellation and use them to decipher ways in which dominant understandings of human rights can be challenged, reinterpreted, and reimagined. In the two examples discussed here, the outcomes of the social praxis constellation can be constructive (as was the case for US reproductive rights feminists participating in the 2008 ICERD review hearing) or frustrating (as was the case for indigenous leaders involved with the negotiations for the Indigenous Declaration). In both examples, the practice of UN citizenship pushes the boundaries of the human rights discussion.

CONCLUSION: ACCESS, INFLUENCE, AND THE PRACTICE OF UN CITIZENSHIP

UN citizenship permits access to government representatives and inclusion in global conversations and diplomatic negotiations. Each "citizen" is entitled to a set of rights because, as social economist Naila Kabeer notes, "to be meaningful, any concept of citizenship carries with it a conception of rights."[103] An assessment of UN citizenship requires a consideration not only of the rights associated with UN membership but also of how those rights are asserted once Member States and NGOs are part of the institution.

One way in which UN citizenship rights are realized is through the adoption of GA resolutions. The themes and topics of the earliest GA resolutions on racism emphasized South African apartheid and other macro forms of racial domination: colonialism and the displacement of native populations by white settlers, specifically in southern Africa. Later resolutions focused on other phenomena, such as migration, violence, foreign occupation, and imprisonment of political dissidents. The GA considered these issues in relation to their disproportionate racial, ethnic, and national impact on diverse groups of people. The handful of resolutions concerning women and antiracism in the 1970s and 1980s did not deal in depth with the gendered dynamics of racial apartheid; rather, they focused on women's activism in antiapartheid freedom struggles. By the 1990s, the GA had begun to account for macro systems of racial oppression by acknowledging gender dynamics. The focus on South Africa in GA resolutions had dissipated by then, and an opportunity to conceptualize an expanded as well as a varied understanding regarding racism occurred during the 1990s, which happened to be consequential years for NGOs at the UN.[104] The recognition of additional manifestations of racism provided feminists with an opportunity to interject their analyses, perspectives, and experiences into considerations about the meaning of racial injustice.

Economic, social, and cultural capital play a substantive role in determining which governments and organizations gain access to the UN and how their membership rights are exercised. Examples of the types of capital that determine the role that an NGO can play at the UN include access to established social networks, fluency in the prescribed languages (English and French), the skills to negotiate and lobby, and the financial ability to afford travel to Geneva or New York City for UN meetings. New and smaller NGOs often find the UN process discouraging because sociopolitical networks take years to establish, and large, established NGOs may consider it strategic to protect their social contacts. The issue of access—"boring, bureaucratic, but important!" in the words of Julie Chen—is particularly critical for NGOs. The existing procedures that govern UN accreditation for NGOs structurally benefit organizations from the global North that have the economic capital to travel to UN headquarters in New York City to answer application questions if needed, the cultural capital to complete application materials in English or French, and the social capital to gain access to NGO networks that can properly guide interested groups through the application process. Securing UN accreditation for NGOs is no easy feat, and it is a highly political experience as well. At the same time, some feminists have been able to seize the opportunity to circumvent the structure of the UN by forming networks of cooperation, demonstrating that the structural impediments at the UN are not always insurmountable.

NGOs that gain UN membership must work with other constituencies at the UN to advance a human rights agenda, and these constituencies have different understandings of the concept of human rights and different approaches to achieving human rights. The three constellations discussed in this chapter—dominant understandings, counterpublic approaches, and social praxis—offer a means of analyzing the advocacy efforts of the different constituencies engaged at the UN. The epistemologies contained in the second constellation represent relational ontologies that move beyond the dualism of the modernist ontologies of the first constellation. Here, "the actions and intentions of social actors"—those who are not UN diplomats or government bureaucrats—are central.[105] Ultimately, it is critical to understand "how rights discourses are understood and used by people living in the world today."[106] This is the "social life of rights" of the third constellation—how human rights are incorporated and made meaningful in everyday life.

The stakes differ for the social actors who attempt to shape the discourse of human rights at the UN. Because of the UN's institutional structure, efforts to advance a human rights agenda at the UN may become complicated and fall short of meeting activists' demands for and on behalf of their constituencies. One cannot lose sight, however, of the fact that discussions about human rights have evolved tremendously since the 1940s. Many of the social actors who are engaged in these discussions are new UN citizens, as are many of those reflected in this research. By consolidating and wielding social and cultural capital, they have been able to secure access to the institution, where efforts to promote their interpretation of human rights have gained visibility and strength.

By the late 1990s, as preparations were underway for the 2001 WCAR, more attention was being given to intersectionality. Until 2000 CERD claimed that its work was gender-neutral, but by shifting from an implicit gender bias to a gender-conscious approach, CERD has ultimately produced a context in which feminists can begin to raise issues that are intersectional.[107] As preparations for the 2001 WCAR were underway, CERD finally acknowledged the usefulness of intersectionality for the first time in its history, which consequently created an opportunity to broaden the discourse of racism to include a consideration of how race and gender intersect. The postapartheid era became a critical moment for activists seeking to reawaken and revisit discourses on racism, which up until then had largely focused on apartheid. Now with many NGOs having UN accreditation, antiracist feminists were poised to make some long-overdue interventions at the 2001 WCAR.

3

A Genealogy of World Conferences against Racism and the Progression of Intersectionality

> Where people worked with [the conference documents] and fought to devise new language, new procedures, new processes for addressing these issues [of racism], the conference really mattered. It mattered that there was a new recognition of discrimination against those of African descent. It mattered that the Roma in Europe would have new opportunities to highlight the discriminations that they suffer under, and so on.
>
> —MARY ROBINSON, FORMER UN HIGH
> COMMISSIONER FOR HUMAN RIGHTS, 2003

THE SUCCESS OF WORLD CONFERENCES, FOR NGOS AND GOVERN-ments alike, is determined in large part by the content of the accords that are known as the Declaration and the Programme of Action. One way to assess the impact of activism is through these official documents. The Durban Declaration and the Programme of Action (DDPA) reflect the determined efforts of antiracist feminists to incorporate the language of intersectionality and address new topics of concern to feminists. A broadened approach to racism is evident by the conclusion of the 2001 World Conference against Racism (WCAR); however, NGOs and governments continued to reference different meanings to the terms "intersectionality" and "gender," and both concepts remained contested. Moreover, the political climate for discussing global racism, as had been done in 2001, became stalled by the end of the decade.

The 2001 WCAR was the UN's third world conference to address racism and the first one to be held outside of UN headquarters in Geneva, Switzerland. Economically powerful governments were openly hostile to each of these conferences, but the 2001 WCAR met especially fierce resistance. Controversy marred each of the conferences but reached a peak during the 2001 WCAR in Durban when the US government delegation staged an apparent walkout, a move that was condemned or commended, depending on one's politics. Recall the US government had boycotted the prior two world conferences of 1978 and 1983 as well.

The purpose of the Durban Review Conference (DRC) in 2009 was to assess the progress that had been made since the 2001 WCAR. Held at UN headquarters in Geneva, the 2009 DRC proved extremely disappointing to activists who sought to pick up where the 2001 WCAR had left off (as I discuss at the end of this chapter). Unfortunately, coordinated and largely successful actions by an oppositional force that had become galvanized by any mention of the Durban conference derailed the 2009 DRC. Therefore the important gains made in increasing the visibility of women's experiences with racism at the UN level, in particular by 2001, felt stalled by the end of the decade.

WORLD CONFERENCE TO COMBAT RACISM AND RACIAL DISCRIMINATION, 1978

On December 16, 1977, the UN General Assembly (GA) passed Resolution 32/129, which approved the organization of the first World Conference to Combat Racism. The resolution passed by a vote of 131 in favor and 1 against (Israel), with 1 abstention (Guatemala). On the same day, the GA also passed Resolution 32/122, which "demanded the release of all individuals detained or imprisoned as a result of their struggle against *apartheid*, racism, racial discrimination, colonialism, aggression and foreign occupation, and for self-determination and independence as well as social progress for their people." The GA's position was that "suppress[ing] the struggle against colonial domination and racist regimes were incompatible with the United Nations Charter and the Universal Declaration of Human Rights." Resolution 32/122 passed by a vote of 97 in favor and 18 against, with 22 abstentions.[1]

Prior to the vote on Resolution 32/122, the United States and Canada (as well as others) had presented arguments cautioning against the direction taken by the first UN Decade to Combat Racism and Racial Discrimination and expressing disapproval of the plans for the upcoming 1978 world conference, which, they argued, steered away from the original intent of the Decade. The United States wanted to "reach a formula whereby only matters in keeping with the original intent of the Decade would be raised during the 1978 World Conference on Racism" and did not vote on Resolution 32/122 because "it had been unable to reach a consensus on such a formula." Canada, voting in support of the resolution, had become increasingly opposed to "recent Assembly sessions" that had resulted in "the inclusion of an alien and unacceptable element in the consideration of various resolutions on the Decade Against Racism and the World Conference Against Racism." Canada wanted to restore the Decade and the conference "to their original purpose, as defined in resolution 3057 (XXVIII) of 2 November 1973." Canada declared that its support for the Decade and the 1978 WCAR would continue if activities during that period remained consistent with the interpretation of "racism" as stated in Article 1 of ICERD.[2]

The first conference was held August 14–25 in Geneva, and representatives of 125 governments and UN observers participated, including representatives from the Commission on the Status of Women, CERD, and national liberation movements. The United States and Israel boycotted the conference from the outset, citing as their reason the 1975 GA resolution equating Zionism with racism (see chapter 2).[3] During the conference fourteen Western nations walked out in midsession "to protest a declaration attacking Israel" that had been proposed by Arab and African governments.[4] Those countries were nine members of the European Common Market—West Germany, Italy, France, Britain, Ireland, the Netherlands, Belgium, Luxembourg, and Denmark—and Australia, Canada, New Zealand, Norway, and Iceland.[5] The West German ambassador stated that the "anti-Israeli texts 'deviated from the purpose' of combating racism" and his country's withdrawal from the conference was therefore "inevitable."[6]

An extensive official report providing an overview about the world conference and other supporting documents, such as fact sheets, are produced by the UN at the conference's conclusion. The boycott is not mentioned in the official report of the 1978 conference nor in fact sheets about the world conference and the UN Decade to Combat Racism. News outlets such as the Associated Press covered the walkout, but its complete erasure from the official conference reports is striking. The remaining delegations continued their negotiations rather than prematurely end the conference, sending the message that the African, Arab, Asian, and Latin American governments did not need the protestors' participation.

DECLARATION AND PROGRAMME OF ACTION, 1978

The GA approved the 1978 Declaration and Programme of Action through the passage of Resolutions 33/99 and 33/100, adopted on December 16, 1978.[7] The primary focus of the documents was on "aspects of racial discrimination, apartheid, and the situation in southern Africa."[8] The Declaration condemned any doctrine of racial superiority and restated the need to further isolate racist regimes through UN sanctions and have the full support of Member States. It expressed support for national liberation movements and the rights of indigenous peoples "to maintain their traditional structure of economy and culture," and recognized "the special relationship of indigenous peoples to their land." The Declaration unequivocally declared that the elimination of racism and racial discrimination required the cooperation and commitment of Member States, international organizations, NGOs, and other local and private organizations and institutions.

The Programme of Action (POA) stated that the Security Council should continue to develop measures to isolate the South African regime, including the imposition of mandatory sanctions and the prohibition of loans and investments. It called for assisting African liberation movements and instituting campaigns supporting the release of political prisoners. The document declared "the UN had a special responsibility to the oppressed peoples and liberation movements in South Africa, Namibia, Zimbabwe, and Palestine." Recommending the initiation of studies on discrimination, the POA also supported the study of the "types of recourse procedures available to migrant workers . . . [with particular attention to] . . . migrant workers who are either stateless or who have no home Government, embassy, or consulate to represent them." This section of the Programme noted the contributions to the conference and studies made by CERD, and stated that the Commission on the Status of Women should produce educational material and studies on the "situation of women living under racist regimes in southern Africa, especially under *apartheid*, and on the women in the occupied Arab and other territories."[9]

The 1978 Declaration and the Programme of Action mention women, with paragraph 22 of the Declaration stating that "special efforts are called for to eliminate the effect of racial discrimination on the status of women," and paragraph 37 of the POA imploring governments, specialized agencies, and NGOs to play a role in ensuring that women have "an active role . . . in the development process" when "redressing the social imbalance between the sexes caused by colonialism or racist regimes," and with the "restructuring of societies." These statements reveal an early acknowledgment of the particular disadvantages that women face when colonialism and racism interact with patriarchy, though the tone is not very compelling.

The 1978 and 1983 world conferences did not have a parallel NGO Forum. In 1978, however, NGOs submitted a statement that pledged their support for the conference's Declaration and Programme of Action, and the Programme of Action for the UN Decade to Combat Racism as well. "Deplor[ing] the slow progress" in eradicating racism and racial discrimination, NGOs faulted the "systematic violations by certain Governments of United Nations conventions, declarations and resolutions outlawing racism, racial discrimination and *apartheid*." The statement committed NGOs to the struggle against racism by having the Non-governmental Organizations Sub-Committee on Decolonization, Racial Discrimination, and Apartheid continue its annual conferences in Geneva, which had started in 1974. In addition to calling for "increased material assistance and moral and political support for national liberation movements," NGOs also demanded "the release of all political prisoners" and condemned "all forms of collaboration with racist regimes, particularly in the political, economic and military fields."[10] In this rather brief statement, NGOs used more forceful language than would commonly be found in UN documents.

WORLD CONFERENCE TO COMBAT RACISM
AND RACIAL DISCRIMINATION, 1983

General Assembly Resolution 35/33 of November 14, 1980, approved the proposal for the world conference in 1983. It stated that the primary purpose of the conference was "the formulation of ways and means and of specific measures aimed at ensuring the full and universal implementation of UN resolutions and decisions on racism, racial discrimination, and *apartheid*."[11] The president of the 1983 conference, Hector Charry Samper of Colombia, said that the topics to be addressed during the conference had to be global because "it was not enough to focus on the most serious cases," such as apartheid.[12]

On November 2, 1982, the Third Committee of the General Assembly approved (with four dissenting votes) the resolution recommending the 1983 conference, which was to be held August 1–12, 1983, in Manila.[13] The venue changed to Geneva after the Philippines withdrew its invitation to host the conference.[14] Though budgetary reasons were cited as the cause for the withdrawal, one of my activist interviewees from San Francisco, who had participated in all three world conferences, said that she and others had lobbied for the change because a world conference "gives a lot of prestige to the government," and President Ferdinand Marcos "was slaughtering the people of Mindanao."[15] The UN tries to host conferences in different regions of the world because everyone has to travel when a conference is in Geneva.[16] But in this case, even though moving the conference to Geneva was unusual, it was a victory for activists who did not want a UN conference in the Philippines.

Given the dramatic walkouts and the boycott of the 1978 world conference, the stakes in 1983 for a successful "consensus-based" conference were high. The conference's secretary-general, James O. C. Jonah of Sierra Leone, strove to ensure that the conflicts that had plagued the first world conference would not affect the second.[17] To put forth his message, Jonah, who was assistant secretary-general for the Office of Field Operational and External Support Activities, "tour[ed] 41 countries representing five United Nations regional groupings, arguing the value of a return to a consensus approach for the anti-racism Decade." In January 1983, eight months before the conference and nine months following the first PrepCom in New York, the GA "revised the provisional agenda to remove paragraphs which were strongly opposed by Western and other countries";[18] this may have been a result of Jonah's outreach.

In addition to the 128 governments that participated in the second world conference, the following liberation movements were invited and sent representatives: the African National Congress (ANC), the Palestinian Liberation Organization, the Pan Africanist Congress of Azania, and the South West African People's Organization (SWAPO).[19] ECOSOC served as the conference's organizing body, as it had in 1978. Of the thirty-four people on the five conference committees, only three were women, representing the countries of Bolivia, Tunisia, and Barbados. Mexico had a representative on the Joint Drafting Group.

On August 9, 1983, the conference observed the International Day of Solidarity with the Struggle of Women of South Africa and Namibia. This was one of the UN's earliest acknowledgments that the racism experienced by women is different *because* they are women. In his remarks during the plenary meeting, Charry Samper said,

> Today, 9 August, has been designated by the General Assembly of the United Nations as the International Day of Solidarity with the Struggle of Women of South Africa and Namibia in order to promote the widest mobilization of world public opinion in support of the righteous struggle of women of South Africa and their national liberation movement, as well as to provide all necessary assistance to them to ensure the speedy triumph of that struggle. This day coincides with the anniversary of the historical demonstration of women in South Africa in 1956 against the discriminatory and humiliating pass laws. It is an occasion to recall the plight of women who suffer particular indignities under *apartheid* and to promote appropriate assistance to them. I am sure I am expressing the view of all participants in this Conference in extending our solidarity to the oppressed women of South Africa and Namibia and assuring them of our support.[20]

These remarks indicate the GA's respect and value for the antiapartheid movement. Though these types of gestures can often be read as largely symbolic or even empty, they establish precedent. Proclamations such as the International Day of Solidarity contribute to an opening for addressing intersectionality more substantially in the future.

DECLARATION AND PROGRAMME OF ACTION, 1983

The Declaration and Programme of Action for the 1983 conference reemphasized the outcomes of the 1978 conference and proposed additional actions to be taken in the fight against racism. The Declaration reviewed topics that had been discussed at the 1983 WCAR, including education, teaching, and training to counter racist attitudes and practices; dissemination of information and the role of mass media in combating racism and racial discrimination; and the implementation of ICERD and related international instruments. Specific areas of action included the "protection of peoples belonging to minority groups, indigenous peoples, migrant workers; recourse procedures for victims of racial discrimination; national legislation and institutions for combating racial discrimination; seminars and studies on combating racial discrimination and *apartheid* and actions by NGOs."[21]

The 1983 POA called for the continued isolation of South Africa, asking governments, the International Monetary Fund, the World Bank, and transnational corporations to cut diplomatic, economic, and political ties. Stressing the importance of education reform to combat racist attitudes and actions, the POA also focused on the role of mass media in disseminating information about liberation movements throughout the world. It declared that mass media "should contribute to making the peoples more aware of the close link between the struggle against apartheid and all forms of racism and racial discrimination and the struggle for international peace and security."[22] By identifying a link between antiracist struggles and international peace and security, this section of the document positioned a national issue—apartheid—as an international concern, signifying that the two realms do not exist in isolation. It also corroborated the evidence of activists who had been working to weaken the apartheid state.

The sovereignty rights of indigenous peoples and the treatment of migrant workers were other topics covered in the POA, and these subjects received a great deal of attention. Stating that indigenous peoples have a right to their own language and customs, the document also called for financial support by national authorities through the establishment of funds for economic and cultural activities, the uses of which were "to be determined with the participation of the indigenous populations themselves."[23] The POA also called for the completion of the international treaty to protect migrant workers and their families,[24] and stated that migrants should not be treated any differently than national citizens in terms of rights and access to courts and tribunals.

The 1983 POA also supported recourse for "victims of racial discrimination," including "just and adequate reparation," and urged nonratifying Member States to adopt ICERD in their respective countries.[25] The POA supported reform in terms of national policy measures as well. It argued for legal reforms and the establishment of "national institutions for the promotion and protection of human rights." One of these national institutions would monitor policy with "a view to ensuring the elimination of all discriminatory laws, prejudices and practices based on race, sex, colour, descent, and national and ethnic origin." Coupled with suggested national policy reforms and legislation, the POA declared that seminars were needed on a range of topics, including the "political, historical, economic, social, and cultural factors leading to racism, racial discrimination, and apartheid" and the "main obstacles to the full eradication of racism, racial discrimination, and apartheid," to name a few.[26]

The POA identified a role for NGOs in combating racism, stating that their involvement in the UN Decade to Combat Racism would be an important contribution, especially because of their ability to reach youth. The POA noted that NGOs "have the opportunity to create and sustain awareness among their members and in society at large of the evils of racism and racial discrimination. Such awareness can be transmitted from a national to an international organization with all the added benefits of the concrete experience of a particular country."[27] Insisting "governments should ensure that non-governmental organizations be enabled to function freely and openly within their societies," the POA called for NGOs to participate to the extent possible in the activities of the UN Decade to Combat Racism.[28] The document concluded with an appeal for the establishment of a second UN Decade to Combat Racism and Racial Discrimination.

There were still disputes about how to appropriately handle the issues concerning South Africa and Israel so that the conference could move forward and achieve consensus. These pertained to paragraphs 19 and 20 of the Declaration and the first section of the POA titled "Action to Combat *Apartheid*." Paragraph 19 charged that Israel was economically and militarily cooperating with South Africa, and paragraph 20 expressed the "deep regret" that those at the conference felt toward the "practices of racial discrimination against the Palestinians as well as other inhabitants." Government delegates disagreed about the wording of the entire apartheid section in the POA, particularly the third paragraph, which called for "support for the national liberation movements of South Africa and Namibia in their struggle against *apartheid*" and reaffirmed the validity of those movements "by all available means, including armed struggle."[29]

Delegates requested separate votes on these disputed sections before the vote on the entire document. For paragraph 19 of the Declaration, the vote was 84 in favor and 15 against, with 16 abstentions.[30] The vote on paragraph 20 generated similar results, with 87 in favor and 17 against, with 14 abstentions.[31] With the two paragraphs approved for inclusion in the text, the final vote on the entire Declaration resulted in 101 in favor and 12 against, with 3 abstentions.[32]

Two votes for the POA occurred—one on the inclusion of paragraph 3, which concerned "armed struggle," and the other on the entire apartheid section, which included a recommendation for sanctions by the Security Council. Paragraph 3 was adopted with a vote of 86 in favor and 20 against, with 2 abstentions. The apartheid section also received approval, with a final vote of 92 in favor and 7 against, with 12 abstentions. The entirety of the POA was accepted with 114 governments in favor (compared to 88 in 1978), 10 abstentions, and no dissenting votes. According to Jonah, the 1983 conference "restor[ed] the consensus which had been evident at the start of the First Decade."[33] The adoption of both the Declaration and the POA occurred in the final hours of the conference, after the clock was stopped so that the voting "could be finished within the mandated time."[34] Having separate votes for specific paragraphs in a document that is not legally binding demonstrates how entrenched the geopolitical divisions on these issues had become. It also shows that the content of these paragraphs prevailed in spite of the fact that the most controversial aspects of the agenda had been removed to appease Western governments.

Unlike the 1978 Declaration and POA, the documents issued for the 1983 conference referenced the UN Decade on Women, which began in 1975.[35] Both the 1978 and the 1983 documents signaled that women's experience with racism differed from that of men. Paragraph 22 of the 1978 Declaration and paragraph 23 of the 1983 Declaration state that "women are often doubly discriminated against" and that "special efforts are called for to eliminate the effects of racial discrimination" on women. The 1983 Declaration was more inclusive than the earlier document: it supported "women's equal participation in the political, economic, social, and cultural life of their societies," whereas the 1978 Declaration mentioned only "political and economic life." The 1983 Declaration also noted that the ratification and implementation of CEDAW "is of particular importance." The language of the conference documents had expanded modestly within just five years to reflect a preliminary understanding of women and racism that acknowledged political, economic, social, and cultural dimensions.

Canada voted against the 1983 Declaration. Referencing two paragraphs about the Middle East, the Canada delegation said that it was "unable to associate itself with the Declaration because of political matters extraneous to the fundamental concerns of the Conference" that had been introduced.[36] Canada also said that statements in reference to South Africa were "drafted in terms that are unacceptable to Canada." Canada did not agree with the POA either, but stated that it "intended to be guided by it in pursuing the policies and measures already introduced to combat racism, racial discrimination, and South Africa's policy of *apartheid*."[37]

By holding the 1978 and 1983 WCARs in relatively close proximity, an overlap of themes and topics was to be expected. What we can glean from the negotiations vis-à-vis the conference records and their corresponding outcome documents is how deeply contested the *idea* of the conferences themselves was for certain countries. Similar to the numerous GA resolutions at this time, the overwhelming focus of both world conferences was the dismantling of South African apartheid. The global conversation on racism remained largely stagnant in this regard for several years following the 1983 WCAR. Nearly twenty years later, with calls for a third world conference underway, the global scene had changed dramatically with apartheid's eventual downfall. The 2001 WCAR was an opportunity to revisit the conversation and renew a global commitment to dismantling racism.

WORLD CONFERENCE AGAINST RACISM, RACIAL DISCRIMINATION, XENOPHOBIA, AND RELATED INTOLERANCE, 2001

General Assembly Resolution 52/111 of December 12, 1997, led to planning for a third world conference in 2001, and South Africa was the only country that asked to host the conference. The 2001 WCAR participants included 170 states, national human rights commissions, and specialized agencies (such as the International Money Fund and the World Bank). Scheduled for August 31–September 7, 2001, the conference officially concluded one day late, on September 8, because of the delegates' inability to reach consensus on the official conference documents.[38]

The 2001 WCAR was unique in that three international PrepComs occurred in Geneva, rather than the standard two.[39] Four regional Prep Coms based on the regional groupings preceded these three Geneva meetings. The first regional PrepCom took place in Strasbourg, France, with the Western Europe and Others Group (WEOG) on October 11–13, 2000, and then the others followed: the Americas PrepCom took place on December 5–7, 2000, in Santiago, Chile; the African PrepCom occurred on January 22–24, 2001, in Dakar, Senegal; and the Asian-Pacific PrepCom happened on February 19–21, 2001, in Tehran, Iran. The United States and Canada are considered part of WEOG, but rather than attend only that PrepCom in France, they sent representatives to Santiago instead. The United States also attended the African PrepCom, a highly unusual and visible move.

The United States' decision to participate in the Americas PrepCom was unprecedented. Roger Wareham,[40] a member of the December 12th Movement International Secretariat, an African American NGO, addressed this point in testimony before the US House of Representatives Subcommittee on International Operations and Human Rights on July 31, 2001, just one month before the Durban conference.[41] Wareham said that the US and Canadian delegations had gone to Santiago to prevent the inclusion of strong language in the declaration of slavery as a crime against humanity, reparations for African descendants, and the economic basis of racism. He added that the US delegation had gone to Dakar because it had received an "advance copy of the language that was being proposed" and was "so appalled by the inflammatory language" that the delegation was intent on persuading the African countries "to tone their language down."[42]

The intentions of the United States and Canada in attending the Prep-Com in Santiago lacked coherence. For example, the United States and Canada proposed language that they rejected during "the last minute . . . of the last meeting" of the PrepCom.[43] This maneuver seemed designed to sabotage negotiations, weaken the language of the documents that would be forwarded to the international PrepComs, and simply stall debate altogether. The United States continued to engage in this kind of behavior throughout the WCAR proceedings. Eva from Mexico recalled witnessing the following incident: "I remember the representative from the Libyan government. . . . At a time when the United States was completely stalling the discussion, he asked, 'What is it that you want from me? I cannot get down on my knees; I am an old man. So we cannot advance if there is not some dialogue among us.'"[44] Given the understanding that the UN fosters a space in which to debate, dialogue, and eventually reach compromise, the US government's actions made it evident that they were not interested in doing any of the three, and this delegate had reached his breaking point. But the US delegation continued its campaign to disrupt and obstruct.

The international PrepComs in Geneva occurred on May 1–5, 2000, May 21–June 1, 2001, and July 30–August 10, 2001. At these meetings the participants discussed the agenda, themes, and logistics of the WCAR, and negotiations regarding the conference documents began. At the first international PrepCom, delegates identified the five themes for the conference:

1. Sources, causes, forms, and contemporary manifestations of racism, racial discrimination, xenophobia, and related intolerance;
2. Victims of racism, racial discrimination, xenophobia, and related intolerance;
3. Measures of prevention, education, and protection aimed at the eradication of racism, racial discrimination, xenophobia, and related intolerance at the regional, national, and international levels;
4. Provision of effective remedies, recourses, redress [compensatory], and other measures, at the national, regional, and international levels;
5. Strategies to achieve full and effective equality, including international co-operation and enhancement of the UN and other international mechanisms in combating racism, racial discrimination, xenophobia and related intolerance, and follow-up.[45]

These five themes are fairly straightforward and linear, from the sources and causes of racism to strategies to overcome it. The term "compensatory" in theme 4 proved problematic for WEOG, which is not surprising, since matters of compensation, which can range from the symbolic (i.e., an official apology for slavery) to the economically redistributive (i.e., forfeiting debt payment from Third World countries) would be directed to the governments in this configuration.

Representatives from NGOs and governments fiercely debated the second theme, and government delegates decided to create a victim list to serve as a document for aiding the finalization of conference documents. A US NGO representative to the regional PrepCom in Santiago described the victim list debate as a competition to determine which group would be classified as the one that had experienced the worst racism:

> All the groups wanted to make sure they were on the list, and there was actually a discussion about which groups had suffered more, what order they should be listed in, and if other groups were worthy of being listed in the group. . . . I was just astonished, listening to this, that there was no sense of "Let's all support one another and make sure that somehow all of us feel represented in this." It was very competitive. Amongst the governments too, it was the same sort of "Well, that's not as important, as egregious. Gypsies and Roma people are not as important as these [other] groups, clearly."[46]

A contentious tone for the 2001 WCAR was established with groups' internal fighting to be recognized as having experienced the worst racism and discrimination and with the spirit of camaraderie and internationalism having faded. This also established an environment in which some new groups could be excluded if not deemed worthy of being on the victim list.[47]

THE NGO FORUM AND THE US "WALKOUT"

The NGO Forum against Racism began on August 28, 2001, at the Kingsmead Cricket Stadium in Durban. A number of plenary sessions and hundreds of workshops comprised the five-day forum. Buses transported participants off-site to other sessions throughout the day. The Forum was extremely disorganized; interviewees referred to it as "a mess."[48] The disorganization impeded people's ability to engage in networking to the extent they desired, and caused stressful days. "It shouldn't be hard to go find your way to a workshop, and you shouldn't arrive there to find out it has been canceled time after time after time," said an interviewee from the United States. She noted that some cancellations had occurred "once or twice," but that she had "helped organize workshops that people couldn't get to because they didn't know that it was happening. So that was extremely frustrating."[49] Adding to the frustration, NGO activists frequently had to translate documents themselves because funds for translators were scarce and the few available translators were difficult to locate.

Despite the chaos, activists and advocates worked hard during the NGO Forum and the 2001 WCAR. The days were long and emotional; it was not uncommon for participants to have only a couple of hours of sleep each night. At the Forum, activists formed and worked in caucuses and commissions to draft position statements, formulate lobbying strategies, and finalize an NGO version of the DDPA to submit to participating governments.[50]

The low-level delegation from the US government arrived in Durban in the middle of the Forum, and it was during the NGO Forum that the US delegation announced that it intended to leave the conference.[51] Whether the United States *officially* walked out is debatable. One US activist asked the head of the NGO Consultation Group every day if the United States had walked out of the conference, and the reply was always "no." "The US government never walked out as far as I know. What they did was go for lunch and never return. I was specifically told that if the US government walked out, they would have had to give their badges in and exit the premises. They did not do that. But the media in the US and everyone assumed that the US government walked out. The government act[ed] with no integrity [by lying] to its people as usual. . . . I mean, it is nothing unusual, but this time they thought it was just okay to lie with no apology."[52] Another interviewee saw the US delegates in Durban after the supposed walkout: "Right after the US did their big 'walkout,' I was over in the hotel where all the diplomats were staying. I was in the hotel and was using e-mail or something, and I looked over to one of the lounge areas and there was the head of the US delegation and the deputy head having negotiations. And they were sitting in the hotel having their negotiations, rather than doing it aboveboard. That captured in some way how disgusting the US position was in the whole process."[53]

Setting aside for the moment whether or not the United States followed protocol for official withdrawal from the 2001 WCAR, their actions set up a context in which the largest number of NGOs coming from the United States now had no official government representation at the 2001 WCAR. This move, to a degree, undermined the efforts of US NGO activists who wanted to confront the US delegation about racism in the United States. However, it also created an opportunity for representatives from US NGOs to lobby government delegates from other countries and in the process realize both the importance of building political relationships outside of the United States and the willingness of other delegates to listen to them.

The US NGO Coordinating Committee and other NGO supporters organized a session for the government delegation to explain its actions to US NGO representatives.[54] A US interviewee described the setting in which hundreds of representatives gathered for the session:

> People were waiting for a really long time for the US official delegates to come out and speak with us. It was a small room, and it was really crowded and packed. But no one came. Then people in the room were informed that we had to go upstairs and relocate to a larger room because the official delegates didn't want to speak in such a small room. So then everybody moved to the bigger room upstairs. . . . People were waiting and waiting and waiting again. And the delegates never came inside. Somebody said the delegates were outside and they weren't feeling good and couldn't come in.

According to my interviewees, the US delegation never entered the room and informed the session organizers that they could not participate in the meeting unless they were guaranteed the absence of the media press. One of the session organizers said that the government delegates were "nervous and almost shaking because, in my opinion, they saw angry black and brown people." A government delegate from the US embassy in Pretoria said he would lose his job "because Secretary of State Colin Powell [had] not made a statement in the US saying that [the delegation was] walking out."[55] Shortly after refusing to speak to the NGO representatives, one of the members of the US delegation "walked across to the CNN office and made a press statement." This move infuriated the meeting organizers.[56]

US NGO representatives quickly formulated a strategy to publicly respond to what appeared to be an imminent walkout following the US delegation's refusal to participate in the NGO meeting. In addition to giving interviews and having press conferences with US media present, NGO representatives organized protests and wore stickers that read "US NGOs here, US government not. Why not?" One person displayed a sign that read, "Colin Powell does not speak for me."

One of the protests, which occurred right after the failed meeting, was one of my interviewee's most memorable experiences at the conference: "People [marched] right after that meeting to the gates of the government conference. [We] started out from [a] building across the street from the NGO Forum [and] marched to the [location of the] government conference. It was nighttime, and while we were marching, people were standing on the sides and cheering us on, too. They were from different countries." Her memory of this protest involves the many non-US supporters condemning the US government. This shows how broad the displeasure with the US government had become and why, in some respects, the US government likely chose to disengage from the Durban proceedings altogether.

Another member of the US NGO Coordinating Committee reflected on the walkout during our interview: "People were really upset. People were trying to figure out what to do. I think one of the things we didn't really have was a substantive, cohesive leadership around the US [NGO] delegation. I think that prevented us from being more strategic about how to respond to the US walkout." She noted that the activism that followed the failed meeting with the US government was important but not necessarily or sufficiently strategic: "I don't think we were strategic enough about getting press statements back to [the] media in the US and putting a better spin on our criticism of the positions or dealing with why the US was walking out in terms of this whole language around the Israeli-Palestinian issue. We could have been more strategic, and we weren't."[57] Her comments suggest that part of the struggle here was also about media image and representation. Not being sufficiently media savvy with messaging proved detrimental to activists because the majority of people in the world learned about the Durban conference through the media reports; and these media reports were overwhelmingly negative and critical.

The US delegation's action was in one sense a performance, because the United States knew that the world media would report it as a walk-out without questioning whether it was official. The supposed "walkout" was an attempt by the United States to exert power over a conference it had lost control over. No one in the NGO community was surprised that the US delegation behaved in the manner it did given the actions of the United States during the PrepComs.

The United States became increasingly isolated from the international community during the 2001 WCAR process, a consequence it had not anticipated (though this changed immediately after the September 11, 2001, terrorist attacks). Though some government delegates tried to appease the United States to keep them engaged, these governments, too, reached their limit and were unwilling to let the United States dictate the topics for discussion at the 2001 WCAR. For example, the United States wanted discussions about the death penalty taken off the table entirely, but some of their fiercest opponents came from European countries that are usually allies. The US government advocated diligently for the removal of any language regarding reparations, but African nations remained steadfast in ensuring that the topic remained on the agenda. In response, the US government released a statement to NGOs participating in the 2001 WCAR about reparations in an effort to quell the momentum (see appendix). The 2001 WCAR, similar to the world conferences in 1978 and 1983, demonstrated how out of touch the United States had become in regard to the global human rights movement against racism.

THE DURBAN DECLARATION AND PROGRAMME OF ACTION

When I interviewed Mary Robinson in June 2003, the former high commissioner for human rights, she referred to the Durban conference as a triumphant achievement, particularly in regard to the advances made on intersectionality. She stated that "very important issues" had been discussed at the conference, "including a much stronger emphasis on the connections between discrimination on the basis of gender and of race." One of the goals of activists at the NGO Forum was to establish the importance of intersectionality in efforts to combat racism, and a system-centered approach to intersectionality (which takes complex systems into account) shaped a number of their advocacy positions during the Durban proceedings.[58]

The NGO version of the DDPA included a description of their approach to intersectionality under the subject heading "gender:" "An intersectional approach to discrimination acknowledges that every person be it man or woman exists in a framework of multiple identities, with factors such as race, class, ethnicity, religion, sexual orientation, gender identity, age, disability, citizenship, national identity, geo-political context, health, including HIV/AIDS status and any other status are all determinants in one's experiences of racism, racial discrimination, xenophobia and related intolerances. An intersectional approach highlights the way in which there is a simultaneous interaction of discrimination as a result of multiple identities."[59] This approach to intersectionality is peppered throughout the NGO DDPA. In the section titled "Africans and African Descendants," historical systems—"slave trade, slavery, conquest, colonization, and apartheid"—and contemporary systems—"racism, discrimination, doctrines and practices of racial supremacy, hate violence and related intolerance"—are identified as shaping the experiences of people of African descent today: "It is the complexity and intersection of these historical and continuing common roots, experiences and struggles to overcome them, that bind Africans and African Descendants together as a world community."[60] The section titled "Asian and Asian Descendant Women" emphasizes "complex systems," noting that the "intersection of sexism, racism and poverty . . . make them [Asian and Asian-descendant women] vulnerable to trafficking for prostitution as mail order brides, domestic workers, low wage or sweat shop workers, and as bonded labour."[61] Sections of the NGO DDPA integrate intersectionality using a system-centered and group-centered approach based on identity categories, including people with disabilities, race, ethnicity, origin, gender, age, and religion.

In general, the language in the WCAR DDPA, issued after the conference, is noticeably weaker than that in the NGO DDPA. The latter strongly condemns globalization:

> We denounce processes of globalisation that concentrate power in the
> hands of powerful Western nations and multinational corporations, and
> that have an impact on every aspect of social life, in every country and

region, as racist and unjust. It widens economic inequalities within and between countries, further impoverishing and marginalizing masses of peoples, and places them at risk to the demand for cheap and informal labour in labour-importing countries. Tools of globalisation such as structural adjustment policies result in poverty, famine, and the collapse of health and educational systems. Globalisation leads to economic and social disintegration, unemployment and marginalisation. It particularly implies both feminisation and racialisation of poverty. Compensatory measures must be extended in this context.[62]

In contrast, the brief paragraph on globalization in the WCAR DDPA talks about its benefits and costs in noticeably subdued language: "While globalization offers great opportunities, at present its benefits are very unevenly shared, while its costs are unevenly distributed."[63]

This globalization language exemplifies how vastly divergent the objectives were for government delegates and NGO representatives as they navigated the political waters of the 2001 WCAR. Yet the 2001 WCAR documents manage to capture a broadened approach to racism that introduces new topics such as gender inequality in access to education, violence against women, freedom of religious expression, modern-day human trafficking, and women migrants. Previous WCARs had not considered these types of issues.[64] The WCAR DDPA states that women and children are disproportionately affected by human trafficking, and government delegations conceded that states should adopt public policies that do not directly or indirectly make women vulnerable to violence or susceptible to trafficking.[65] In alignment with international law, the document also acknowledges that sexual violence is systematic and is used as a weapon of war, and that states are fully aware of the grave situation,[66] and Article 54(a) states that "the intersection of discrimination on grounds of race and gender makes women and girls particularly vulnerable to [sexual] violence, which is often related to racism, racial discrimination, xenophobia and related intolerance."

Debates about the meaning of gender are definitely contentious at the UN, especially because of pressure from conservative states. As education scholar Jennifer Chan-Tiberghien contends, the approach to gender in the 2001 WCAR documents is based largely on a colonial or neocolonial view of womanhood: "While it is important to acknowledge feminist success in putting gender on these UN agendas, the term 'gen-der' has little significance outside the traditional category of 'women'; in almost all cases it signifies non-indigenous, non-migrant, able-bodied, and heterosexual women."[67] During the final days of negotiation at the 2001 WCAR, the Moroccan government delegation briefly proposed that all the text referencing "gender" in the official conference documents be placed in brackets, to signify disagreement among the negotiating parties,[68] a move that may have been a response to activists' efforts to persuade government delegations to consider the fluidity of gender and sexual diversity.[69] The "gender compromise" is noted in a footnote in the WCAR DDPA, which states, "The term 'gender' refers to the two sexes, male and female, within the context of society. The term 'gender' does not indicate any meaning different from the above."[70] The feminist en-gagement in the Durban proceedings made an impact in the sense that the final WCAR documents acknowledge that women experience racism differently than men in a far more expanded way than previous world conferences had done. However, more work lies ahead in terms of offer-ing a richer interpretation of both intersectionality and gender.[71]

The NGO DDPA generated far more controversy than the WCAR DDPA. NGOs adopted controversial language about Israel and Zionism, which forced Robinson to reject the NGO documents. Her decision upset many NGO activists, who viewed her as a liaison to the government del-egations, not as someone with authority to approve decisions made by NGOs. Patricia from a lesbian rights group in Peru, was extremely critical of Robinson's decision:

> I thought it was terrible that she refused to receive the document from
> civil society. It's not what she wants or what she doesn't want. It's
> that she has to receive the document that civil society presents to her.
> She cannot put conditions on it. Up until the end she said to us, if we
> remove that part (regarding Palestine and Israel) that she would endorse
> the document. We said no. No, no, no! In other words, we weren't going
> to change our decision or our proposal because she didn't feel like re-
> ceiving the document. To hell with it then. She had no right to do that.[72]

Robinson was in a difficult political position, however. She told me that NGOs had given her no alternative:

I refused to endorse the NGO document, which was a great pity, because there were some very good things in that document, far superior to some of the official text. Normally, as high commissioner, with my links in society, I would have strongly recommended the NGO text to an intergovernmental conference. That would have been the general expectation. I didn't decline to receive it; I did receive it. But I made it clear that I wasn't going to endorse it or recommend it to Member States because it contained language that tried to reopen [the] "Zionism as racism" [debate] and other language [that] was unacceptable.[73]

Another activist from the United States believed that Robinson truly had no choice but to reject the documents "given the circumstances." The result was the loss of "all the good things in the NGO document . . . all the stuff about the Dalits, all the stuff on criminal justice. All the great stuff in the NGO document got lost, and that is clearly a disadvantage for everyone."[74]

Robinson was personally blamed for the controversies surrounding the Durban conference, and paid a heavy price for of it: she was not reappointed as high commissioner in 2002. Yet her engagement with the issues and her leadership at the Durban conference ultimately opened up a space in which new understandings of racism could be globally debated for the first time in nearly twenty years. In fact, Robinson spent four of her five years as high commissioner focused on the 2001 WCAR.[75]

THE 2009 DURBAN REVIEW CONFERENCE

The terrorist attacks of September 11, 2001, just a few days after the 2001 WCAR concluded, exacerbated the difficulties feminists faced upon their return home as they tried to pursue an agenda to combat racism. During my interviews, which began in 2003, it was difficult, if not impossible, to talk about the Durban proceedings without discussing the inflammatory responses of the US government and the political policies that emerged in the wake of the attacks. At the same time, the 2001 Durban conference had started an overdue, albeit imperfect, conversation about racism and the ways in which racisms have expanded and transformed. Importantly, the official adoption of feminist language began to provide an opening for new discussions on racism, and an acknowledgment of intersectionality began to be incorporated into the discourse of antiracism. It is always true, however, that several steps backward often follow even slight progress. The 2009 DRC did not move the conversation started at the 2001 Durban conference forward. Instead, the goals of the conference were undermined by conflict and political posturing, emboldening the forces that did not want to have the conversation at all.

The review conferences, which are mandated by UN protocol, are essential for assessing the impact of the world conferences.[76] The principal objective of the 2009 DRC was to revisit and evaluate the implementation of the DDPA.[77] After about two years of preparation, the UN convened a four-day conference beginning on April 20, 2009, in Geneva. The 2009 DRC had four main objectives:

> To review the implementation of the DDPA by all stakeholders at the national, regional, and international levels. The review would include an assessment of contemporary manifestations of racism, racial discrimination, xenophobia, and related intolerance through an inclusive, transparent, and collaborative process. It would also identify concrete measures and initiatives for combating and eliminating all manifestations of these phenomena.

> To assess the effectiveness of the existing Durban follow-up and other relevant UN mechanisms dealing with the issues of racism, racial discrimination, xenophobia, and related intolerance in order to enhance them.

> To promote the universal ratification and implementation of the International Convention on the Elimination of All Forms of Racial Discrimination and the proper consideration of the recommendations of the Committee on the Elimination of Racial Discrimination.

> To identify and share good practices achieved in the fight against racism, racial discrimination, xenophobia, and related intolerance.[78]

The intent of the DRC was to pick up where the 2001 WCAR had left off. The DRC's objectives predetermined a fairly mild and standard undertaking. The fire that had ignited in the lead-up to the 2001 WCAR had largely died down by this point, but rapidly reemerged when the UN announced the 2009 DRC. Yet the rather mild objectives of the DRC proved too controversial, and critics of the DRC tried to prevent the conversation from even starting.

The UN Office of the High Commissioner for Human Rights (OHCHR) knew early on that the public relations campaign for the 2009 DRC would face strong and well-organized opposition. Revisiting issues that had been debated at the 2001 WCAR or introducing new issues would be unacceptable to these forces—even the *idea* of the conference would be opposed. Navi Pillay from South Africa, who followed Robinson as the high commissioner for human rights, did not want a repeat of the controversies that had embroiled the 2001 WCAR and had cost Robinson her position. One observer noted that "the battle over perceptions" mattered more to Pillay than the concrete outcomes of the 2009 DRC.[79] Pillay's office went to great lengths to abide by the requests of the United States and the nations in the European Union. Canada and Israel had already indicated that they would not participate in the 2009 DRC, but the United States, having just elected President Barack Obama, was wavering.

Pillay's efforts notwithstanding, on the night before the opening of the conference, the United States, joined by its European allies, decided to boycott. The primary controversies had to do with the possible inclusion of the Middle East conflict in the DRC outcome document, and the scheduled address by Iranian president Mahmoud Ahmadinejad, the only head of state to attend the conference.[80] Ahmadinejad's outlandish but completely predictable comments on the first day of the DRC finished the process of derailing the conference, much to the delight of the groups and governments that had endorsed the boycott. Opposition to the UN's antiracism agenda also contributed to the ideological warfare waged by the governments that did not support the conference. When it became apparent that the DRC gathering would address reparations, land rights, violence against women, indigenous sovereignty, caste, state violence, imperialism, and apartheid, the opposition began to focus on how to weaken the outcome document.

Contributing to the political turmoil were newly formed conservative NGOs such as NGO Watch and NGO Monitor, which had become increasingly concerned with political organizing in the UN's antiracism forums after the Durban conference. Formed in 2003 by two conservative US think tanks to monitor NGOs' impact on UN policies, NGO Watch had become inactive by 2007, but it reactivated for the 2009 DRC. NGO Monitor, founded in 2001 by Gerald M. Steinberg, an Israeli academic, closely scrutinizes funding sources of progressive NGOs. The Ford Foundation, which provided the largest amount of the financial support for NGO activists from around the world to participate in the 2001 WCAR and NGO Forum, was one of their targets.[81] The Ford Foundation came under intense pressure and criticism for supporting NGOs that were loosely or broadly identified as pro-Palestinian. The foundation board subsequently voted to discontinue funds for any follow-up work that was in any way related to the 2001 WCAR. The impact of this decision was monumental, given the substantial number of organizations and advocates that the foundation supported.[82] NGO Monitor regularly scrutinizes the groups that receive Ford Foundation funding to determine if they merit support. Some members of the US House of Representatives even considered having the Ford Foundation investigated for allegedly supporting "anti-Israeli" groups.[83]

The division between those NGOs that wanted the 2009 DRC to be a success and those that attended as a tactic to undermine it was readily apparent during Pillay's meeting with NGOs at the DRC. As Pillay started to field questions, a young woman asked, rather defiantly, "What did *you* learn from this conference about what you should do differently next time?" Clearly sensing the hostility in her voice, Pillay asked, "What did I learn, you ask?" "Yes," the young woman replied. "Did you learn a lesson here?" Pillay responded, "Yes, I learned you show up. You do not boycott an international conference, especially the day before. You show up, you negotiate."[84] Pillay's frustration stemmed from the fact that the OHCHR had made incredible concessions to appease the governments that opposed the 2009 DRC. The outcome document had been significantly weakened, and all references to Palestine or the Palestinian struggle removed. The United States, joined by its European allies, indicated satisfaction with this outcome, so Pillay and the other UN members who had acquiesced to the demands were understandably dismayed by the United States' last-minute decision to not attend. The reason given by the United States was that the final 2009 DRC document would endorse the 2001 DDPA—a logical and expected endorsement given the conference's title and objectives. The United States' action constituted a stunning display of disrespect to the high commissioner.

In the first press release that followed the announcement of the United States' withdrawal, Pillay stated that she was "shocked" and "deeply disappointed" by the news: "A handful of states have permitted one or two issues to dominate their approach to this issue, allowing them to outweigh the concerns of numerous groups of people that suffer racism and similar forms of intolerance."[85] Acknowledging the sensitive nature of racism and the difficulty of talking about it, Pillay also maintained that the reasons given for not participating in the conference could have been dealt with following standard UN procedures: "It would have been possible to make it clear in a footnote that the US had not affirmed the original document and therefore is not in a position to reaffirm it, which is a routine practice in multilateral negotiations to enable consensus-building while allowing for individual positions to be expressed. And then we could have all moved on together, and put the problems of 2001 behind us."[86] Pillay said she "had to face a widespread and highly organized campaign of disinformation." The effectiveness of this campaign cannot be overstated. When a number of people, including Ministers, informed Pillay that the DDPA was anti-Semitic, she denied the charge and pointed out that 182 states had approved the document. She noted, "It was clear that either they had not bothered to read what [the document] actually said, or they were putting a cast on it that was, to say the least, decidedly exaggerated."[87]

In her final press release, Pillay criticized the "bizarre behavior" of states in the negotiation process: "Because of this campaign [of disinformation] that was so determined to kill the conference, some countries decided to boycott it, although a few days earlier, they had actually agreed on what is now the final text. I consider this bizarre. You agree to the text on Friday evening, and walk out on Sunday. I think it was unfortunate that a few states disengaged from the process. Although almost all of them had agreed to this text, they are not part of the consensus that adopted it."[88] Pillay stated she hoped that the boycotting governments would "come back into the process [and] add their names to the list of 182 states that have adopted the outcome document."[89] Frustrated by the "many mainline newspapers who incidentally declined many [of her] op-eds" to set the record straight, Pillay thanked the Geneva Press Corp for having "seen through the propaganda."[90] She was also forthright about the offensive personal attacks she had encountered, which referred to her as the "dangerous" and "ludicrous" high commissioner for human rights.

Governments are aware that the documents and proposals issued at the conclusion of a UN conference carry some political weight. The positions stated can shape discourse and global perception of an issue as well as establish important precedents. Because of the pressure applied by the governments that opposed the 2009 DRC, the nineteen-page outcome document does not refer in detail to the 2001 DDPA, and it does not propose anything new. It was a document approved in haste in an effort to save the credibility of the conference. In fact, it was approved before the conference had officially concluded. NGO representatives were stunned: those who had traveled to Geneva to influence the document were no longer able to do so. The dialogue had abruptly and officially ended.

The 2009 DRC outcome document includes a mere five sections, and its contents are not at all inspiring. The first two sections summarize the 2001 WCAR; the third section describes ICERD implementation and CERD recommendations; the fourth and fifth sections discuss the "sharing of best practices" and identify "concrete measures and initiatives" to encourage the "implementation" of the DDPA. The outcome document is a stark reminder of how maligned the process had become.[91]

The particular indignities experienced by racially marginalized women are not mentioned until paragraph 70 of the document; the discussion of the intersection of gender and racial discrimination from an analytical perspective does not go beyond the mere acknowledgment that gendered dimensions to racial discrimination exist. Furthermore, the debate about the meaning of gender had not changed: paragraph 88 reaffirms the footnote about gender that was inserted into the DDPA. The UN's efforts to combat global racism were still stuck in 2001. Yet 182 Member States adopted the 2009 DRC outcome document, only 7 fewer states than those that had approved the 2001 DDPA. Delegates from all over the world still wanted to discuss racism, intolerance, and xenophobia; they still wanted to talk about the Durban conference. To say that the 2009 DRC was a disappointment in comparison to the 2001 WCAR is an understatement. In Geneva, UN conferences have a completely different energy. In addition, the conference did not include a meeting space for NGOs.

President Obama's administration had signaled its desire to have a different relationship with the UN early on (Obama appointed Susan Rice as UN ambassador and elevated the position to cabinet level, for example[92]). With links to family still in Kenya and remaining childhood friendships formed during his time in Indonesia, President Obama is uniquely positioned to understand the importance of multilateralism.

His decision to not send a US delegation to the 2009 DRC deeply angered US racial justice activists who had anticipated, and even expected, a more cooperative experience than they had with the administration of George W. Bush.[93] President Obama may understand the importance of the UN better than his predecessor, but when it came to Durban and its legacy, nothing had really changed.[94]

Over five years have passed since the 2009 DRC, and many questions remain. How can antiracist feminists who are committed to uplifting women and their communities not lose ground in the fight against racism? How can we heed the "Where are the women?" chant from the NGO Forum in Durban? Discussing racism is not easy or comfortable; it should not be. As frustrating as UN protocols can be, they are structured to encourage and stimulate dialogue, debate, and, ultimately, negotiation and compromise. Not showing up is an easy escape from a difficult dialogue. Perhaps more important is the observation that the conservative opposition would not be so well organized if they did not feel a threat from progressive antiracist groups and activists.

CONCLUSION: MOVING FORWARD AND THEN BACKWARD

The UN's interest in combating racism began in the 1960s. Of particular significance in this history are the World Conferences against Racism, held in 1978, 1983, and 2001. The Declaration and POA originating from each world conference presented consensus-based strategies to combat racism, ranging from a call for mandatory sanctions against racist regimes to supporting national liberation and decolonization movements, including armed struggle. The question of South Africa was particularly divisive in the 1978 and 1983 WCARs because governments embraced different approaches for appropriately dealing with apartheid. The same was true of the Israeli-Palestinian issue. There should be no impression, though, that global North or Western governments wanted these world conferences to take place at all. They were entirely opposed to the idea of them, and their subsequent boycotts and obstructionism were a dramatic reflection of this opposition.

By the time a third WCAR became a possibility in 2001, the downfall of South African apartheid and the independence of Namibia were the new realities, and tensions then evolved into disputes between governments and their citizens, as well as between different governments, over the purpose of a third WCAR. Like its predecessors, the controversies stemming from the 2001 WCAR and the 2009 DRC were directly connected to the actions of certain governments, including the United States. Particularly egregious was the alleged US "walkout" during the 2001 WCAR, which received a tremendous amount of media press coverage. This should have been an embarrassment for the US government, which has yet to participate in a WCAR. It is not so much that its absence leaves something amiss—in fact, the United States' absence can reduce the imposition of barriers meant to severely limit the discussion—but that its actions reveal a profound disdain for the work of US-based anti-racist activists.

Mary Robinson told me that despite these extreme difficulties she faced as high commissioner, she remained committed to the 2001 WCAR and to what it tried to achieve. She believed that the topics discussed—"racism, discrimination, treatment of minorities" and the recognition of intersectionality—comprised an "extraordinarily serious agenda."[95] For Robinson, "Durban must be a beginning, not an end."[96] As a result, the challenges, debates, and eventual outcomes of the world conferences have come to represent the terrain of struggle over power, representation, and a voice for the future.

4

Making the Intersectional Connections

I think it was an extraordinarily difficult conference to prepare for. It was in fact the most difficult task that I had as high commissioner, because I took the theme of the conference seriously to be a conference against racism, discrimination, xenophobia, and related intolerance.

—MARY ROBINSON, FORMER UN HIGH
COMMISSIONER FOR HUMAN RIGHTS, 2003

A TREMENDOUS AMOUNT OF STRATEGIZING AND PREPARATION preceded the successes achieved by feminist activists at the Durban conference. The nearly two-year preparatory period provided women with opportunities to form new transnational coalitions and to develop collective strategies on how to most effectively lobby their advocacy positions against racism at a global level. As Margaret, a young African Canadian feminist activist, stated in our interview, preparing for a world conference is a "moment in time that focuses people."[1] The transnational coalitions that developed and the new articulations of particular issues that resulted from those alliances had an impact not only on the outcome documents that were issued after the conference—the DDPA and the parallel DDPA document issued during the NGO Forum—but also on the activists themselves.

The process of preparing for world conferences, as scholar Charles Henry says, serves "as a place of discovery, of expressing meanings and creating new identities."[2] It is within the "transnational spaces" shaped by the UN and, more specifically, informed by the occasion of the world conferences, that a continual remapping of "the geographical as well as ideological boundaries" occurs.[3] The remapping of boundaries signifies that "the moment" Margaret identified for the 2001 WCAR was a time for antiracist feminist activists to consolidate, negotiate, and debate their agendas for UN-based advocacy.

In this chapter, I address "the moment" by focusing on the organizing efforts of feminists from Canada, the United States, Mexico, and Peru during the nearly two-year preparatory period for the Durban conference. During the activist meetings and gatherings that led up to the world conference, feminists from these countries advocated for an expanded approach to overcoming racism that directly addressed the particular needs of women in their communities. In advancing an intersectionality approach, antiracist feminist activists paid attention to context when complicating dialogues about racism by pushing the boundaries of universalism. As such, antiracist feminists' voice and agency solidified an acknowledgement at the UN level of the interactional dynamics of race and gender. It merits mentioning that the activist deployment of intersectionality had far more nuance than the official records suggest, which is one of the limitations of relying solely on official records to tell a story.

INTERSECTIONALITY IN CONTEXT

As I discussed in the introductory chapter, intersectionality is a theoretical concept that signifies the indivisibility of interlocking forms of oppression that can exist at the level of an individual's identity or can reference structural forms of subordination that exist in society at large.[4] The term can refer to the moment in which racism, sexism, or classism collide to form a "matrix of domination"; it can also refer to how race, class, gender, and sexuality (among other social categories) influence the structural forms of subordination.[5] In the first context, the language of "double discrimination" or "multiple jeopardy" is commonly used. The second assesses how the "systematic forces" of racism, classism, and sexism "shape societies";[6] here intersectionality is about structures and systems rather than the experiences of individuals or groups of people.[7]

For the concept of intersectionality to have transnational salience, an awareness of social location and power relationships must be incorporated into its application so that multiple understandings of intersectionality can meaningfully coexist. When reading power backward and forward, as Cynthia Enloe suggests, intersectionality does not become limited to its primary use by US activists. In fact, diverse invocations of intersectionality at the transnational level present ideal opportunities for cross-border tactics that draw on regionally based realities.

For many antiracist feminist scholars and activists, identity categories "shift with a changing context."[8] An essentialist or universal conceptualization of, for example, global antiblack racism is problematic because the contexts vary: antiblack racism in the United States is unlike antiblack racism in Peru. These variances are situated "at the crossroads of different systems of power and domination."[9] Working "at the crossroads" can present opportunities for new feminist coalitions, as was the case for the women included in this research. The Durban conference and its corresponding NGO Forum each offers a venue in which to understand how transnational relationships formed, evolved, and even became contested.

Canadian education scholar Jennifer Chan-Tiberghien argues that a "gender-as-intersectionality" paradigm prevailed at the Durban conference. This paradigm, informed by a "'difference' and 'differences' strategy," was meant to signify the diversity of women's experiences "in their specific racial or other locations."[10] Inadequate recognition of this rich diversity among women was one of the controversies that arose during the 1995 UN World Conference on Women in Beijing.[11] By contending that women experience racism in a sundry manner, these antiracist feminist activists advanced an approach to intersectionality that did not take context for granted. Rather than relying on false universalisms, antiracist feminists worked toward the "new universality of cosmopolitanisms," the direction that Boaventura de Sousa Santos has urged the larger field of human rights to take (see chapter 5).

However, tensions amongst NGO activists across the region are also very tangible, especially because US women of color have experienced a political climate that has positioned them as complicit in US foreign policies and as representatives of the state. US antiracist activists were taken to task for not understanding the full extent of US imperialism and US foreign policies during the Durban conference. Women in the global South even formed the South-South Initiative in March 2001, a space open only to women from African, Asian-Pacific, Latin American, and

Caribbean NGOs.[12] At the same time, power infuses the politics of the global South as well, including in the ways select people from the global South became involved in the 2001 WCAR proceedings. Power is by no means unidirectional.

A synthesis of giving voice and moving toward an interactive, rather than additive, understanding of oppression is most prevalent in these UN-based advocacy efforts. These political objectives are important points of departure on which antiracist feminist activists can continue to build in the future. The outcomes of the efforts discussed in this chapter suggest that adopting an intersectionality approach for the 2001 WCAR led to an explicit recognition that men and women do not experience racism in the same way, and that to effectively address women's experiences with racism at the UN level, a gender-neutral approach could no longer be acceptable. These realizations and positions did not emerge in isolation. Arturo Escobar notes "the growing Latin American and global transnational networks of indigenous women and Afro Latin-American women's networks" and "particular social movements" as the critical spaces in which women have been able to "articulate gender perspectives" and "embark on challenges to patriarchal constructions of indigeneity on a day-to-day basis," respectively.[13] The 2001 WCAR is an example of this critical space.

THE FOUR NATIONAL CONTEXTS OF THE AMERICAS

Canadian activists function within a space in which multiculturalism is celebrated and the discourse of multiculturalism and its policies preempt honest discussions about racism. A human rights activist from British Columbia pointed out, "Multiculturalism here in Canada has been perceived to be all about food and dance. And when it comes to talking about sharing power and sharing money and making the society more egalitarian . . . multiculturalism hasn't helped that discourse of talking about antiracism."[14]

In Mexico, the framework for understanding racism has been narrowed to its de jure form. Because legal segregation never occurred in Mexico (as it did in the United States), the position of the Mexican government is that the nation does not have a "race problem," and the prevailing discourse denies the very existence of racism. Discourse on race is dominated by discussions of *mestizaje*—the Spanish term for racial mixing. In Mexico, *mestizaje* refers to the mixing of Spanish and indigenous peoples following Spain's conquest of Mexico. These discussions have failed to acknowledge that conflicts concerning indigenous peoples can be race-based, and it has made invisible the existence of Afro-Mexicans.[15] Discussions of *mestizaje* tend to underscore nationalist universalisms—"we are all Mexicans"—which produces a challenging environment for antiracist activists, who contend that people are socially stratified based on racial difference.

The Peruvian context, while somewhat similar to that of Mexico in terms of embracing a *mestizaje* discourse for the purposes of nationalism, includes racial and gender dynamics that are deeply tied to a Spanish colonial legacy that privileges whiteness (or Spanish ancestry) and demeans the existence of indigenous communities as well as Afro-descendants.[16] Racial stratification has become normalized, and antiracist feminist activists work against a deeply entrenched racial ideology that is seen as a problematic colonial relic. Afro-Peruvian and Asian-Peruvian communities are treated as "foreign," and the importance of whiteness in Peruvian national identity can be clearly seen in the media, where gross caricatures of indigenous peoples and African descendants function as the comedic foil to white characters. Examples are the popular characters of Paisana Jacinta and Negro Mama on Latin Frequency (Frecuencia Latina), a widely watched Peruvian television channel.[17]

The United States resides, both literally and figuratively, between the Canadian and Latin American contexts. The United States' attitude toward racism embraces neither the wide acceptance of multiculturalism found in Canada nor the negation of racism's existence that is prevalent in Mexico and Peru. The election of President Barack Obama has elevated a problematic rhetoric of postracialism that serves as a tactic for nonengagement with persistent racial disparities in the areas of labor, health, and education, among others. Although the widely accepted "melting pot" and "salad bowl" models of national identity recognize, albeit awkwardly, the multicultural and multiracial nature of US society, the theories are not translated into a sustained commitment to combat racism and other inequalities.

Unlike the governments of Mexico, Peru, or even Canada, the US government played a particularly deliberate role in undermining the WCAR's proceedings, which complicated the work of all of the feminists I interviewed, not just activists from the United States. As much as the US government tried to publicly distance itself from the 2001 WCAR, it became invested in controlling the language of the conference and the discourse emanating from the preparatory stages when it became evident that the conference agenda would directly challenge the United States and its allies by focusing on issues such as slavery, colonialism, violence, genocide, and US imperialism. The new coalitions forming among activists and allied Third World government delegations, voices that could legitimately challenge the power (or empire) of the United States, also became a concern and a force that the United States (and its allies, including Canada) needed to quell.

Interviews with feminist activists from the Americas suggest that national contexts shaped their objectives for the 2001 WCAR and that they experienced challenges when they organized as antiracist feminists. Women from Canada planned to counter the false image of domestic racial harmony in Canada that originates from the discourse of multiculturalism by spotlighting gendered racism at the international level. Women of color in the United States had to be mindful of national privilege—hence, they had to be particularly attentive to not control the political discussions with other activists so as to avoid replicating the tendency of the US government to dictate and dominate. Because many of the Mexican women's groups were not actively engaged in the Durban proceedings, the women from Mexico that I interviewed largely worked in isolation from mainstream feminist organizations based in Mexico. They had to foster new transnational collaborations with other regional networks, such as those centered on the rights of indigenous peoples and gays and lesbians. The Peruvian activists I interviewed adopted a similar approach. They sought regional networks focused on the rights of African descendants and gays and lesbians to prepare for the 2001 WCAR and the NGO Forum. Even though the national contexts of Mexico and Peru were not conducive to nationally based antiracist feminist organizing, these activists managed to engage the Durban proceedings in meaningful ways.

The Canadian Paradox

A wide array of Canadian activists involved in the 2001 WCAR began with preparing for the conference in the late 1990s. These women attempted to reveal the falsity of the racial harmony imagery produced by the Canadian government and transmitted globally. Audre, who worked in the area of Canadian Aboriginal women, and Margaret, who engaged in work with black youth, were just two of the many women I interviewed committed to disrupting the illusion of racial democracy, a task undertaken in coalition with members of other domestic and international activist communities and networks. Their goal was to develop a new framework with which to understand the plight of indigenous and African Canadian women.

The UN has hailed Canada's multiculturalism legislation as a global model, in part because it is viewed as being in compliance with ICERD, of which Canada is a signatory.[18] The intention of Canada's multiculturalism policy, first adopted in 1971, was to encourage the full realization of the multicultural nature of Canadian society through programs designed to promote the preservation and sharing of ethnocultural heritages. These programs were intended to facilitate mutual understanding and appreciation among all Canadians. This policy was the forerunner of the Canadian Multiculturalism Act, which became law in 1988. For people of color—referred to as "visible minorities" in Canada—the struggles were not about culture but race. In other words, recognizing or even celebrating aspects of different cultures is not the same as dismantling structural racism and inequality.[19]

Audre acknowledged the historical struggles of indigenous peoples working at the UN level and pointed to the significance of the Durban conference: "I think it was the first time that Aboriginal people took that much space and place [at a UN world conference]. That recognition was there because the major regions in the world had the chance to speak on Aboriginal issues and the speakers were all indigenous peoples. And, for me, it's been a long, long, long fight, or a seed that was [planted] a long time ago by indigenous peoples."[20] Audre acknowledged the lengthy history and contentious battles that indigenous communities have faced at the UN. She admitted that that recognition has been a long time coming, and moreover, suggested that indigenous peoples had taken their rightful place within the conference space.

Audre stood out as a forceful and knowledgeable voice on the issue of Aboriginal women, and the Canadian government invited her to join the official government delegation. Accepting this position, in her view, was crucial to facilitating activists' access to decision makers in the Canadian government as well as in the UN. Others from the NGO community were confused by her role, however, and many believed that she was working *for* the government. When she realized that misinformation was circulating about her role on the delegation, Audre quickly worked to counter it by facilitating introductions between Native activists and the powerful people that they wanted to lobby. Audre understood that her privileged position on the Canadian delegation should be used to help not only her own organization but also as many indigenous communities as possible. Audre's experience on the government delegation was a mixed bag, especially, she said, since government delegates treated her as "a secretary" until she asserted her role as clearly as possible to her fellow government delegates: "I'm here also on behalf of Aboriginal women in Quebec, so I have to do my job."[21] For her, this meant repeatedly raising the issues faced by Aboriginal women in Canada to anyone who would listen to her, whether they were members of the Canadian delegation, other government delegates, UN officials, or other activists.

During an NGO meeting with indigenous leaders in Santiago, indigenous activists discussed issuing a statement on behalf of the world's indigenous peoples. Audre voiced concern regarding the proposed text for the statement because "nothing was there for Aboriginal women, nothing was mentioned that we have to protect our women." She continued,

> We need real public security in our communities, safety, [and] promote
> nonviolence because the violence is the main problem for aborigi-
> nal women, and then poverty. And they are really . . . closely linked
> together. . . . And so I raised my hand and I spoke . . . somebody was
> translating in Spanish . . . and I [said] I think it's a wonderful declara-
> tion, and that's what we need, to stick together. . . . But one thing is
> sure . . . [that] when I read that declaration, it's mostly towards men. [I]
> feel that everything . . . was built on a male perspective. [It] would be
> nice [if] the first paragraph introducing [the indigenous] declaration . . .
> mentioned that every article in [this] declaration will apply equally to
> indigenous women and indigenous men regardless . . . of religion or sex
> or whatever.

Understanding that a document on behalf of indigenous peoples was a public record of their position as indigenous peoples, Audre knew the importance of ensuring women were explicitly mentioned here. This statement would be used later to lobby government delegations during the negotiations at Durban.

After Audre stated her view about the exclusion of women, a Canadian national chief approached her to express his displeasure. He accused her of having a problem with him personally, and they had the following uncomfortable exchange:

National chief: How come every time I speak for Canada . . . or outside of Canada, you're always after me? Do you have something against me?

Audre: [You think] that I have something against you? No way. You're our national chief.

National chief: No? You always bring up the women . . . every time I speak. . . . You have something against me.

Audre: But in fact and in the reality—on a day-to-day [basis] . . . on a reserve or a community, do you think that women are equal to men? [The] rights are there, you know, the human rights declaration, the international conventions are saying that, yes, we're equal, but in fact, [that's not] the reality.

National chief: Well, you'll have all the gay people, lesbian people . . . the young people, and [other] people, [who will] all want their space in that declaration.

Audre: Well, why not? I don't mind. I'm open [to it]. They're not here today. They [couldn't] afford to come and . . . claim their [space] or whatever, [to tell us] what they need. [But] I am here.[22]

Initially stunned that a modest suggestion to modify the opening lines of an introductory paragraph for an indigenous peoples statement could result in such an exchange with her national chief, Audre realized resistance to intersectionality could also come from her "own brothers and sisters." Her experience was not unique in this regard. Many participants believed that intersectionality steered primary attention away from an authentic discussion about racism.

Margaret was part of an NGO committed to the empowerment of

Canadian youth. She believed the importance of the preparatory period was to network, build coalitions, and begin early lobbying efforts with Canadian government delegates. To apply her analysis of intersectionality to a global forum was a thrilling opportunity for her. Margaret had prior experience working at the UN level, and saw herself as a mentor to other youth, in particular young women of color, who shared the goal of making the world conference work for their needs. As she became further involved with organizing youth for the 2001 WCAR, Margaret began to work with a group of young Canadian women of color. She said, "The group of women I came to surround myself with in [the national preparatory] process were predominantly black. They were young women of color, very strong, very knowledgeable about the issues."[23]

Margaret attended the 2001 WCAR as part of a program for young women that she helped build in her organization. The program's objective is to bring young women in Canada together to talk about "life at the intersection of race and gender, particularly in the areas of violence and poverty." Margaret also involved herself in working with the African-descendant community. Therefore, she also had some involvement in the reparations movement from Canada, because reparations became an issue that united black Canadians. She stated that the reparations movement was an "important starting point" for inserting a "gender component" into analyses of antiblack racism in Canada.[24]

The process of forming coalitions is about building a structure for fostering a dialogue about intersectionality among activists, which allows them to conceptualize issues in a new way. Social movements in Canada, including those for labor, youth, and women, "are quite progressive," according to Margaret, but incorporating matters of race within them can be extremely difficult. Margaret said that it is "the hardest" element to incorporate, "the one we pay the most lip service to and actually never do anything [about], and the most divisive." For her, the 2001 WCAR provided key opportunities to work with other Canadian-based progressive social movements that had not adequately grappled with racism.[25]

Canadian activists preparing for the Durban conference were just as focused on participation as they were on stimulating an overdue national dialogue about the intersection of gender and race in Canada. The months of preparation gave feminists an opportunity to think about how to articulate the intersection of race and gender within a Canadian context and how to do so in coalitions that were not exclusively feminist or made up only of women. According to the women I interviewed, their work was challenged by a national discourse of multiculturalism that focuses on less threatening aspects of culture and subsequently silences critical discussions about racism.

Grappling with the Breadth of US Power

The sociopolitical position of US feminist activists, who routinely outnumber participants from other countries at world conferences, was unique in relation to the Durban proceedings because of the explicit and aggressive nature of the US government's efforts to undermine the conference. Unlike the Canadian government, which initially openly supported the 2001 WCAR (including providing substantial sponsorship for several activists to travel to Durban, and hosting national consultations throughout the country), the US government was not enthusiastic about the occasion of a world conference focused on the subject of racism.[26] This hostility produced a unique situation for US people of color who identified as antiracist activists and as critics of the US government: they found themselves on the receiving end of other activists' anger triggered by the US government's actions throughout the world.

A number of US feminists of color, some of whom had gone to the 1995 UN World Conference on Women in Beijing or had participated in other UN world conferences or meetings, had some understanding of the challenges they would face as US women (regardless of racial or ethnic background) at the Durban conference. US women of color had to consider how their privileged status as US citizens distinctively situated them in relation to other participants at the Durban conference, including other women.

Forming coalitions proved enormously challenging for US racial justice activists who did not interrogate the link between national privilege and global manifestations of racism, undermining potential transnational alliances. An interviewee from the United States expressed frustration about other US activists on this point. She said, "You don't want to think about yourself as American, but you are. Even though you are a person of color and you identify as a person of color who is racially oppressed, you are an American, and that means something when you are going outside of the country. And that means something about the way people perceive you, and that means something about how you behave in being real conscious about the national privilege you have as an American citizen. I think that stuff informs the way that people interact with each other in both direct and indirect ways."[27] Having led a racially diverse delegation of women to the Durban conference, this Asian American feminist understood that having her delegation fully appreciate the challenges of being US women of color in a global setting was critical to having any chance of fostering transnational feminist links to other women not from the United States.[28]

In essence, US activists of color were caught between a rock and a hard place, constantly having to negotiate their positionality in every organizing space. Of course, many US activists of color were not sensitive to or conscious of national privilege. Unfortunately, negative encounters with a few US activists triggered resentment that created difficulties for other activists. Lisa Crooms, who attended the Durban conference as part of the Women's Institute for Leadership Development (WILD) for Human Rights group, stated, "As feminists of color, many of us failed to be reflexive, opting, instead, to re-create hierarchy by not relinquishing our privilege vis-à-vis our sisters from the global South. Many of us clung to the fallacious notion of our own universal and permanent victim status in a context where we were often oppressive."[29] For many activist delegations, US people of color embodied and represented US power. This was a profoundly upsetting realization, particularly for those US activists who had not previously experienced the depth and breadth of vibrant anti-US imperialism movements.

The realities of being from the United States and the maneuverings of the US government to weaken the Durban conference played a role in determining the content of some of the training sessions for US NGO delegations. Organizations such as the now defunct Women of Color Resource Center based in Oakland, California, and MADRE, an international human rights organization based in New York City,[30] contributed tremendous organizational resources to prepare their NGO delegations. Since the staff of these two organizations had experience working at the UN level, they understood the long-term benefits of having coordinated and organized delegations. They also knew that entering a global space without a consciousness about how the United States is perceived internationally would hinder the formation of transnational coalitions. The Women of Color Resource Center's training sessions, which focused on "meeting political objectives as a delegation and helping people meet their individual goals at the conference," aided their delegates tremendously. For MADRE's leadership, training US participants to better "understand the UN system . . . [and] the difference between one [UN] body and another" was critical, particularly because the MADRE organizers wanted their delegates to "understand the relationship between issues of economic justice and issues of gender, and the intersection of those issues" in conversation with aspects of the UN system that could be useful to their organizing efforts.[31]

For US activists, grappling with the breadth of US power was absolutely essential to deciphering how to develop sustainable transnational coalitions and even to fully understand the extent and depth to which US foreign policies affect people's lives, oftentimes without our even knowing about it until decades later. As such, intersectionality can prove useful for uncovering not only the scope of US power but also how national privilege can obscure or even skew our approaches to racism at the global level.

Challenging the Denial of Racism's Existence

The 2001 WCAR offered feminists the opportunity to rupture the silence about racism in Mexico that had been upheld by the *mestizaje* nationalist discourse. In 2000 the Academia Mexicana de Derechos Humanos and the Rigoberta Menchú Tum Foundation hosted, respectively, a cross-regional NGO conference on racism across Mexico and Central America and a meeting for indigenous Mexican youth in Mexico City. Most speakers at the Academia Mexicana conference sought to highlight the racial injustices faced by indigenous groups and immigrants, and, to an extent, the discussions acknowledged that women experience racial injustice differently than men.

A Mexican feminist lesbian organization wanted to foster a deeper understanding of racism by highlighting the intersection of racism and sexuality.[32] Eva, who is part of this organization, talked about her participation in preparatory meetings that led up to the Durban conference. During this period, she garnered support for her work on lesbian rights.

For instance, she attended the regional PrepCom meeting in Santiago, Chile, in December 2000. There she became involved in an alliance between feminists and gay and lesbian networks. She also connected with a coalition of organizations from throughout Mexico and other parts of Latin America that drafted an NGO declaration about the intersection of racism and sexual orientation at the Foro de las Américas, a conference held a few months prior to the 2001 WCAR in Quito, Ecuador. The declaration urged governments to incorporate sexual orientation in final WCAR documents and to investigate and prosecute acts of violence directed at gay and lesbian communities of color. The declaration also called on NGOs to "create gathering spaces, reflection, analysis and action, that permits understanding and deconstructing the connections among diverse forms of discrimination and intolerance."[33]

According to Eva, it was during the several months of meetings before the WCAR that "the process became very, very rich." Seeking networks outside of Mexico helped Eva realize some of her own shortcomings as a Mexican feminist in regard to antiracism, and she realized how the formation of alliances could be effectively deployed in a world conference setting because of the multiple social movements and governments engaged in the process. Pointing out how the work of feminist alliances influenced conference proceedings, she said, "We managed to impact very strongly and effectively other social movements [in Santiago] and even at the WCAR itself: the governments of Brazil and Canada were raising the issues of gender and sexual diversity constantly. So those successes were the best that we've ever had in our history as lesbians."[34] Indeed, an articulation of the intersection of racism and sexuality or sexual diversity had never before occurred at the UN.

The preparatory period enabled activists and advocates from Mexico to begin long-overdue dialogues about racism, both nationally and regionally, within Mexico. The participation of unexpected organizations such as the one advocating for lesbian rights further complicated the discussion in antiracism forums. The Durban conference itself, while relevant, was not as critical for Eva as the preparatory gatherings. In Santiago she managed to become part of influential international alliances that were able to advance an understanding of racism that considered sexuality and sexual diversity, among other issues.

Establishing New Transnational Alliances for Peruvian Women

The Peruvian feminists who participated in the Durban conference represented African-descendant, indigenous, and lesbian communities, indicating a varied intervention from Peruvian activists despite the low number of organizations in attendance. The women I interviewed had collaborated with diverse Latin American organizations whenever possible while preparing for Durban. One venue in which this collaboration proved extremely beneficial was at the Foro de las Américas in Quito.

Foro participants eventually produced their own Programme of Action (POA) to combat racism in Latin America.[35] The opening paragraph sets the tone for the remainder of the Programme: it states that the struggle to eradicate racism in the Americas requires a collective consideration of how racism affects women, displaced people, African and Asian descendants, the LGBT community, migrants, the Roma, children, and many other marginalized groups and communities. The document, which contains 188 paragraphs, discusses racism in a comprehensive way, with nearly every page mentioning the intersection of racial injustice with gender, sexuality, class, ethnicity, displacement, age, nationality, or ancestry.

The day before the Foro convened, Patricia, one of the representatives of a lesbian rights group from Peru, and representatives from other Latin American–based gay and lesbian groups held a satellite meeting to strategize. Patricia found this meeting enormously useful because it allowed gay and lesbian groups from South America to develop a document based on an intersectional, integrated analysis that considered racism and sexuality together. Patricia expressed how meaningful the Foro experience was for her politically, emotionally, and spiritually: "Because of months of work, various working groups adopted articles against discrimination based on sexual orientation. So it didn't just come from one working group or one commission. So in the final conference document from the Foro de las Américas, it was clear that everyone opposed discrimination based on sexual orientation."[36] The explicit inclusion of discrimination directed at lesbian and gay communities in working groups or caucuses that were not directly focused on sexual rights was a remarkable step forward (see table 4.01 for a list of caucuses and commissions for the 2001 WCAR). Sexual rights were no longer viewed as having nothing to do

TABLE 4.01   NGO Caucuses and Commissions for the 2001 WCAR

CAUCUSES		COMMISSIONS	
An opportunity for people who share interests in particular issues to strategize, network, and lobby as a collective		Thematic forums for exchanging information, discussing issues, and strategizing	
African/African Descendants*	Immigration/ Migration*	African Descent	Globalization/ Militarization/ Environmental Racism
Arab/Middle East*	Indigenous Peoples*	Colonialism	Hate Crimes
Asian	Race and Poverty*	Criminal Justice	Health (HIV/AIDS)
Caste	Refugees/Internally	Dalits	Indigenous Peoples
Class	Displaced	Disabled Persons	Information Media
Criminal Justice*	Religious	Displaced Persons	National Ethnic
Education*	Intolerance*	Education	Minorities
Environmental Justice	Reparations/ Compensatory	Ethnic Cleansing	Palestine
Globalization*	Measures*	Foreign Occupation	Religious Intolerance
Health	Sexual Orientation*	Gender	Reparations
	Women*		Roma/Travelers
	Youth*		Sexual Orientation
			Trafficking
			Youth and Children

* Author interviewed participants from these caucuses.
Source: WILD for Human Rights, handout from WCAR training for delegation,
    January 2001.

with indigenous or African-descendant communities, for example. More important, opposition to discrimination based on sexual orientation represented a significant expansion of understanding racism, moving the conversation beyond a narrow conceptualization of race.

At this Foro, women of African descent from the Americas issued a declaration statement to participants. The Afro-Peruvian women I interviewed for this research contributed to the drafting of this declaration. The statement chastises states that have denied women of African descent "the right to build and affirm our identity as afrodescendant [sic] peoples of the Americas and Caribbean." For these activists, the failure to recognize African descendants within their respective national contexts is the result of state policies "that deny diversity and promote a false national identity based on homogeneity."[37] These women acknowledged the diversity of women, stating, "Without a vision that includes women it will be impossible to eradicate racism, racial discrimination, and xenophobia." The declaration notes further that the authors represent "various nationalities, sexual orientations, languages, physical conditions, ages and [those] living in rural and urban areas," and that they considered themselves promoters of "a transformational struggle for equality and respect." Addressing human rights issues ranging from sexual, reproductive, and other health rights to economic and education rights, the declaration states that a gendered analysis of racism is essential; hence the authors propose "that all anti-racism policies systematically include a gender perspective, designing specific actions and strategies that address the particular situation of afro-american and afro-caribbean women [*sic*]."

When I interviewed Natalia at her office in September 2003, she described leaving the conference with a renewed sense of her African heritage, a feeling experienced by many participants of African descent, whose motto became "We went to Durban as Blacks and left Durban as African descendants." The 2001 WCAR was Natalia's first UN world conference. She explained the importance of terminology during the negotiations: "In the entire Durban process, we [African descendants] had a leading role, much more of a leading role than any of the states would have wanted. Because to assert that you are African descendants, to use that word, well, the states were very resistant. There were problems in the second preparatory committee meeting in Geneva because you are talking about Africa, about the slave trade and trafficking, and you're talking about reparations. You reach a critical point regarding reparations [when you talk in terms of African descendants]."[38] In Peru, a country that is highly conscious of skin color, the term "black" (*negro* in Spanish) is used differently than it is in the United States. No "Black Power" movement ever existed in Peru, and *negro* is commonly hurled as an insult. Afro-Peruvians do not conceptualize blackness in the same way as African Americans because their vastly different historical trajectories. The different meanings of "black" are issues of translation to some degree, but they are also about arriving at forms of self-identity that have distinct local and national contexts.[39]

With the development of a transnational consciousness regarding African descendants emerging from preparation for the Durban conference proceedings, Natalia and other women of African descent wanted to ensure that the issue of gender would not be lost. "The first struggle was to introduce gender in general," she said. "We were winning that struggle because there was space for it. [But] we needed to make the gender perspective transversal within documents regarding African descendants."[40] Natalia and other women worked diligently to ensure the integration of a gender perspective into, for example, any lobbying papers or position statements about African descendants.

Some of the Peruvian women I spoke with worked in coalition with other Latin American activists to advance a comprehensive conceptualization of human rights at the Foro. The Foro's Programme of Action is an illustration of how the strategies developed in collaborative settings are strikingly distinct from the top-down approach carried out by, for instance, large established organizations such as Amnesty International, which tends to privilege civil and political rights over economic, social, and cultural rights.

The political benefits realized during preparations for the Durban conference indicate that the process can sometimes be more valuable than the outcome reflected in the final conference documents. For many activists, the activities that preceded Durban were instrumental to their organizing efforts, as Patricia pointed out: "The process of participating in the Durban preparations influenced me a great deal in that I came to understand the interrelationship of rights and the interrelationship of different forms of discrimination, too. And this has helped me realize, too, that we need to link up to other movements—in other words, movements having to do with human rights, indigenous peoples, African descendants, etc.—because we have a common objective. So for me, it wasn't just Durban [that influenced me the most], but the entire process surrounding Durban, of thinking about Durban."[41] Natalia explained how her conference preparations led to shifts in her thinking, which modified the work she was doing as part of the director of an Afro-Peruvian organization. Given the restraints the women of Peru experienced due to their small number of participants, weak government support, and travel and funding limitations, several moments during the preparatory process and the conference itself proved instrumental.

Women from around the world descended on Durban, South Africa, to make visible their views on racism. Two ways in which women accomplished this visibility were through drafting advocacy position statements for public release and organizing sessions for the NGO Forum. This section focuses on two advocacy statements that merit particular attention in reflecting an intersectional analysis of racial injustice: the statements from the Women's Caucus and from the Indigenous Women of the Americas. Both statements offer a perspective on racism that centers on an intersectional analysis. This section also focuses on two human rights hearings organized by US women's groups to advance an important understanding of what is gained through an intersectional analysis.

The Women's Caucus statement, "Women Standing at the Intersection of Race and Gender: Women's Caucus Statement to the WCAR," released on September 4, 2001, first identifies the "root causes of racism" as the result of "slavery, colonialism, racist immigration policies, globalization, [and] armed conflict." The text emphasizes the interrelationship of all human rights principles and recognizes the causes of racism as "a fundamental source of [the] feminization of poverty and violence against women."[42] It emphasizes the interconnected nature of different forms of discrimination and offers a perspective on matters ranging from foreign occupation, migration, and poverty to violence and seeking asylum.

The statement from the Indigenous Women of the Americas was similar in content and intent, but particular attention was given to how globalization has devastated the livelihoods of many indigenous communities in the region. Maintaining that globalization "has institutionalized racism and as a consequence led to a greater marginalization and racial discrimination against women, indigenous people, blacks, and migrants," the indigenous women's groups that endorsed this statement defined globalization as "the internationalization of the labor force, the reduction of the role of states, the increase of economic power of private, nonstate actors, and the absence of international laws that promote codes of conduct and the right of association and expression."[43]

This statement concludes by offering a host of suggestions on how to diminish the negative effects of globalization on indigenous communities, blacks, and migrants. These range from legal proposals for the ratification of international human rights law to the role of the media and the promotion of education and cultural diversity in deterring the negative effects of globalization. The statement notes that a "reorientation of globalization towards a model based on solidarity" that has "as its goal an equitable social development" is essential to end economic globalization that privileges corporations over human sustainability.

Both documents should be read as examples of transnational feminist interventions that analyze social conditions as by-products of neocolonialism, globalism, and racism. More important, those who endorsed these documents recognized that the effects of neocolonialism, globalism, and racism are not limited to the struggles of indigenous peoples. Feminist activists also identified other communities, such as African descendants and migrants, for instance, that have been marginalized. Both position statements show that activism for human rights must reach far beyond legal considerations. Human rights are concerned with social rights—that is, a right to community development that does not further impoverish communities and the creation of alternative goals for globalization. These women are re-creating a discourse on human rights that merges legal, social, cultural, economic, and political dimensions.

WILD for Human Rights organized a two-hour forum on September 1, 2001, titled "Jeopardizing Human Rights: Revealing the Racist Links in U.S. Foreign and Domestic Policy." The objective was to show how seemingly distinct policy issues are actually interconnected and relational in the global context. Speakers addressed the systematic and structural nature and effects of racism, emphasizing the interconnectedness of civil, political, and economic rights. The session juxtaposed domestic and international issues by coupling US and international speakers. In one pairing, Rinku Sen of the Applied Research Center (in Oakland, California) spoke on the consequences of public benefit restrictions in US welfare reform, and Sarah Mukasa of Akina wa Mama Africa (based in the United Kingdom, with regional offices in Uganda and Nigeria) discussed the impact of structural adjustment programs on women in Africa. In doing so, Sen and Mukasa revealed how these different policies on poverty are strikingly similar in objective and intent. In another pairing, Manuel Piño, an environmental activist and director of Indian studies at Scottsdale Community College (in Scottsdale, Arizona) spoke of the environmental degradation resulting from uranium mining near the Acoma

Pueblo in New Mexico, and Wassan Al-Khudairi, an Iraqi woman living in the United States, described how the uranium extracted from US Native reservations is used in bombs that are dropped on Baghdad and other parts of Iraq. The other two pairings in the forum dealt with the assault on reproductive rights in the United States and its parallel connection to the prohibition of expanding family planning programs in Third World countries, and the links between US state-sanctioned violence directed at the criminalization of US youth on the US mainland and the years of mistreatment of the people of Vieques, Puerto Rico, due to extensive US military training on the island.[44]

By showing that domestic and foreign policies do not operate in isolation, the WILD for Human Rights forum encouraged participants to think creatively about local-global coalitions. In making the case that, for example, discussions about US welfare reform should occur in relation to structural adjustment policies or that the diminishment of reproductive rights in the United States should be considered in relation to the cutting of funds for family planning programs in the Third World, the WILD forum illuminated possibilities for new transnational feminist alliances. The forum revealed how seemingly dissimilar issues can be differently contextualized when an intersectionality lens is used, because this perspective can uncover policy relationships that had previously been overlooked.

For WILD for Human Rights, the hearing was one of its "greatest achievements" in Durban. My interviewee stressed the significance of the hearing in getting members of the WILD delegation to really "understand the links," noting that even the eighteen-month training period was not enough time to adequately address the interrelationship dynamics of these various issues. She said that the hearing advanced an important feminist analytical perspective that "re-creates human rights," and that the limitations on human rights stem, in part, from how the discourse of human rights is misused politically through an overemphasis on civil and political rights.[45] One of the goals of the hearing was to elevate a racial and gendered analysis that places the social and economic dimensions of human rights at the center of discussion.

The Center for Women's Global Leadership (CWGL) also organized a human rights hearing, with an approach to intersectionality that centered the subjectivities of women.[46] Titled "Women at the Intersection:

Indivisible Rights, Identities, and Oppressions," the hearing investigated three topics: bodily integrity and sexuality; migration and immigration; and war, conflict, and genocide. Women from every region of the world provided moving testimonies of their experiences. CWGL has a solid record of organizing hearings at world conferences that, according to my interviewee, are always about the intersection of racism and sexism: "To me, if you are bringing women together from around the world, dimensions of race and class and other issues are always present." Organizers of the hearing "worked intuitively for a while" to identify the appropriate testimonials for inclusion, but they knew that intersectionality would be, as my interviewee stated, "the focus of the stories told."[47]

During the course of the hearing, intersectionality became more than a theoretical or political approach. The women's moving testimonies transformed the issue into a matter of urgency when they revealed how frequently the role of gender was ignored or invalidated in conversations about race. One example was the negation of gender's role in understanding racialized violence. Maria Toj Mendoza, from Kiche, Guatemala, relayed her story about military and state-sponsored violence:

> What happened to me took place in 1982, when we were attacked by the army. I was in Joyabaj, in Kiche province. When they saw us from a distance, they began to fire grenades with shrapnel at us. When one of them exploded, the left side of my body was hit. My ear was affected. I fainted, and when I regained consciousness I was covered with blood and a lot of matter was coming out of my ear. My whole family was separated by the war. I didn't see two of my sons for seven years. Can you imagine what it would be like to not see your children, not to know how they are, not to see them grow up, not to be able to give them a mother's love and affection? I had to separate from my husband. I was alone in my community. The women of the community helped me when they found me abandoned. It is thanks to them that I had the strength to recuperate from those difficult moments. Although I did not die, I did not completely recover. I remained deaf in one ear. And more than anything else, I remained traumatized.[48]

The room remained completely silent during Maria's testimony, as it did during the testimonies of the other women who had had similarly devastating experiences. Many of us in the audience were visibly shaken. The hearing format is powerful precisely because the stories are so moving, and because they stay with the audience long after the hearing's conclusion. Although not mentioned in Maria's testimony, US government documents declassified in the late 1990s reveal that the US government was fully aware of the massacre and abuses aimed at the indigenous peoples of Guatemala. US citizens, as a result of violently aggressive US foreign policies in Central America, were arguably complicit in Maria's suffering.[49]

The position statements by the Women's Caucus and the Indigenous Women of the Americas as well as the NGO Forum events organized by WILD for Human Rights and CWGL reveal the benefits of using an intersectionality lens. They offer important insights about the intersection of gender and racial violence as well as illuminate critical links between domestic and US foreign policies, for instance. These contributions, too often overlooked in previous settings, remain fundamental to understanding transnational feminist interventions in UN forums and in world conferences focused on racism.

CONCLUSION: MORE THAN JUST CONFERENCE DOCUMENTS

The full story of Durban cannot be understood solely through its final outcome document, the DDPA. It was the preparatory process that mattered most to many women activists from the Americas. They formed various networks—for youth, women, lesbian, and indigenous and African-descendant peoples—at local, national, and regional levels. In establishing these networks, activists groups were able to reconceptualize human rights from the vantage point of their new coalitions. Although building new coalitions can be difficult for people who have not worked together before, especially when time is limited, the problems that arise can be productive to work through for the sake of future collaborations. An occasion such as the world conference forced activists to grapple with how to translate and consolidate their agendas, requiring them to conceptualize their strategies more clearly and to define their platforms against racism more broadly.

US activists were the most widely represented of all national constituencies in the 2001 WCAR. This disproportionately high representation, coupled with the US government's efforts to dilute the UN's antiracism agenda, meant that other participants frequently regarded US feminists of color as privileged. US participants had to negotiate multiple pluralities and subjectivities within a transnational space. Many Canadian, Mexican, and Peruvian interviewees also had to wrestle with questions of power because of their access to capital that facilitated their involvement with the Durban proceedings, but "being" from the United States tended to overshadow the privilege (perceived or real) of women attendees from Canada, Mexico, or Peru, mostly because of US imperialism.

For Mexico and Peru, it was the intervention more than the number of participants that was significant. The approach to intersectionality by lesbian rights groups was based on the interrelationship between sexuality and racism, and being able to link to other feminist and gay and lesbian networks in the region validated their efforts. Even though no mention of sexual diversity can be found in the DDPA, Eva and Patricia were able to pursue their agendas in satisfying ways by forming regional coalitions outside of Mexico and Peru. It was the formation of new coalitions that proved critical to these activists because coalitions can be maintained long after a world conference has concluded.

Even though the Peruvian contingent was the smallest when compared to the other countries included in my research, its intervention had a critical effect on local activism, particularly in terms of solidifying transnational connections for African descendants in the region. For Peruvian women of African descent, forming coalitions with women of African descent from other parts of South America proved eye-opening and empowering. Coalitions allowed these activists to link domestic racism to regional realities, and this in turn shaped their larger objectives for the conference.

The statements resulting from the preparatory period and the two human rights hearings highlight the beneficial aspects of intersectionality. At the 2001 WCAR feminists recast locally based agendas in ways that aligned their goals of building broader transnational alliances. These revitalized agendas shaped the participants' collective understanding of the meaning of "local" and "global," leading participants to consider the critical nature of transnational feminist engagement, which subsequently informed the production of progressive statements and the content of human rights hearings. Feminists engaged in political organizing at the global level contribute to the vital role of transnational feminist solidarity in their engagements with UN mechanisms; in other words, to overcome obstacles presented by powerful entities such as the United States, feminists had to envision ways to disrupt government alliances to make progress in advancing intersectionality.

The use of intersectionality in activist spaces toward its integration in UN discourse is noteworthy. Not every activist position has resonance at the UN level, which does not suggest that these other analytics are any less compelling. Rather, the concept of intersectionality advanced in such a way that feminist interventions in the UN discourse about racism validated arguments that a gender analysis matters when it comes to understanding racism in its totality. It is a perspective that has penetrating benefits for future antiracist feminist advocacy.

5

Intersectionality as the New Universalism

A problem or condition that disproportionately affects a subset of
women may be framed solely as a women's problem. Aspects of the
issue that render it an intersectional problem may be absorbed into
a gender framework and there may be no attempt to acknowledge
the role that some other form of discrimination, such as racism, may
have played in contributing to the circumstance. In this context, the
full scope of problems that are simultaneously products of various
forms of discrimination, such as on the basis of race and gender,
escapes effective analysis. Consequently, efforts to remedy the
condition or abuse in question are likely to be as incomplete as is the
analysis upon which the intervention is grounded.

—RADHIKA COOMARASWAMY, FORMER UN SPECIAL
RAPPORTEUR ON VIOLENCE AGAINST WOMEN, 2001

THE PARTICIPATING GOVERNMENT DELEGATES AT THE 1945 UNCIO
could likely not have predicted that many of the racial and gender tensions that surfaced at that time would still exist today. The UN has grown
in size as well as in bureaucracy, and remains a difficult and messy institution to navigate. Yet new social actors today—such as the antiracist
feminists interviewed in this book—form what I believe are essential
counterpublics to ensure that discourses, meanings, and advocacy do not
remain stagnant or reflective of the political interests of the relatively
few. Their coming together is not always tranquil, easy, or straightforward, but it is essential in the terrain of struggle over representation,
power, and voice that exists at the UN. These counterpublics are not unprecedented. Chapter 1 locates counterpublics at the UN from the very

beginning in the voices of those excluded from the spaces of power occupied by the "great powers." These counterpublics challenged the presumption that the "great powers" knew what they were doing in 1945. It is in that same spirit that antiracist feminists also challenge the UN today.

This coming together is also complicated by the unevenness pertaining to the practice of UN citizenship that can at times be inclusionary or exclusionary, depending on the situation. Yet entities with less economic capital have made important strides in the UN's agenda on racism in part because economically powerful governments had no "moral authority" upon which to assert their views in this regard. If anything, their actions have exacerbated racial animosity and continue to do so. As the UN has grown in size, new meanings and understandings of human rights have entered the landscape. New social actors enter this political arena with their own interpretations of what human rights mean. As discussed in chapter 2, ICERD makes no mention of reproductive rights in the treaty, but US feminist activists offered a convincing interpretation of the treaty in which reproductive justice has now become a matter of racial justice and thus a matter of concern for CERD. What happened at this hearing furthered the antiracist feminist work of the Durban conference in a different, but equally important, venue. As activists strategize to advance their own human rights agendas, they do so in a human rights constellation I refer to as "social praxis" because they strive to reconcile modernist and relational ontologies through their UN-based advocacy efforts. It is within the social praxis constellation that intersectionality comes to the fore.

The UN has become the meeting location for activists and representatives from NGOs engaged in a range of political struggles. World conferences, in particular, have been sites of promise for activists.[1] As detailed in chapter 3, these WCARs have been extremely contentious gatherings. Tracing this genealogy reveals the multiple levels of hostility directed at them. The WCARs were not welcome gatherings, a fact that should not be surprising given geopolitical power. But the WCARs demonstrate the seriousness of the UN agenda against racism. This seriousness put powerful governments in positions they were unaccustomed to—with the result being that eighteen years elapsed before the convening of the third WCAR.

The critical historical narrative of the UN (chapters 1 and 3) forms a foundation for understanding the complex terrain and the agency exerted regarding representation, voice, and power (chapters 2 and 4). By coupling the critical historical analysis with antiracist feminist activism, we can see how intersectionality has progressed. The historical narrative details glimmering moments at the UN in which the category "women" was situated in relation to racial discrimination. Antiracist feminists took these glimmering moments even further, resulting in what I consider the new universalism of intersectionality that has taken hold in certain spaces of the UN. But, of course, the work remains unfinished, and is as much about strengthening an intersectionality analysis at the UN as responding to the "identity crisis" of the UN.

Antiracist feminists had an opportunity to influence "the international struggle against racism" that has been considered "the most important human rights campaign waged by the UN over its half-century existence"[2] because a number of critical shifts had taken place in the years just before the 2001 WCAR. These dramatic shifts included the end of South African apartheid and the independence of Namibia in the mid-1990s; the appointment of Mary Robinson, a strong advocate for civil society organizations, as high commissioner for human rights in 1997 and later as president of the Durban conference in 1998; and CERD's General Recommendation 25 on gendered dimensions to racial discrimination in 2000.[3] These shifts did not happen in isolation; a rich history of voices and movements from the margins of dominant power found ways to challenge the status quo and be assertive. Topics discussed as part of the UN agenda against racism began to expand; as such, the politics of antiracist feminists was poised to make an important intervention on the existing discourse.

The United States, Canada, and Western Europe have not dominated the UN agenda against racism as they have other agendas at the UN in part because they did not consider the antiracism campaign important enough to vie for control of its discourse or to insist on shaping its agenda. This left an opportunity for other governments—Third World nations empowered by social and cultural capital, for instance—to explore subjects through the GA that economically powerful governments did not want discussed. This same opportunity did not necessarily emerge with regard to the UN agenda on women, which has been largely shaped by the interests of economically powerful nations and has incorporated the dominant discourse of Western liberalism in terms of women's liberation or women's rights. Consequently, UN spaces focused on racism offered a more appropriate context for the work of antiracist feminists.

NGOs, particularly feminist NGOs, substantially increased their participation at the UN during the world conferences on women in the 1980s and 1990s.[4] NGO advocates realized that these conferences presented a valuable opportunity—direct and unprecedented access to the delegates of world governments—if UN accreditation could be secured. Today, thousands of NGOs send representatives and delegations to the UN world conferences and the corresponding NGO Forums, as well as treaty compliance review hearings, and these nonstate actors have increasingly applied pressure on the UN to respond to their demands.[5]

Amrita Basu has suggested that the global or international feminism at the UN from the 1970s through the 1990s can be grouped into two broad phases: "The first phase, between 1975 [and] 1985, was marked by bitter contestation over the meaning of feminism and over the relationship between the local and global. The second decade-long phase, which began with the Nairobi conference in 1985, and culminated in the Beijing conference in 1995, was marked by a growth of networks linking women's activism at the local and global levels."[6] The feminist practices described by the research presented in this book represent a third phase—from about the late 1990s through the 2000s—in which UN-based feminism evolved into a practice of transnational feminism. In focusing on advocacy beyond UN forums explicitly focused on women, this research uncovers a transnational feminism that developed in UN spaces directly addressing racism.[7]

I maintain that the activism explored in this research is transnational feminist in character because of the ongoing navigation between advocating for and translating local realities for a transnational context and audience. Numerous NGO statements from the Durban conference were usually not nation-specific, though some were region-specific. Since NGOs organize themselves into caucuses and networks, this structure can lend itself to formulating positions that account for and recognize transnational links. Transnational feminism as an antisubordination logic, as a theory that aims to understand hegemony, and as a politics of internationalist solidarity (i.e., not global sisterhood) was central to their antiracist advocacy efforts. This activism also emerged in concert with intersectionality. Since the transnational feminist practice shown in this research is mutually constructed with intersectionality, both of these frameworks converge in the case of the activism corresponding to the Durban conference.

Boaventura de Sousa Santos refers to a "new universality of cosmopolitanism" in reclaiming human rights from the powerful. Transnational feminism must be central to this reclaiming as an "emancipatory political practice."[8] As such, intersectionality—with its consideration of geopolitical spaces, historical narratives, and political situations together—becomes essential as efforts to transform human rights are initiated worldwide.[9] This concluding chapter explores the "new universalism of intersectionality" that materialized in the third phase of feminist engagement at the UN and summarizes the views of the antiracist feminist activists who played a role in its development about the importance of the UN.

SIMULTANEOUSLY NAVIGATING PARTICULARISM AND UNIVERSALISM THROUGH INTERSECTIONALITY

With preparations well under way for the 2001 WCAR by the late 1990s, antiracist feminist activists maintained that a more complex framework would be needed to address matters of racism that were not adequately reflected in the prevailing discourse of the time. One way that antiracist feminists intervened was through the articulation of a new universalism. This may appear to be paradoxical, since much of their advocacy efforts speak to disrupting a universalism based on perceived commonalities with regard to gender-based discrimination. But antiracist feminists introduced what I term a "new universalism of intersectionality." This perspective advances a paradigm about racism that acknowledges—rather than flattens—differences that can be attributed to structural, institutional, systematic, geopolitical, and individual factors. A universalism of intersectionality, which considers sociopolitical and geopolitical contexts, including intragender dynamics, allows for flexibility and nuance in shaping discourses about gender and racism.

The women interviewed for this book conveyed experiences and perspectives that would have been missed without an intersectional approach. For Canadians, intersectionality based primarily on subjectivities informed by the national context proved effective for working domestically and then translating those agendas internationally. For US feminists, a consideration of subjectivities and the intersection of structural policies created an opportunity to advance a new image of US feminist activism that acknowledged the effects of US power. For women from Mexico and Peru, intersectional subjectivities were linked to projects of democracy and human rights. Sexual rights were considered less in the context of the individual than in changing societal institutions and structures. In addition, women of African descent in Peru worked with other women of African descent in the region to integrate a gendered analysis of racial discrimination. In each setting, invocations of intersectionality were distinctive because they corresponded to local contexts and realities.

By approaching the subject of racism from an intersectional feminist perspective, activists from the Americas have been able to advocate for an approach to racism that is not meant to undermine existing discourses or understandings about racism; rather, their intent is to enhance and expand them. Their efforts to build relationships of solidarity in a transnational capacity have promoted a holistic approach to eventually overcoming racism and racial discrimination through UN mechanisms. As discussed in this book, these efforts have not always been well received by some activists or advocates who have struggled to have their own voices heard. Moreover, any shift in institutional discourse is bound to encounter some resistance. Yet the period before the Durban conference, in particular, produced a series of critical opportunities for antiracist feminists from the Americas to advance an intersectionality-based agenda that better addressed their lives.

The post-Durban period has been far more complicated. The 2001 WCAR resulted in the formation of well-organized and well-funded conservative NGOs that made their presence known at the 2009 Durban Review Conference. These watchdog groups, which were set up to monitor and essentially limit the effectiveness of socially progressive NGOs, have forced unwelcome changes in the way that NGOs are funded. The UN has also been a frequent target of those who seek to undermine its initiatives.[10] World-systems theorist Immanuel Wallerstein writes that the 9/11 terrorist attacks allowed some conservatives to "attempt to undo the cultural evolution of the world-system that occurred after the world revolution of 1968 (particularly in the fields of race and sexuality)." He notes that they "have sought to liquidate many of the geopolitical structures set in place after 1945, which they have seen as constraining their politics."[11] One of these geopolitical structures is the UN.

Despite ongoing efforts to undermine the UN, when the UN recognizes an issue as a human rights matter and as an issue that merits international attention, this acknowledgment aids activists' work tremendously. Achieving visibility at the UN remains an instrumental and strategic objective for many human rights activists, including most of the antiracist feminists whose voices are recorded in this book.

THE CONTINUING IMPORTANCE OF THE UN

The women I interviewed described the UN and the status of human rights within it as being "in crisis," stating that the UN has lost its sense of purpose and its moral compass. These women faulted the United States for exacerbating this crisis with its ongoing campaign to restructure the global order, yet they remain committed to engaging with the UN, determined to make it a responsive, democratic, participatory, and viable multilateral global institution. Even when disappointed in the UN's failures, these feminists were largely unwilling to relinquish their right to participate at the UN. The women I spoke with did not have overly optimistic views about the institution's future, but they argued that the UN provides excellent opportunities for networking at the local and global levels, interacting with government delegates, and influencing global discourses.[12]

Since initiatives on global human rights and international law converge at the UN, some observers misconstrue the UN's ability to hold governments accountable through punitive action. A longtime US human rights lawyer and advocate noted this problem, saying, "I think activists need to have a clear view of the UN as a collective, not a super-structure. We need to understand that like any other collective, the individual members retain their independence and, to a good and bad degree, their autonomy of action."[13] Another US interviewee conceded that the UN is a "daily disappointment from the point of view of what one would like the UN to be able to be," but noted the importance of "a realistic view of what the UN is and is not" to understand "the spaces that it provides for engagement and struggle." According to her, the "problems at the UN" cannot be solved without addressing the underlying issue of governmental reform: "We can't change what we want in the world through the UN if we aren't also changing governments."[14] A US interviewee who represented a women's economic justice coalition pointed out the UN's limitations in the following manner: "We sometimes talk as if the UN were [former Secretary-General] Kofi Annan and some Secretariat and some structure that had some kind of autonomy, but they don't have a lot of autonomy beyond what the member governments are demanding, and so it is going to reflect the geopolitics of the moment. And we are all aware of what those geopolitics are and where power is right now. And the UN doesn't have the power to extract itself from that reality."[15] All of these women spoke about the structural limitations of engaging the UN. It is not an autonomous entity disconnected from governments' problematic actions and politics; moreover, when we view the UN as a collective, as my interviewee above suggests, then it becomes clearer to activists what the UN can and cannot do. As feminists know very well, working in collectives can be rewarding as well as time-consuming and frustrating. But a collective, even if flawed, is typically the preferred model when the goal is full participation.

Many interviewees pointed out that despite the problems inherent in the UN's structure, no other institution offers similar opportunities for influencing global discourse. One longtime US feminist activist stated, "I would say that the UN has become more important post-9/11 precisely because it's more under attack. The importance of a place that at least holds up the ideals and provides a space for interaction and discussion in the face of the power of the US government, of multinational corporations, of global media. . . . It seems to me even more important that progressives, antiracists, and feminists enter that space, because I think we are just much poorer without it. What else do we have [that can] influence that global discourse?"[16] As this interviewee points out, the legitimacy of the UN became challenged post-9/11, which suggests the UN's importance in trying to uplift some sense of human rights ideals that can come into direct conflict with the belligerence of some governments' actions. If the UN acts as a counterbalance to governments' unwieldy power, then the UN can represent a promising space for activists' engagements.

Mexican and Peruvian interviewees stressed that the UN remains significant because it provides a crucial space for negotiations and carries "moral authority."[17] The representative from a Mexican lesbian rights NGO pointed out that without the UN, "the possibilities for negotiation between the different regions would be even more severely limited. The divisions become strengthened."[18] Mexican activists agreed that greater division could further empower the United States. Peruvian interviewees were less optimistic about the future of the UN as an overall institution, but they also believed that the UN world conferences were useful. As citizens of the poorest country in my comparative research, they felt that Peru had the greatest disadvantage at the UN because it has the least political and economic power.

Women repeatedly stated the importance of supporting and strengthening multilateral spaces such as the UN, a point made by a former director of a Mexican human rights organization: "We also have clarity here . . . not just me, but as an organization, that we have to strengthen multilateral spaces. In other words, for us, it is not an option for the United Nations to disappear. It is not an option because it would be like permitting that hegemony becomes formally installed. It is not just about being, but about a right. And good or bad, it is an intergovernmental space, multilateral, that can permit certain accords."[19] She saw the strength of international structures and pressure from the UN as being influential in efforts to hold the Mexican government accountable for its systematic record of human rights violations.

Interviewees also discussed the importance of having an outside international body that supports global activism for human rights. The representative of a US women of color–led organization, for example, said, "There comes a point . . . [where a] country's rule of law in itself is not enough. People have to come in and step in, and there has to be an international body that is accountable."[20] The representative from a gay and lesbian group in Canada made a similar point: "I think the UN has a role because there needs to be something outside of national borders as an ideal, as a mark, as a dialogue space as well [as] a space of influence."[21] The representative of an indigenous peoples organization in Peru stated that the moral weight of the UN and the corresponding international pressure that it can leverage provides support for activists' goals when their own governments ignore their concerns: "I think anything related to the

United Nations carries moral weight. We have a space to say, 'Look, there are countries which violate the human rights of indigenous peoples.' And there is a space where you can go and say, 'My country is doing [x] . . .' And in some way, it is pressure for the nation-states to respect and to take notice."[22] She further noted that indigenous peoples have access to a number of UN conventions and initiatives that offer protection because national governments can be pressured to respect them.

Women frequently reiterated the importance of the UN itself, stating that a world without this institution was unimaginable, "even with all its problems," because activists would be "in a much worse place . . . today."[23] Another interviewee noted that the UN cannot be abandoned "for the very reasons" that make it weak, meaning that just because power at the UN can be wielded undemocratically, it should not result in activists relinquishing that advocacy space entirely.[24] A longtime human rights advocate from the United States emphasized that it is the only place where activists "can force governments to sit around the table and talk about human rights. And I think you've got to start with that, and we've got to work on that."[25] The UN, she continued, has "never worked the way it was envisioned to work because of global politics." Another US interviewee offered a similar point: "It is one of the few places where governments can come together to voice concerns about issues . . . and Southern countries can come as a bloc to try and change something. Some of them are effective. . . . So the fact that you can walk up to the government delegate and give them something to lobby for is [possible] only at the UN. It is not just governments having access, but also NGOs having access to governments."[26] Her point about forming political blocs correlates with the early actions of Latin American governments discussed in chapter 1 at the UNCIO, where these governments formed a bloc to counter the efforts of the "great powers." In the case of the 2001 WCAR, NGO activists formed similar blocs and released various position statements to reflect their collective concerns. Preparing for a UN world conference facilitates this critical process of coming together to enact change. It speaks to the importance of "the moment" (see chapter 4).

My interviewees noted that the UN cannot be the institution it is meant to be without the active participation of NGOs. Global civil society has a responsibility to ensure that the UN functions properly by continuing to challenge the intentions and actions of economically powerful governments at the UN. The executive director of an indigenous rights organization in Mexico City stated that the world's citizenry must apply pressure to strengthen the UN. If civil society abrogates this responsibility, "who will defend us . . . our community?" she asked. "We have to insist that somebody be there to defend us."[27] A member of a lesbian rights group from Peru also considered the role that global civil society must play, especially in light of the UN's limitations: "I think the United Nations has been terribly debilitated and in the control of the United States. But I think that is due to the lack of pressure for citizens, because if each citizenry would push their representatives that they don't have to pay attention to the United States whenever they feel like it, then I think the composition of the United Nations could change."[28] These women make a case for active citizen engagement with the UN to pressure the institution into not acquiescing so easily to demands from powerful governments, such as the United States. If the UN is to be improved, then global citizens must play a role in that process. US activist may in fact play a particularly crucial role here. As one US human rights activists stated, "I think that the more important question we all have to really ask ourselves is what are we going to do as American citizens about US imperialism. And how we handle and address that question will then determine to some extent what the UN can be or can't be."[29]

Many activists wondered whether energy should be put into the increasingly popular World Social Forums instead of the UN world conferences. One US interviewee rightly observed that people "are trying to create something" at the World Social Forums, and that "the UN is not [as] exciting." Yet she noted that the "solidarity work" that occurs at the UN is critically important.[30] One of my Canadian interviewees put it this way: "I don't see the argument around how futile these [UN world conferences] are. . . . If these things are futile, it is because of how they have been abused."[31]

In sum, the antiracist feminist activists I spoke with largely agreed about the continued importance of the UN as a site for their political activism. They expressed a desire to change the UN to better reflect their realities and experiences with racism, and they voiced the hope that it will one day evolve into a more participatory and democratic institution. The greatest obstacle, as one US interviewee noted above, is the influence wielded by the economically powerful countries, particularly the United

States. Her point emphasizes the especially important role US citizens play in preventing the US government from acting without consequence in the world. The antiracist feminists I interviewed were conscious of the limitations of the UN as an institution, yet they acknowledged the importance of the unique opportunity that the UN provides for debates and negotiations regarding the world's most urgent problems.

CONCLUDING THOUGHTS

Every UN discussion or forum devoted to the issue of racism since the early years of the institution has been challenging, contentious, and provocative. Antiracist feminist activists nonetheless have succeeded in expanding the dialogue on racial discrimination at the UN to consider and acknowledge the confluence of race- and gender-based discrimination. As a result, even though racism continues to be deeply embedded worldwide, what the UN considers racially unjust in the 2010s is much broader than what it considered racially unjust in the 1970s. The reason for this— and one of the keys to strengthening the fight against racism around the globe—is intersectionality.

As discussed in this book, world conferences are significant not just because of their outcomes, but also because of the critical process that develops due to the extensive preparation involved. Political scientist Charles Henry argues, "The benefits of the [world conference] process" is that "they can serve as incubators of change."[32] A blanket assessment of ineffectiveness and inadequacy when it comes to anything UN-related, then, is inaccurate. Much of what happens within that space is neither a total success nor a complete failure, and some of the concrete shifts happen before the official UN gathering even takes place. If feminists wed themselves to this binary (success versus failure), we will become politically paralyzed.

Many of the activists I interviewed expressed a perspective similar to Henry's, emphasizing that their work was aided in important ways by opportunities that could only be afforded by the UN. Almost all said that their participation in the 2001 WCAR had generated renewed enthusiasm for work that was often embattled at home. Among those who cited the importance of the networks created during the conference was Natalia, an Afro-Peruvian feminist activist: "An NGO can become strengthened through the world conference process. . . . Not so much because we were working with different definitions, but because the process and the dynamic of those types of reunions expands your thinking. So things that may appear disconnected [may not be]."[33] When communities who typically do not work together or know each other have an opportunity to collaborate, the interaction leads to shifts in thinking. In the case of the 2001 WCAR, this coming together produced moments of clarity for activists as they strategically organized to envision how to overcome contemporary manifestations of global racism without dismissing racism's historical legacies.

The world conference experience also crystallizes the dynamics of power in a way that cannot be learned in textbooks. A woman of color from Canada said, "I am just struck by, overall, how much Durban changed my life. I go to many conferences and do things locally in terms of politics. I don't know if it's Durban or the world. If 9/11 hadn't happened, would I still get that sense? But this acute awareness that I do have to think about how power is organized internationally, which is such a simple thing and probably lots of people on the front lines know this in their bones, but for me . . . that was a change . . . [and] that means a particular thing is happening in the international [realm] in my name. That is what Durban did."[34] Her point is a striking reminder of what we have to gain analytically and politically by reading power backward and forward and by participating in these types of events. This life-changing experience occurred not only for this interviewee but for the numerous participants of the world conference whom I had the privilege to interview and likely for many I wish I had been able to talk to.

Cynthia Enloe reminds us of the profound implications of linking the personal and the international when she states, "The implications of a feminist understanding of international politics are thrown into sharper relief when one reads 'the personal is international' the other way round: *the international is personal.* This calls for a radical new imagining of what it takes for governments to ally with each other, compete with and wage war against each other."[35] Applying this "radical new imagining" to feminists instead of governments, the "international is personal" paradigm nurtures an opportunity to generate new thinking and new energies toward the goal of transnational feminist solidarity. Transnational feminism is about struggle, resilience, and hope.

The welcome message on the home page of the United Nations website provides a fitting close for this exploration of antiracist and feminist activism inside the UN. The message, repeated in all of the UN's official languages, reads, "United Nations. It's Your World!" How would the meaning change if the slogan instead read, "It's *Our* World"? When the UN is viewed as ours, then we understand our right to be heard and represented there. The antiracist feminist activists I interviewed consider the UN "ours"—and because of this, they place demands on it, engaging its imperfect mechanisms in their efforts to make the institution a space of participatory democracy, a place where the most marginal of voices matter as much as the most powerful ones.

APPENDIX

Copy of the E-mail and Non-Paper Sent by the US Government to US NGOs during the Preparatory Period of the 2001 WCA

Subject: US Government "Non-Paper" on the WCAR
Date: Tue, May 15, 2001

Demarche
World Conference against Racism

We wanted to engage you on an urgent basis concerning the world conference against racism, scheduled to be held in Durban, South Africa[,] in four short months (Aug. 31–Sept. 7). Key preparatory meetings for the world conference resume next week in Geneva. It is our hope that those meetings can set a positive tone for the world conference to help it be the success that we all want it to be.

Our objectives for Durban have remained consistent: a forward-looking conference that acknowledges historical injustices and their modern legacy and results in a balanced final document that will serve as a blueprint for fighting present-day manifestations of racism and related intolerance.

We would like the WCAR to focus on the current form and manifestations of racism as it was intended to do by the UNGA, rather than to apportion blame for past injustices or to seek to exact compensation for these acts. While we acknowledge the importance of recognizing the role we all played in past injustices, it is equally important for us to focus on ways to end deplorable practices that continue today. We cannot miss this opportunity.

We would like, in particular[,] to call your attention to the remarks of High Commissioner Robinson to the opening ceremony of the 57th commission on human rights on March 19, when she noted that "during the past month alone hundreds have been killed in Borneo, Burundi and countless other parts of the world on the ground of ethnicity. Ethnic conflict has surfaced . . . in Macedonia. . . . And the insidious, subtle forms of discrimination continue to operate. . . . Combating these abuses, working to end the wretched practice of trafficking in humans, focusing on the gender dimension of racism, respecting the rights of indigenous peoples and minorities in deed as well as word, extending human rights education to inform everyone, especially young people, about where intolerance leads—these are the issues that go to the heart of the world conference. We can and must tackle them."

Also speaking before the CHR, UN Secretary-General Kofi Annan made an equally important statement, noting: "And while we have built up an impressive array of laws, institutions and independent watchdog groups, the people who suffer most from the denial of their human rights are often unaware of their rights and beyond the reach of these mechanisms. So we must take our effort to a higher level. That is the heavy burden facing the WCAR. The UN conferences of the 1990's have given the people of the world a series of dynamic blueprints for progress on key issues . . . and not least human rights. The WCAR has similar potential to reach deeply into the lives of people and give them both help and hope."

Finally, we wish to call your attention to the text of CHR resolution 2001/5 on "racism, racial discrimination, xenophobia and related intolerance" that was adopted unanimously at the CHR on April 18; the USG co-sponsored this resolution. We believe that the WCAR sections (operative paragraphs 48–71) strike the right balance and should serve as a model for the dialogue and cooperation that we are looking forward to in Durban.

The key recommendation is in paragraph 62, which "recommends that the world conference adopt a declaration and program of action containing concrete and practical recommendations to combat racism, racial discrimination, xenophobia and related intolerance."

We look forward to close cooperation at the upcoming inter-sessional meeting in Geneva and to working with your delegation to achieve a balanced document for consideration at the second PrepCom.

With a view towards facilitating a positive outcome both in the Geneva preparatory meetings and the world conference itself, we wanted to make clear to you our thinking concerning the conference, and some of the key issues.

We have done so in the form of a non-paper that we would like to share with you, and to which we invite your attention. We look forward to receiving your reactions to this paper, and to continue discussions with your authorities as the world conference approaches.

Non-Paper
World Conference against Racism
Background

—The preparatory process for the world conference against racism is entering a crucial phase in Geneva. The second, and final, meeting of the preparatory committee for the conference is scheduled for May 21–June 1 in Geneva.

—The 2nd PrepCom session is to be preceded by a May 7–11 working group meeting, a continuation of the one originally convened March 6–9 but which foundered over differences concerning draft synthesis documents prepared by the WCAR secretariat in the Office of the High Commissioner for Human Rights (OHCHR) and on how to proceed. Several delegations from different regional groups felt that the secretariat's drafts had not sufficiently taken into account provisions on certain subjects that had been developed in their regional meetings.

—We, too, were disappointed that many of the wide array of issues that we believe to be of key importance to the WCAR were addressed inadequately in the secretariat document. At the same time, we must say that on the more highly politicized issues, the high commissioner attempted to steer the right course in order for the WCAR to be the success that we all want.

—In any event, a dispute developed at the working group meeting as to how to best proceed[:] Using the secretariat's texts as the basis for negotiation, or basically starting from scratch and creating entirely new texts which would be drawn only from a compendium of WCAR documents produced by the various regions.

—It appears that this dispute is now on the way to resolution, as a result of the position taken by Secretary-General Annan at the commission for human rights annual meeting that negotiations should, in fact, proceed on the basis of the secretariat's draft texts, with other documents being looked to for reference.

—We hope all Geneva participants will come together to support this approach so that there is no further delay due to procedural wrangling—especially since preparatory time for the world conference is growing short—and so that we can move on to a consideration of substantive matters.

—Moving forward on this matter will not prejudice the ability of delegations to make substantive proposals to modify or add to the secretariat's drafts at the working group and the PrepCom.

—On substance, we wanted to give you a clear idea of how the U.S. views the world conference against racism.

U.S. view of the world conference

—We hope you share our basic view that the world conference against racism provides a unique opportunity to address the full range of racism-related matters that plague the world today—from genocide, ethnic cleansing and xenophobia to denial of equal rights and opportunities to certain people and groups.

—There is much that citizens and nations can take to Durban in terms of sharing experiences and ideas for the future. Likewise, there will be much to take away from Durban in terms of strategies to combat racism and related intolerance.

—We must not let this unique opportunity to collectively address these issues escape us.

—We understand that some countries have a much more limited view of this conference. For example, there are some who believe that this gathering should address current crises such as the Middle East conflict. It appears that some are attempting to resurrect the "Zionism is racism" style of language rejected by the United Nations several years ago.

—The U.S. has from the very beginning rejected this or like language. We are of the strong opinion that it is especially inappropriate to disrupt this conference by returning to a discussion which was concluded a decade ago.

—It is clear and generally understood that world conferences are not meant to address country-specific situations. To do so would polarize discussion in the conference and could seriously jeopardize prospects for achieving consensus on common approaches to combating racism throughout the world.

—Finally, there are other countries (and many individuals) that believe the primary issue for the conference is some form of international compensatory scheme for the 17th–19th century trans-Atlantic slave trade, or for colonialism.

—This issue is addressed in more detail below, but we would like to make a few fundamental points:

—We agree that slavery and the slave trade of the distant past must be acknowledged, discussed, learned from and condemned.

—We believe, moreover, that each country must take it upon itself to confront its own past, and to provide effective recourse and remedies to address the legacy of slavery.

—However, we simply do not believe that it is appropriate to address this history—and its many and vast aspects—through such measures as international compensatory measures.

—We also believe that focusing on this issue—rather than the wide-ranging, racism-related problems with varying root causes that occur everywhere in the world and affect people's lives today—works to distract attention and would dilute efforts to address these problems in meaningful ways. One of these problems which, in fact, is present-day slavery and slavery-like practices.

—In this regard, we are very much in agreement with the views of Senegalese President Abdoulaye Wade, as expressed in his speech that opened the Africa regional meeting for the world conference held in Dakar in January. President Wade argued passionately for African states to approach the world conference against racism as a way of finding practical solutions to current problems. In the same connection, we draw your attention as well to the heart-wrenching remarks of the Rwandan delegate to the Dakar conference concerning the recent genocide in that country.

—We hope that you share this view of a forward-looking, practically-oriented world conference, and look forward to working with you to make it a success.

The slavery issue

—We wanted to focus particularly on this issue with you and to make clear how we view it.

—First, the United States fully agrees that slavery, no matter how distant in the past it has been, is relevant to racism-related issues in the world today and is relevant to the WCAR.

—We believe, in this regard, that the world conference should acknowledge that the legacy of slavery, as well as that of conquest and colonialism, is among the sources and causes of racism and racial discrimination as they exist in the world today.

—We believe, further, that this legacy must be condemned, and the practices involved labeled morally reprehensible.

—We are also willing to join others in expressing regret for involvement in those historical practices.

—Moreover, we believe it important to find appropriate ways of honoring and paying tribute to the legacy of the enslaved, both in terms of what they and their families endured and their important role in helping to build many of the countries of the world today.

—In this connection, we note that there are serious moves afoot in the United States today to create the first national museum devoted exclusively to the history and culture of Africans and African Americans, and also to nominate New York City's African burial ground which holds the remains of over 20,000 enslaved from the 1600–1700s to the world heritage list.

—We also note proposals made in the Americas regional meeting and elsewhere for memorialization and educational activities of this nature.

—Again, however, we are not willing to agree to anything that suggests present-day liability on the part of one state to another for that historical situation.

—The convention on the elimination of racial discrimination requires that states provide access to a remedy and redress for individuals who are victims of unlawful discrimination. We vigorously support measures contemplated in the convention.

—But there is no comparable basis for addressing the historical internal situation concerning slavery, including through reparations or some other international compensatory scheme.

—Having said that, we are fully in accord with the proposal in the African regional document for the enhancement and progressive development of national remedies for victims of racial discrimination, and the widest possible dissemination of information concerning such matters.

—We also believe that the United States has much to share in terms of our own, often painful experience[,] both historical and current[,] and steps that have been taken to overcome the effects of slavery and racism and to correct wrongs in a wide range of areas, from education to the administration of justice. Although much has been done that we are proud of, much remains to be done and we intend to go to the world conference to listen and learn as well as to share information of our own best practices.

—The United States for many years has sought to address the developmental/ economic needs of African countries in a variety of substantial ways. The U.S. has carried out, in many African countries, as much as 40 years of bilateral assistance, as well as making contributions through international development agencies. More recently, we have undertaken the most massive debt relief program in history, totaling more than 1 billion dollars in Africa.

—We will continue to do what we can to address those needs.

—In sum, we recognize that the historical slavery/slave trade issue is an important one that must be addressed. We are trying to be as flexible and creative as possible within the framework of the basic position that we have outlined.

—We sincerely hope that you will recognize that effort and join with us in dealing with this issue in a way that recognizes its importance, but without jeopardizing the achievement of the overall goals of the conference.

NOTES

INTRODUCTION: THE CHALLENGING ROAD TO THE DURBAN CONFERENCE

1 Maxine Baca Zinn, Pierrette Hondagneu-Sotelo, and Michael A. Messner, eds., *Gender through the Prism of Difference*, 3rd ed. (New York: Oxford University Press, 2005). See also Linda Alcoff and Elizabeth Potter, eds., *Feminist Epistemologies* (New York: Routledge, 1992); and Nira Yuval-Davis, *Gender and Nation* (London: SAGE Publications, 1997).

2 Please note that I use the term "Durban conference" to refer to both the WCAR and the NGO Forum. However, I use "2001 WCAR" or "NGO Forum" when needed for clarity.

3 Charlotte Bunch and Susana Fried, "Beijing '95: Moving Women's Human Rights from Margin to Center," *Signs: Journal of Women in Culture and Society* 22, no. 1 (1996): 200–204; Mallika Dutt, "Reclaiming a Human Rights Culture: Feminism of Difference and Alliance," in *Talking Visions: Multicultural Feminism in a Transnational Age*, ed. Ella Shohat (Cambridge, MA: The MIT Press, 1998), 225–46; Esther Ngan-Ling Chow, "Making Waves, Moving Mountains: Reflections on Beijing '95 and Beyond," *Signs: Journal of Women in Culture and Society* 22, no. 1 (1996): 185–92.

4 William Armaline, Davita Silfen Glasberg, and Bandana Purkayastha, eds., *Human Rights in Our Own Backyard: Injustice and Resistance in the United States* (Philadelphia: University of Pennsylvania Press, 2012).

5 *United Nations Chronicle*, "Conference Against Racism: Preparations," New York, May 1983, 54. All UN documents and resolutions about racism either italicize or underline the word "apartheid."

6 Tom Lantos, "The Durban Debacle: An Insider's View of the UN World Conference Against Racism," *Fletcher Forum of World Affairs* (Winter/Spring 2002): 31.

7 Lantos, "Durban Debacle," 52.

8 A search on LexisNexis Academic about the 2001 Durban conference identifies hundreds of newspaper articles, well over half of which discuss Israel.

9   A public opinion survey conducted by Pew Research Center's Global
     Attitudes Project found that Europeans are far more sympathetic to
     Palestinians than are citizens of the United States. Pew Research, "Ameri-
     cans and Europeans Differ Widely on Foreign Policy Issues," April 17,
     2002, accessed August 12, 2014, http://www.pewglobal.org/2002/04/17/
     americans-and-europeans-differ-widely-on-foreign-policy-issues/.

10   Carol Anderson, *Eyes Off the Prize: The United Nations and the African Ameri-
     can Struggle for Human Rights, 1944–1955* (New York: Cambridge University
     Press, 2003).

11   Italics mine. Feminist Majority Foundation, "Campaign for Afghan Women
     and Girls," accessed September 16, 2013, http://www.feminist.org/afghan/
     aboutcampaign.asp.

12   Ibid. Information on the Revolutionary Association of the Women of Af-
     ghanistan, go to http://www.rawa.org/index.php (accessed September 19,
     2013).

13   The notion that the US military could somehow play a role in respecting
     women's rights is an outrageous assertion because of the hypermasculin-
     ity and rampant violence structurally inherent to military culture and its
     institutional establishment.

14   As stated on INCITE!'s website, "Since the U.S. invaded Afghanistan in 2001,
     INCITE! has used political art to express and strengthen a movement to end
     violence against women of color and our communities. Wonderful women
     of color artists, including Favianna Rodriguez, Samia Saleem, and Cristy C.
     Road, have created beautiful and powerful images and posters for INCITE!
     projects." See http://www.incite-national.org/page/posters. INCITE! links
     interpersonal violence to "larger structures of violence, including militarism,
     attacks on immigrants' rights and Indian treaty rights, the proliferation of
     prisons, economic neo-colonialism, [and] the medical industry." See INCITE!
     Women of Color Against Violence, "INCTE! Analysis," accessed December 17,
     2013, http://www.incite-national.org/page/analysis.

15   Paola Bacchetta, Tina Campt, Inderpal Grewal, Caren Kaplan, Minoo Mo-
     allem, and Jennifer Terry, "Transnational Feminist Practices against War,"
     Meridians: feminism, race, transnationalism 2, no. 2 (2002): 307 and 303.

16   Reviewing the list of accredited NGOs registered to attend the 2001 WCAR
     from the UN website confirms this point.

17   Both monetary contributions came during the Clinton administration.
     The Bush administration did not contribute at all to the 2001 WCAR. See
     United Nations, Office of the High Commissioner for Human Rights, "An-
     nual Appeal 2000: Overview of Activities and Financial Requirements,"
     accessed September 20, 2013, http://www.ohchr.org/Documents/AboutUs/
     annualappealo.pdf; and United Nations, Office of the High Commissioner
     for Human Rights, "Annual Report 2001: Implementation of Activities and
     Use of Funds, 2002," accessed September 20, 2013, http://www.refworld
     .org/docid/47fdfbodo.html.

18 It was widely believed that former US Secretary of State Colin Powell would attend the 2001 WCAR, especially because he had expressed an interest in attending the conference. However, the prospect of his attendance quickly faded.

19 Eduardo Galeano, *Open Veins of Latin America: Five Centuries of the Pillage of a Continent* 25th anniversary ed. (New York: Monthly Review Press, 1997).

20 Manisha Desai, "Transnationalism: The Face of Feminist Politics Post-Beijing," *International Social Science Journal* 57, no. 2 (2005): 322.

21 Charlotte Bunch and Niamh Reilly. *Demanding Accountability: The Global Campaign and Vienna Tribunal for Women's Human Rights* (East Brunswick, NJ: Center for Women's Global Leadership, Rutgers University, 1994), 5.

22 Ibid.

23 See also Michael G. Schechter, ed., *United Nations-sponsored World Conferences: Focus on Impact and Follow-up* (Tokyo: The United Nations University Press, 2001); and Michael G. Schechter, *United Nations Global Conferences* (London: Routledge, 2005).

24 The Women's Institute for Leadership Development (WILD) for Human Rights sponsored my participation. I had served on the youth advisory board of WILD for Human Rights in the mid-1990s. WILD for Human Rights, formerly located in San Francisco, has now transitioned into being an initiative program of the UC Berkeley School of Law. See the organization's website, accessed February 2, 2013, at http://www.law.berkeley .edu/8227.htm. Because of the limited number of NGO passes, only a small group from our delegation was able to participate in the 2001 WCAR.

25 In Durban, massive public protests were staged by South Africans, many of whom had traveled to Durban to raise their voices about the worsening conditions in postapartheid South Africa. See Ashwin Desai, *We Are the Poors: Community Struggles in Post-Apartheid South Africa* (New York: Monthly Review Press, 2002).

26 For the Beijing conference, the final official document was called Platform for Action rather than Programme of Action.

27 Sylvanna M. Falcón, "Invoking Human Rights and Transnational Activism in Racial Justice Struggles at Home: US Antiracist Activists and the UN Committee to Eliminate Racial Discrimination," *Societies without Borders* 4 (2009): 295–316.

28 Elora Chowdhury, "Locating Global Feminisms Elsewhere: Braiding US Women of Color and Transnational Feminisms," *Cultural Dynamics* 21, no. 1 (2009): 72.

29 Margaret E. Keck and Kathryn Sikkink, *Activist Beyond Borders: Advocacy Networks in International Politics* (Ithaca, NY: Cornell University Press, 1998); Sonia E. Alvarez, "Advocating Feminism: The Latin American Feminist NGO Boom," *International Feminist Journal of Politics* 1, no. 2 (1999): 181–209, and "Translating the Global: Effects of Transnational Organizing on Local Feminist Discourses and Practices in Latin America," *Meridians:*

feminism, race, transnationalism 1, no. 1 (2000): 29–67; Bunch and Reilly, *Demanding Accountability.*

30 See Escárcega for a useful discussion about the role of the global indigenous movement (GIM) and the United Nations. Sylvia Escárcega, "The Global Indigenous Movement and Paradigm Wars: International Activism, Network Building, and Transformative Politics," in *Insurgent Encounters: Transnational Activism, Ethnography, and the Political*, ed. Jeffrey S. Juris and Alex Khasnabish (Durham, NC: Duke University Press, 2013).

31 Chowdhury, "Locating Global Feminisms Elsewhere," 59.

32 Sandra Whitworth, *Feminism and International Relations: Towards a Political Economy of Gender in Multilateral Institutions* (New York: MacMillan Press, 1994), xii.

33 See Chowdhury, "Locating Global Feminisms Elsewhere," 55.

34 Charles P. Henry, *Long Overdue: The Politics of Racial Reparations* (New York: New York University, 2009).

35 Vijay Prashad, *The Darker Nations: A People's History of the Third World* (New York: New Press, 2007). See Chowdhury, "Locating Global Feminisms Elsewhere," 67.

36 Mexico is part of both configurations.

37 For example, Bandana Purkayastha contends that religion, and our assumptions about religion, should be considered in an intersectionality framework transnationally. See Bandana Purkayastha, "Intersectionality in a Transnational World" *Gender & Society* 26, no. 1 (2012): 55–66.

38 Leslie McCall, "The Complexity of Intersectionality," *Signs: Journal of Women in Culture and Society* 30, no. 3 (2005): 1771–800. See also Kathy Davis, "Intersectionality as Buzzword: A Sociology of Science Perspective on What Makes a Feminist Theory Successful," *Feminist Theory* 9, no. 1 (2008): 67–85; Jennifer C. Nash, "Re-Thinking Intersectionality," *Feminist Review* 89 (2008): 1–15.

39 Expert seminars are UN-sponsored meetings at which experts in a subject field meet with interested parties to learn more about a particular topic.

40 Kimberlé Williams Crenshaw, "Gender-Related Aspects of Race Discrimination," paper presented at the Expert Seminar Group Meeting on Gender and Racial Discrimination, Zagreb, Croatia, November 21–24, 2000, 7. This definition builds on Crenshaw's earlier work in which she contended that intersectionality had to do with how the intersection of race, class, and gender determine (or predetermine) women of color's access to housing, employment, and education, to name a few. See Kimberlé Williams Crenshaw, "Mapping the Margins: Intersectionality, Identity Politics, and Violence against Women of Color," in *The Public Nature of Private Violence: The Discovery of Domestic Abuse*, ed. Martha Albertson Fineman and Roxanne Mykitiuk (New York: Routledge, 1994).

41 Lisa A. Crooms, "'To Establish My Legitimate Name Inside the Consciousness of Strangers': Critical Race Praxis, Progressive Women-of-Color Theo-

rizing, and Human Rights," *Howard Law Journal* 46 (2003): 243–44.

42 In the second edition of her seminal book *Black Feminist Thought*, Collins attempts to apply her matrix framework to the transnational level with mixed results. Collins compares African women and African American women by highlighting structural adjustment policies and US welfare programs:

"In both cases [referring to poor African women and poor African American women], the poverty of Black children was traced back to the sexuality and reproductive capacities of their mothers. But whereas African women's poverty was deemed permanent and thus unresponsive to aid, African American women were deemed unworthy recipients of aid that maintained their status as permanent beggars. In both cases, the best action was to let them starve." (Patricia Hill Collins, *Black Feminist Thought: Knowledge, Consciousness, and the Politics of Empowerment*, 2nd ed. [New York: Routledge 2000], 241)

But Collins's useful comparison of US welfare and structural adjustment policies does not analyze the structural (and intersectional) links between structural adjustment policies and welfare reform (see Robin Levi and Eve McCabe, "Rights and Reform: The Impact of Structural Adjustment and Welfare Reform" [San Francisco: Women's Institute for Leadership Development (WILD) for Human Rights, 2001]). WILD for Human Rights released a paper that delved into how structural adjustment policies and welfare reform are constructed similarly in their objectives (ibid.). In the paper, they called for the coalition of advocates for the progressive reform of welfare and structural adjustment policies to work together because of the ways global and local levels of poverty are linked. By viewing structural adjustment policies and welfare reform as linked, then poverty can be viewed in a relational context, opening new possibilities for transnational feminist solidarity.

43 Gloria Anzaldúa, *Borderlands / La Frontera: The New Mestiza*, 2nd ed. (San Francisco: Aunt Lute Books, 1999). See also Sylvanna M. Falcón, "Mestiza Double Consciousness: The Voices of Afro-Peruvian Women on Gendered Racism," *Gender & Society* 22, no. 5 (2008): 660–80.

44 Nash, "Re-Thinking Intersectionality."

45 See Linda Martín Alcoff, "The Problem of Speaking for Others," accessed December 17, 2013, http://www.alcoff.com/content/speaothers.html.

46 Hae Yeon Choo and Myra Marx Ferree, "Practicing Intersectionality in Sociological Research: A Critical Analysis of Inclusions, Interactions, and Institutions in the Study of Inequalities," *Sociological Theory* 28, no. 2 (2010): 129–49.

47 Choo and Ferree, "Practicing Intersectionality," 129.

48 Ibid., 136; see also McCall, "Complexity of Intersectionality."

49 Christine E. Bose, "Intersectionality and Global Gender Inequality," *Gender & Society* 26, no. 1 (2012): 70.

50 Sylvanna M. Falcón, "Transnational Feminism and Contextualized Intersectionality at the 2001 World Conference Against Racism," *Journal of Women's History* 24, no. 4 (2012): 99–120.

51 Purkayastha, "Intersectionality in a Transnational World"; Bandana Purkayastha, Anjana Narayan, and Sudipto Banerjee, "Constructing Virtual, Transnational Identities on the Web: The Case of Hindu Student Groups in the US and UK," *Journal of Intercultural Studies* 32 (2011): 495–517.

52 Purkayastha, "Intersectionality in a Transnational World," 62.

53 Choo and Ferree do not argue that one type of intersectionality is better than the others, but they prefer the complexity of the third model.

54 Falcón, "Transnational Feminism"; Vivian May, "Speaking into the Void"? Intersectionality Critiques and Epistemic Backlash," *Hypatia* 18, no. 1 (2014): 96–97.

55 Sandra Soto, "Where in the Transnational World Are U.S. Women of Color?" in *Women's Studies for the Future: Foundations, Interrogations, Politics,* ed. Agatha Meryl Beins and Elizabeth Lapovsky Kennedy (New Brunswick, NJ: Rutgers University Press, 2005): 111–24.

56 Inderpal Grewal and Caren Kaplan, *Scattered Hegemonies: Postmodernity and Transnational Feminist Practices* (Minneapolis: University of Minnesota Press, 1994), 17.

57 According to Caren Kaplan, Norma Alarcón, and Minoo Moallem, "The discourses of 'international' or 'global' feminism rely on political and economic as well as cultural concepts of discrete nations who can be placed into comparative or relational status, always maintaining the West as the center." Caren Kaplan, Norma Alarcón, and Minoo Moallem, eds., *Between Woman and Nation: Nationalisms, Transnational Feminisms, and the State* (Durham, NC: Duke University Press, 1999), 12.

58 Daiva K. Stasiulis, "Relational Positionalities of Nationalisms, Racisms, and Feminisms," in Kaplan, Alarcón, and Moallem, *Between Woman and Nation,* 194.

59 Chandra Talpade Mohanty, Ann Russo, and Lourdes Torres, eds., *Third World Women and the Politics of Feminism* (Bloomington: Indiana University Press, 1991), 13.

60 Ella Shohat, "Introduction," in *Talking Visions: Multicultural Feminism in a Transnational Age,* ed. Ella Shohat (Cambridge, MA: MIT Press, 1998), 38.

61 Jacqui M. Alexander and Chandra Talpade Mohanty, eds., *Feminist Genealogies, Colonial Legacies, Democratic Futures* (New York: Routledge, 1997).

62 *Meridians,* "Ama Ata Aidoo, Edna Acosta-Belén, Amrita Basu, Maryse Condé, Nell Painter, and Nawal El Saadawi Speak on Feminism, Race, and Transnationalism," *Meridians: feminism, race, transnationalism* 1, no. 1 (2000): 1–28.

63 Chandra Talpade Mohanty, *Feminism without Borders: Decolonizing Theory, Practicing Solidarity* (Durham, NC: Duke University Press, 2003).

64 Ibid.

65 Valentine M. Moghadam, "Globalizing Women: An Introduction and Overview" in *Globalizing Women: Transnational Feminist Networks* (Baltimore:
The John Hopkins University Press, 2005), 1–20.

66 Keck and Sikkink, *Activist Beyond Borders*, 12–13.

67 Amrita Basu, "Globalization of the Local/Localization of the Global:
Mapping Transnational Women's Movements," *Meridians: feminism, race,
transnationalism* 1, no. 1 (2000): 68–84.

68 Janet Conway, "Geographies of Transnational Feminisms: The Politics of
Place and Scale in the World March of Women," *Social Politics: International
Studies in Gender, State, and Society* 15, no. 2 (2008): 212.

69 Stasiulis, "Relational Positionalities," 196.

70 Desai, "Transnationalism."

71 Kaplan, Alarcón, and Moallem, *Between Woman and Nation*, 12.

72 Mohanty, *Feminism without Borders*.

73 Grewal and Kaplan, *Scattered Hegemonies*.

74 See Sylvanna M. Falcón and Jennifer Nash, "Shifting Analytics and Linking
Theories: A Conversation about the 'Meaning-making' of Intersectionality and Transnational Feminism," *Women's Studies International Forum* 50
(2015): 1–10.

75 Canadian interviewees informed me that it is expected that the govern-
ment will fund activists attending conferences. When I informed them that
I could not imagine the US government funding activists attending the
Durban conference, many were surprised.

76 Paolo G. Carozza, "From Conquest to Constitutions: Retrieving a Latin
American Tradition of the Idea of Human Rights," *Human Rights Quarterly*
25 (2003): 281–313; and Mary Ann Glendon, "The Forgotten Crucible: The
Latin American Influence on the Universal Human Rights Idea," *Harvard
Human Rights Journal* 16 (2003): 27–39.

77 Bobby Vaughn, "Afro-Mexico: Blacks, Indigenas, Politics, and the Greater
Diaspora," in *Neither Enemies nor Friends: Latinos, Blacks, and Afro-Latinos*,
ed. Anani Dzidzienyo and Suzanne Oboler (New York: Palgrave Macmillan,
2005).

78 See Dan Collyns, "Peru's Minorities Battle Racism," BBC News, June 13,
2010, accessed March 9, 2014, http://www.bbc.co.uk/news/10205171; and
BBC News, "Peru Apologises for Abuse of African-origin Citizens," November 29, 2009, accessed December 17, 2013, http://news.bbc.co.uk/2/
hi/8384853.stm.

79 See "Alert/ Press Release: Peru/Peruvian Government Sanctions TV Station
$27,000 for Racist Programming," accessed September 17, 2013, http://
afrolatinoproject.org/2013/08/28/alert-press-release-peru-peruvian-
government-sanctions-tv-station-27000-for-racist-programming/.

80 Strikingly, Mexico and Peru combined received significantly more slaves in
total than the United States, suggesting that the erasure of the existence
of populations of African descent is intense. Henry Louis Gates, "Blacks

in Latin America," accessed December 17, 2013, http://www.pbs.org/wnet/
black-in-latin-america/featured/full-episode-mexico-peru/227/. For a critique of Gates' documentary, see Christina A. Sue and Tanya Golash-Boza,
"More Than 'A Hidden Race': The Complexities of Blackness in Mexico and
Peru," *Latin American and Caribbean Ethnic Studies* 8, no. 1 (2013): 1–7.

81   During the interview process, I wanted to be mindful that the United
     States is not the only nation that has experienced a devastating terrorist
     attack, and that is why I often add the clause "in the United States" when I
     reference September 11. In Latin America, for example, one has to be clear
     to indicate *which* September 11 is being discussed, because September 11,
     1973, marked the death of President Salvador Allende of Chile, the world's
     first democratically elected Marxist head of state, who was succeeded by
     the brutal dictator General Augusto Pinochet. I mention this other Sep-
     tember 11 not to minimize the tragedy in the United States but to begin
     to decenter (for myself personally, and in the context of this research) the
     United States while not negating its very real power and control in the
     world. Adding the clause may seem like a tiny gesture within the realm of
     activist research, but those rhetorical manoeuvres matter and contribute
     to an important and appropriate decentering of the United States.

82   Nikki Jones, *Between Good and Ghetto: African American Girls and Inner-City
     Violence* (New Jersey: Rutgers University Press, 2009), 166.

83   Ibid., 167.

84   Manisha Desai, "The Possibilities and Perils for Scholar-Activists and
     Activist-Scholars: Reflections on the Feminist Dialogues," in *Insurgent En-
     counters: Transnational Activism, Ethnography, and the Political*, ed. Jeffrey S.
     Juris and Alex Khasnabish (Durham, NC: Duke University Press, 2013),
     106.

85   In all of these UN spaces, WILD for Human Rights facilitated my ability to
     participate, for which I am truly grateful.

86   Nancy A. Naples, "Changing the Terms: Community Activism, Globaliza-
     tion, and the Dilemmas of Transnational Feminist Praxis," in *Women's
     Activism and Globalization: Linking Local Struggles and Transnational Politics*,
     ed. Nancy A. Naples and Manisha Desai (New York: Routledge, 2002).

87   Jennifer Suchland, "Is Postsocialism Transnational?" *Signs: Journal of
     Women in Culture and Society* 36, no. 4 (2011): 837–62.

1. RACE, GENDER, AND GEOPOLITICS

1   Some of these haunting images can be viewed at "Pictures from World War
     II" in the National Archives, http://www.archives.gov/research/military/
     ww2/photos/ (accessed October 25, 2013).

2   The tragedy here is that the atomic bombs dropped in the Japanese cities
     of Hiroshima and Nagasaki by the United States occurred *after* the partici-
     pating delegates signed the Charter of the United Nations in August 1945.

3   See Stephen C. Schlesinger, *Act of Creation: The Founding of the United Nations* (Boulder: Westview Press, 2003). The research conducted for this chapter received generous funding support from the University of California Center for New Racial Studies.

4   Anthony Anghie, *Imperialism, Sovereignty, and the Making of International Law* (Cambridge: Cambridge University Press, 2007). See also W.E.B. Du Bois, "The Negro and Imperialism," in *W.E.B. Du Bois on Asia: Crossing the World Color Line*, ed. Bill V. Mullen and Cathryn Watson (Mississippi: University Press of Mississippi, 2005), 37–47; and chapters 5 through 7 of R. M. Douglas, Michael P. Callahan, and Elizabeth Bishop, eds., *Imperialism on Trial* (Lanham, MD: Lexington Books, 2006).

5   Quoted in C. Anderson, *Eyes Off the Prize*, 37–38.

6   Millie Thayer, *Making Transnational Feminism: Rural Women, NGO Activists, and Northern Donors in Brazil* (New York: Routledge, 2009), 26.

7   Anibal Quijano, "Coloniality of Power, Eurocentrism, and Latin America," *Nepantia: Views from South* 1, no. 3 (2000): 533–80.

8   Ibid., 533–43.

9   Walter D. Mignolo, "Citizenship, Knowledge, and the Limits of Humanity," *American Literary History* 18, no. 2 (2006): 312.

10 Walter D. Mignolo, "Who Speaks for the 'Human' in Human Rights?," *Hispanic Issues On Line* 5, no. 1 (2009): 14.

11 Ibid., 7.

12 Cynthia Enloe, *Bananas, Beaches, and Bases: Making Feminist Sense of International Politics*, 2nd ed. (Berkeley: University of California, 2000), 196.

13 The segregation of African Americans of course was not the only form of racism in the United States at this time. The internment of Japanese Americans on a massive scale during World War II (which included the rendition of people of Japanese descent from different Latin American countries, including Peru, for the purposes of trading them for US civilians held by Japan) also occurred during this time. See Thomas Connell, *America's Japanese Hostages: The World War II Plan for a Japanese-Free Latin America* (Westport, CT: Greenwood Publishing Group, 2002).

14 Some of these rights existed for women in colonies where there had been vibrant women's rights movements for decades. Under colonial rule, however, their rights were taken away. See Amrita Basu, ed., *Women's Movements in the Global Era: The Power of Local Feminisms* (Boulder, CO: Westview Press, 2010); Barbara Callaway and Lucy Creevey, *Women, Religion, and Politics in West Africa: The Heritage of Islam* (Boulder, CO: Lynne Rienner Publishers, 1994); and Radha Kumar, *A History of Doing* (New Delhi: Zubaan Books, 1990).

15 The "codification of the difference between conqueror and conquered" that Quijano discusses in terms of race fundamentally created these racial divisions (Quijano, "Coloniality of Power," 533).

16 C. Anderson, *Eyes Off the Prize*, 38 and 41; see also 41n133 and 41n134.

17 The text of the charter is available on the UN website, accessed February 2, 2012, http://www.un.org/en/documents/charter/chapter1.shtml.

18 United Nations, Conference on International Organization, "Amendments to the Dumbarton Oaks Proposals Submitted by the Delegations of Brazil, the Dominican Republic, and the United States of México," May 5, 1945, doc. no. 2 G/25, in *Documents of the United Nations Conference on International Organization, San Francisco, 1945* (hereafter cited as *Documents of UNCIO*), vol. 2, *General* (London: United Nations Information Organizations, 1945), 602; United Nations, "Documentation for Meetings of Committee I/1," May 11, 1945, doc. no. 215 I/1/10, in *Documents of UNCIO*, vol. 10, *Commission 2—General Assembly*, 536.

19 United Nations, "Verbatim Minutes of Opening Session," April 25, 1945, doc. no. 8 G/5, in *Documents of UNCIO*, vol. 1, *General*, 111 and 123.

20 See C. Anderson, *Eyes Off the Prize*, 41.

21 See Mignolo, "Who Speaks for the 'Human'?," 8.

22 C. Anderson, *Eyes Off the Prize*. The Soviet Union wanted to be granted an additional two votes, and the United States eventually agreed to this arrangement. See Virginia Crocheron Gildersleeve, *Many a Good Crusade: Memoirs of Virginia Crocheron Gildersleeve* (New York: The Macmillan Company, 1955), 330.

23 C. Anderson, *Eyes Off the Prize*, 40. Members of forty-two national organizations served as consultants, and ranged from very conservative to liberal; see Dorothy B. Robins, *Experiment in Democracy: The Story of U.S. Citizen Organizations in Forging the Charter of the United Nations* (New York: Parkside Press, 1971).

24 W.E.B. Du Bois concluded the Dumbarton Oaks proposals structurally advantaged economically powerful countries and therefore, the UN's very foundation is undemocratic. See Du Bois, "Negro and Imperialism."

25 Bethune was vice president of the NAACP.

26 See Robins, *Experiment in Democracy*, 207–10.

27 For a list of the groups that were opposed to the ratification of the UN Charter, see Robins, *Experiment in Democracy*, 231–32.

28 Mignolo, "Who Speaks for the 'Human'?," 15.

29 Quijano, "Coloniality of Power," 565–66.

30 See Gordon W. Morrell, "A Higher Stage of Imperialism? The Big Three, the UN Trusteeship Council, and the Early Cold War," in Callahan, Douglas, and Bishop, *Imperialism on Trial*.

31 France was not part of the original "great powers" configuration. In the course of the conference, however, France's status changed to that of a great power. Subsequent references to the "great powers" in this chapter thus include France. Although some conference records mention four powers, later records indicate that there were five.

32 Yehuda Z. Blum, "Proposals for UN Security Council Reform," *American Journal of International Law* 99, no. 3 (2005): 638.

33 Patrick Worsnip, "U.N. Launches Talks to Expand Security Council," Reuters News Service February 19, 2009, accessed September 25, 2011, http://www.reuters.com/article/2009/02/19/us-un-council-idUSTRE51I71V20090219.

34 United Nations, "Invitation of the United States of America to the Conference," April 26, 1945, doc. no. 3, G/2, in *Documents of UNCIO*, vol. 1, *General*, 1–2.

35 United Nations, "Summary Report of Eighteenth Meeting of Committee III/I," June 12, 1945, doc. no. 936, III/1/45, in *Documents of UNCIO*, vol. 11, *Commission 3—Security Council*, 471–76; United Nations, "Summary Report of Nineteenth Meeting of Committee III/I," June 13, 1945, doc. no. 956, III/1/47, in *Documents of UNCIO*, vol. 11, *Commission 3—Security Council*, 486.

36 United Nations, "Summary Report of Seventh Meeting of Committee III/1," May 16, 1945, doc. no. 338, III/1/14, in *Documents of UNCIO*, vol. 11, *Security Council*, 290–91.

37 United Nations, "Verbatim Minutes of Fourth Meeting of Commission III," June 22, 1945, doc. no. 1149 III/11,in *Documents of UNCIO*, vol. 11, *Commission 3—Security Council*, 122.

38 United Nations, "Summary Report of Fourth Meeting of Commission III/3," May 11, 1945, doc. no. 231 III/3/9, in *Documents of UNCIO*, vol. 12, *Commission 3—Security Council*, 295–96.

39 Ibid., 296.

40 See appendix 21 in Robins, *Experiment in Democracy*.

41 United Nations, "Statement by Mr. John Sofianopoulos, Chairman of Technical Committee III/1, on the Structures and Procedures of the Security Council," June 8, 1945, doc. no. 852 III/1/27, in *Documents of UNCIO*, vol. 11, *Commission 3—Security Council*, 711–14.

42 United Nations, "Verbatim Minutes of Fourth Meeting of Commission III," 124.

43 Gildersleeve, *Many a Good Crusade*, 337. Although France was not a sponsoring host government for the UNCIO, during the pre-UNCIO proceedings, which likely began at Dumbarton Oaks, France was granted veto authority. Therefore, France, too, had a vested interest in ensuring that the power structure remained intact.

44 Focus on the Pacific region is not within the scope of this book, but it bears mentioning that because of the issue of trusteeship and colonial territories, this region was of vital military interest to the great powers. Because of postwar rebuilding efforts, the stakes for the future of the Pacific Rim, and for what it would look like, were extremely high in comparison to other regions.

45 United Nations, "Summary Report of the Eleventh Meeting of Committee III/1, 21 May 1945May 22, 1945, doc. no. 486, III/I/24, in *Documents of UNCIO*, vol. 11, *Commission 3—Security Council*, 352.

46 United Nations, "Summary Report of Eighteenth Meeting of Committee III/I," 473.

47 United Nations, "Amendments to the Dumbarton Oaks Proposals Presented by the Delegation of Mexico," May 5, 1945, doc. 2, G/7 (c) (1), in *Documents of UNCIO*, vol. 2, *General*, 184. Of note is that Latin American governments held their own meetings in Mexico prior to the UNCIO to begin the formulation of a unified regional agenda. Arab governments also formed a bloc, recognizing that it would be an important strategy to counter the five permanent members.

48 United Nations, "Verbatim Minutes of Fourth Meeting of Commission III," 129.

49 United Nations, "Summary Report of Nineteenth Meeting of Committee III/I," 486.

50 United Nations, "Documentation for Meetings of Committee I/1," 529.

51 Gildersleeve, *Many a Good Crusade*, 348–49.

52 Ibid., 338.

53 *United Nations Conference on International Organization Journal*, no. 42 (Jun. 12, 1945): 133. A journal was published during the conference proceedings to summarize the previous day's activities.

54 However, these governments were unsuccessful when it came to limiting the scope of discussion by the General Assembly. An amendment to the Dumbarton Oaks proposal "empowered the Assembly to discuss any international question at any time," in direct defiance of the opposition of the "Big Five." See Mary McLeod Bethune Papers, reel 9: Scrapbooks cont., "Big 5 loses in Committee Vote, 27 to 11: Assembly Empowered to Discuss Any International Topic," (date and newspaper unknown), folder #17 (Scrapbook), frame 0057 in microfilm [also in folder #18, no name, frame 00133 in microfilm], The Bethune Foundation Collection, Part 1: Writings, Diaries, Scrapbooks, Biographical Materials, and Files on the National Youth Administration and Women's Organizations, 1918–1955, Stanford, CA: Hoover Institute, Stanford University.

55 John R. Crooke, "U.S. Views on UN Reform, Security Council Expansion," *American Journal of International Law* 99, no. 4 (2005): 906–8. See also Miguel d'Escoto, "The United Nations Is Beyond Reform . . . It Has to Be Reinvented," interview with the former UN General Assembly president, Democracy Now!, April 26, 2010, accessed May 26, 2010, http://www.democracynow.org/2010/4/26/the_united_nations_is_beyond_reformit.

56 See chapter 1 of C. Anderson, *Eyes Off the Prize*.

57 United Nations, "Verbatim Minutes of Third Meeting of Commission II," June 21, 1945, doc. no. 1144, II/16, in *Documents of UNCIO*, vol. 8, *Commission 2—General Assembly*, 131.

58 According to Carol Anderson, "Indeed, the Americans were not opposed to colonial rule at all, they just wanted to be more coy and subtle about their ambitions than the British, who flaunted Empire at every turn" (C. Anderson, *Eyes Off the Prize*, 35).

59 United Nations, "Analysis of Papers Presented by Australia, China, France, United Kingdom, and United States," May 11, 1945, doc. no. 230, II/4/5, in *Documents of UNCIO*, vol. 10, *Commission 2—General Assembly*, 642.

60 The UN Trusteeship Council suspended its operations on November 1, 1994, following the independence of Palau in October 1994, the last remaining United Nations trust territory.

61 Quoted in C. Anderson, *Eyes Off the Prize*, 50; see also 50n161.

62 Ibid., 50.

63 Mignolo, "Who Speaks for the 'Human' in Human Rights?," 16.

64 Quijano, "Coloniality of Power," 534.

65 C. Anderson, *Eyes Off the Prize*, 35.

66 Gildersleeve, *Many a Good Crusade*, 323. Gildersleeve was hoping to be assigned to the trusteeship at the UNCIO, which she found fascinating, but instead Stettinius and Stassen became the key negotiators on this issue.

67 This debate occurred at a time when authority had started to shift from Western Europe to the US.

68 United Nations, "Verbatim Minutes of Third Meeting of Commission II," 128.

69 Mary McLeod Bethune Papers, reel 9: "Scrapbooks cont.," "Report Negro Shut Out of World Organizations" by Edgar G. Brown (date and newspaper unknown), folder #17 (Scrapbook), frame 00078 in microfilm, The Bethune Foundation Collection, Part 1.

70 United Nations, "Verbatim Minutes of Third Meeting of Commission II," 145. Italics mine.

71 Ibid., 146.

72 Ibid., 133–34.

73 Ibid., 152.

74 United Nations, "Proposed New Part (C) to Be Added to Working Paper Submitted by the Delegation of Australia," May 25, 1945, doc. no. 575, II/4/12 (a), in *Documents of UNCIO*, vol. 10, *Commission II—General Assembly*, 695.

75 United Nations, "Section B of Chapter on Dependent Territories and Arrangements for International Trusteeship," June 17, 1945, doc. no. 1044 II/4/37 (2), in *Documents of UNCIO*, vol. 10, *Commission 2—General Assembly*, 711.

76 The defined criteria only applied to 3 percent of the colonial territories; see C. Anderson, *Eyes Off the Prize*, 50.

77 See C. Anderson, *Eyes Off the Prize*, 41; Anderson provides a rich history of the NAACP's transition from a human rights organization in the 1940s to a civil rights one by the 1950s.

78 See Daniel W. Aldridge III, "Black Powerlessness in a Liberal Era: The NAACP, Anti-Colonialism, and the United Nations Organization, 1942–1945," in Callahan, Douglas, and Bishop, *Imperialism on Trial*. This agenda changed, however, post-UNCIO. See C. Anderson, *Eyes Off the Prize*.

79 Mary McLeod Bethune Papers, reel 2: "Biographies, Oral Histories, and Interviews cont.," "News Service, NCNW: Dr. Mary McLeod Bethune Speaks on the San Francisco Conference," folder #26, frame 00850 in microfilm, The Bethune Foundation Collection, Part 1. This speech appears to have been given on June 1, 1945, at the Asbury Methodist Church.

80 Mary McLeod Bethune Papers, reel 9: "Scrapbooks cont.," "Noted Negro Spokesmen Interviewed" (May 1, 1945, newspaper unknown), folder #17 (scrapbook), frame 0003 in microfilm, The Bethune Foundation Collection, Part 1.

81 Mary McLeod Bethune Papers, reel 9: "Scrapbooks cont.," "Mrs. Paul Robeson Speaks" (date and newspaper unknown), folder #17 (scrapbook), frame 00026 in microfilm, The Bethune Foundation Collection, Part 1.

82 Signing the UN Charter was not a requirement for all participating delegates.

83 Anges E. Meyer, "Frank, Fearless, and Internationally Experienced: Dean Gildersleeve Popular Choice," *Washington Post*, March 11, 1945.

84 June E. Hahner, "The Beginnings of the Women's Suffrage Movement in Brazil," *Signs: Journal of Women in Culture and Society* 5, no. 1 (1979): 200–04 and Ellen DuBois and Lauren Derby, "The Strange Case of Minerva Bernardino: Pan American and United Nations Women's Right Activist," *Women's Studies International Forum* 32 (2009): 43–50.

85 All four women who signed the UN Charter addressed the conference. Two men addressed the conference as well: Francis M. Forde from Australia, and Jan Masarynk, the minister of foreign affairs of Czechoslovakia.

86 Gildersleeve, *Many a Good Crusade*, 353.

87 Spurgeon may have been Gildersleeve's longtime partner; they lived together for several decades. A biography of Gildersleeve is available on the Columbia University website, http://www.columbia.edu/cu/alumni/Magazine/Summer2001/Gildersleeve.html (accessed April 11, 2012).

88 Gildersleeve, *Many a Good Crusade*, 353.

89 Mary McLeod Bethune Papers, reel 2: "Biographies, Oral Histories, and Interviews cont.," "News Service, NCNW: Dr. Mary McLeod Bethune Speaks on the San Francisco Conference," folder #26 (speeches & writings, undated [2]), frame 00853 in microfilm, The Bethune Foundation Collection, Part 1.

90 United Nations, "Report of the Rapporteur (General) of Committee I/2 on Chapter IV," May 21, 1945, doc. no. 464 I/2/28, in *Documents of UNCIO*, vol. 7, *Commission 1—General Provisions*, 64.

91 This final text appears in the UN Charter, Chapter 3, Article 8. See United Nations, "Charter of the United Nations," accessed September 25, 2011, http://www.un.org/en/documents/charter/chapter3.shtml.

92 United Nations, "Summary Report of Twentieth Meeting of Committee II/3," June 7, 1945, doc. no. 833 II/3/57, in *Documents of UNCIO*, vol. 8, *Commission 2—General Assembly*, 213.

93   The Iranian delegation supported Brazil and inquired if "it would be acceptable to omit the specification that the Commission be composed entirely of
women"; the delegate suggested that the commission could consist of half
women and half men. See ibid., 213.

94   United Nations, "Summary Report of Twentieth Meeting of Committee
II/3," 213.

95   The UN Human Rights Commission no longer exists. The Human Rights
Council replaced the commission on March 15, 2006.

96   United Nations, "Summary Report of Twentieth Meeting of Committee
II/3," 213.

97   UN special committees receive a mandate and are established temporarily,
unlike UN councils or commissions, which are permanent.

98   See United Nations, "Commission on the Status of Women Founding Resolution," ECOSOC resolution 11 (II), June 21, 1946, *United Nations Journal
of the Economic and Social Council* 29, July 13, 1946, accessed September 25,
2011, http://www.un.org/womenwatch/daw/csw/pdf/CSW_founding_
resolution_1946.pdf; and United Nations, Commission on the Status of
Women, "Overview," accessed September 25, 2011, http://www.un.org/
womenwatch/daw/csw/index.html#about. For Commission on the Status of Women's history, see UN Women, "Commission on the Status of
Women," accessed September 25, 2011, http://www.un.org/womenwatch/
daw/csw/index.html#about.

99   United Women's Conference, *Women's Share in Implementing the Peace*
(San Francisco: Executive Committee of the United Women's Conference,
1945), 41. Based in Washington, DC, GFWC claims to be an international
organization, hence the eventual dropping of the word "national" in their
original moniker. The presidents of GFWC have always been from the
United States and all have been privileged white women. Photos of all
past presidents are available on the organization's website. See General
Federation of Women's Clubs, "GFWC International Past Presidents:
1890–2014," accessed June 13, 2015, http://www.gfwc.org/who-we-are/
history-and-mission/gfwc-international-past-presidents/. The website
states the following about the symbolism of the organization's emblem:
"GFWC's emblem depicts a circular band signifying eternity. In the center
of the circular band, the crusader's shield emerges from a darkened world
(represented by the field of darkness), which represents enlightenment.
The enameled colors—red, white, and blue—are the colors of the United
States of America. The red implies courage, the white equals purity, and
the blue stands for constancy." See General Federation of Women's Clubs,
"Logos, Emblems, Icons," accessed June 13, 2015, http://www.gfwc.org/
membership/gfwc-resources/logos-emblems-icons/.

100 These organizations remained segregated organizations well into the 1950s.
See Julie A. Gallagher, "The National Council of Negro Women, Human
Rights, and the Cold War," in *Breaking the Wave: Women, Their Organiza-*

tions, and Feminism, 1945–1985, ed. Kathleen A. Laughlin and Jacqueline L. Castledine (New York: Routledge, 2011), 82.

101 United Women's Conference, *Women's Share*, 42.

102 Ibid., 12 and 86.

103 Mignolo, "Who Speaks for the 'Human' in Human Rights?," 9.

104 Quoted in United Women's Conference, *Women's Share*, 13.

105 Ibid.

106 Ibid., 23.

107 Ibid., 26.

108 Ibid., 28.

109 Ibid., 32.

110 Ibid.

111 Ibid., 39.

112 Ibid., 61.

113 Gildersleeve, *Many a Good Crusade*, 332.

114 United Women's Conference, *Women's Share*, 63.

115 Ibid.

116 Ibid., 64.

117 Ibid., 65.

118 Ibid., 100. For a history of the Inter-American Commission of Women, see Organization of American States, "Brief History of the Commission," accessed March 12, 2012, http://www.oas.org/en/cim/history.asp.

119 Unfortunately, no archives exist for the last hour of the conference, due to technical problems with the transcription recorders.

120 DuBois and Derby, "The Strange Case of Minerva Bernardino."

121 For an excellent and succinct history of the Dominican Republic, see Light Carruyo, *Producing Knowledge, Protecting Forests: Rural Encounters with Gender, Ecotourism, and International Aid in the Dominican Republic* (University Park: Penn State University Press, 2008).

122 Ultimately this struggle was about the inherent rights to which all human beings are entitled, an issue that was not sufficiently addressed by the UN Charter and that led to the UN's adoption of the Universal Declaration of Human Rights in 1948. See Mignolo, "Who Speaks for the 'Human' in Human Rights?"

123 Prashad, *Darker Nations*.

124 Mignolo, "Who Speaks for the 'Human' in Human Rights?"

2. UN CITIZENSHIP AND CONSTELLATIONS OF HUMAN RIGHTS

Epigraph: Boaventura de Sousa Santos, "Toward a Multicultural Conception of Human Rights," in *Moral Imperialism: A Critical Anthology*, edited by B. Hernández-Truyol, 54. New York: New York University Press, 2002.

1 See "Growth in United Nations Membership, 1945–Present," accessed October 24, 2013, http://www.un.org/en/members/growth.shtml.

2　Andrea Smith has identified some important concerns about US racial justice movements organizing around a human rights paradigm. See Andrea Smith, "Human Rights and Social-Justice Organizing in the United States," *Radical History Review*, no. 101 (2008): 211–19.

3　For more on ECOSOC, see United Nations, Economic and Social Council, "About ECOSOC," accessed March 7, 2012, http://www.un.org/en/ecosoc/.

4　See Falcón, "Invoking Human Rights."

5　Evelyn Nakano Glenn, *Unequal Freedom: How Race and Gender Shaped American Citizenship and Labor* (Cambridge, MA: Harvard University Press, 2002).

6　See for example, John Foran and Richard Widick, "Breaking Barriers to Climate Justice," *Contexts* 2013 (Spring): 34–39.

7　Article 13 of the 2001 WCAR's Programme of Action states "that slavery and the slave trade are a crime against humanity." Negotiations involved being very careful in the wording here so that the issue of reparations could not have momentum. See United Nations, "Report of the World Conference Against Racism, Racial Discrimination, Xenophobia, and Related Intolerance," 2001, doc. no. A/CONF.189/12, 11.

8　This idea of constellation is influenced by Susanne Zwingel's work as she writes about three "constellations of norm translation" as it pertains to the women's convention: "global discourse translation, impact translation and distorted translation." See Susanne Zwingel, "Translating International Women's Rights: CEDAW in Context," accessed March 2, 2014, http://graduateinstitute.ch/files/live/sites/iheid/files/sites/genre/shared/conference_october_2010/Susanne%20Zwingel.pdf. See also Susanne Zwingel, "How Do Norms Travel? Theorizing International Women's Rights in Transnational Perspective," in *International Studies Quarterly* 56, no. 1 (2012): 115–29.

9　Dana Collins, Sylvanna Falcón, Sharmila Lodhia, and Molly Talcott, "New Directions in Feminism and Human Rights: An Introduction," *International Feminist Journal of Politics* 12, no. 3–4 (2010): 304; and Eva Brems, "Protecting the Human Rights of Women," in *International Human Rights in the Twenty-first Century*, ed. G. Lyons and J. Mayall (Lanham, MD: Rowman & Littlefield, 2003).

10　Deepest thanks to Molly Talcott, who was of great assistance with this framing.

11　Dangerous incarnations of human rights have clearly emerged, as Leela Fernandes powerfully documents in her discussion about the "militarization of human rights" as part of US state practices. See chapter 2 in Leela Fernandes, *Transnational Feminism in the United States* (New York: New York University Press, 2013).

12　Margaret Somers, "Rights, Relationality, and Membership: Rethinking the Making and Meaning of Citizenship," in *Public Rights, Public Rules: Constituting Citizens in the World Polity and National Policy*, ed. Connie L. McNeely (New York: Routledge, 1998), 155–56, 158, 166.

13 Naila Kabeer, ed., *Inclusive Citizenship: Meanings and Expressions* (London: Zed Books, 2005), 23.

14 The UN Human Rights Council superseded the commission in 2006.

15 Phyllis Bennis, *Challenging Empire: How People, Governments, and the U.N. Defy U.S. Power* (New York: Olive Branch Press, 2005), 198.

16 Pierre Bordieu, "The Forms of Capital," in *Handbook of Theory and Research for the Sociology of Education*, ed. John G. Richardson, trans. Richard Nice (New York: Greenwood Press, 1986), 242 and 241–58.

17 Important debates have taken place about understanding citizenship, what it is and what it means. See, for example Kabeer, *Inclusive Citizenship*.

18 Walden Bello, "As Obama Arrives in London for G20, Tens of Thousands Gather to Protest in the Streets," *Democracy Now!*, April 1, 2009, accessed April 14, 2010, http://www.democracynow.org/2009/4/1/as_obama_arrives_in_london_for.

19 Leslie Sklair, *Globalization: Capitalism and Its Alternatives* (New York: Oxford University Press, 2002), 317.

20 Thayer, *Making Transnational Feminism*, 86. "Intangible political resource" includes leadership ability and experience, and differs from my use of "social capital," which refers to social relationships and networks.

21 Claude E. Welch Jr., ed., *NGOs and Human Rights: Promise and Performance* (Philadelphia: University of Pennsylvania Press, 2000).

22 Interview with author, November 18, 2008, New York City.

23 A review of the résumés and curricula vitae of UN staff and officials highlights the qualifications desirable for those working at the UN.

24 Max Weber, *The Methodology of the Social Sciences*, ed. Edward Shils and Henry Finch (New York: Free Press, 1949), 90.

25 Sally Morphet, "Multilateralism and the Non-Aligned Movement: What Is the Global South Doing and Where Is It Going?," *Global Governance* 10, no. 4 (2004): 517.

26 To clarify, the title of the resolution would initially indicate whether it had a connection to antiracism efforts at the UN. Closely reviewing the content of the resolution would then validate this initial assessment.

27 "World Racism Conference Calls for Action against Multinationals," *United Nations Chronicle* 15, no. 9 (1978): 52.

28 During the 1970s and even the 1980s, the GA repeatedly issued resolutions about "activities of foreign economic and other interests which are impeding . . . efforts to eliminate colonialism, *apartheid*, and racial discrimination in southern Africa." See, for example, United Nations, General Assembly, "Resolution 2873: Activities of Foreign Economic. . .," Twenty-sixth Session, December 20, 1971. All General Assembly resolutions are available on the United Nations website at http://www.un.org/documents/resga.htm (accessed March 8, 2012).

29 United Nations, General Assembly, "Resolution 3151: Policies of Apartheid of the Government of South Africa," Twenty-eighth Session, December

14, 1973, 30. GA Resolution 3379 also highlights an outcome of the first World Conference on Women, which was held in Mexico City in 1975, a few months prior to the resolution's adoption. The outcome document from the Mexico City conference stated, "International co-operation and peace require the achievement of national liberation and independence, the elimination of colonialism and neo-colonialism, foreign occupation, zionism, *apartheid*, and racial discrimination in all its forms."

30 Associated Press, "Fourteen Western Nations Walked Out of a U.N. Conference," August 25, 1978. The actions of the state of Israel vis-à-vis Palestinians and the racialist nature of Zionism have persisted as contentious issues. Italics in source.

31 For example, paragraph 418 of the NGO Declaration and Programme of Action for the World Conference Against Racism, Racial Discrimination, Xenophobia, and Related Intolerance, in Durban, South Africa, August 27–September 1, 2001, states the following: "Also call for the reinstitution of UN resolution 3379 determining the practices of Zionism as racist practices which propagate the racial domination of one group over another through the implementation of all measures designed to drive out other indigenous groups, including through colonial expansionism in the Occupied Palestinian Territories (in the Gaza Strip, the West Bank, including Jerusalem), and through the application of discriminatory laws of return and citizenship, to obliterate their national identity and to maintain the exclusive nature of the State of Israel as a Jewish state to the exclusion of all other groups." The full NGO Declaration and Programme of Action can be found at http://academic.udayton.edu/race/06hrights/WCAR2001/NGOFORUM/index.htm (accessed April 12, 2012).

32 United Nations, General Assembly, "Resolution 37/1: Appeal for Clemency in Favour of South African Freedom Fighters," Thirty-seventh Session, December 7, 1982, 14. Italics in source.

33 United Nations, General Assembly, "Resolution 37/68: Further Appeal for Clemency in Favour of South African Freedom Fighters," Thirty-seventh Session, December 7, 1982, 28.

34 United Nations, General Assembly, "Resolution 38/11: Proposed New Racial Constitution of South Africa," Thirty-eighth Session, November 15, 1983, 22.

35 United Nations, General Assembly, "Resolution 47/96: Violence against Migrant Women Workers," Forty-seventh Session, December 16, 1992, 178.

36 United Nations, General Assembly, "Declaration on Apartheid and Its Destructive Consequences in Southern Africa," December 14, 1989, doc. no. A/RES/S-16/1, accessed March 18, 2012, http://daccess-dds-ny.un.org/doc/RESOLUTION/GEN/NR0/210/34/IMG/NR021034.pdf?OpenElement.

37 United Nations, General Assembly, "Resolution 45/176: Policies of *Apartheid* of the Government of South Africa," Section D, Forty-fifth Session, December 19, 1990, 43; and United Nations, General Assembly, "Resolution

46/79: Policies of *Apartheid* of the Government of South Africa," Section D, Forty-sixth Session, December 13, 1991, 32.

38 Morphet, "Multilateralism," 525. On the Belgrade summit, see Prashad, *Darker Nations*. The Bandung Conference in 1955 was another significant gathering and a precursor to Belgrade, which led to the official founding of the NAM movement.

39 Phyllis Bennis, *Calling the Shots: How Washington Dominates Today's U.N.* (New York: Olive Branch Press, 1996), 13.

40 Ibid., 16–17.

41 Morphet, "Multilateralism," 525. Membership in the G-77 and NAM can overlap meaning that nations may be represented in both configurations.

42 United Nations, "Secretary-General Says Non-Aligned Movement's Mission More Relevant than Ever in Light of Growing Gulf between Rich and Poor Countries," accessed March 7, 2012, http://www.un.org/News/Press/docs/2006/sgsm10636.doc.htm.

43 South Africa, for example, possesses a large amount of social and cultural capital, which it had developed during the battle against apartheid and the subsequent adoption of progressive social policies and a progressive constitution. Even though post-apartheid South Africa is increasingly turbulent, the country's social and cultural capital made it extremely difficult for other governments to reject its request to host the third WCAR and its corresponding NGO Forum (see Desai, *We Are the Poors*). Moreover, even though UN officials and NGO advocates felt it fitting that the Durban conference proceedings take place there, South Africa was also the only country to volunteer to host the conference.

44 United Nations, Economic and Social Council, "List of Non-Governmental Organizations in Consultative Status with the ECOSOC as of 1 September 2011," accessed March 7, 2012, http://csonet.org/content/documents/E2011INF4.pdf.

45 See United Nations, "NGOs in Consultative Status, by Region (2007 & 1996)," accessed April 13, 2012, http://www.un.org/esa/coordination/ngo/about.htm.

46 According to Article 62 of the UN Charter, the policy recommendations are "with respect to international economic, social, cultural, educational, health, and related matters."

47 See United Nations Economic and Social Council, "About ECOSOC."

48 This procedure is stated in the UN Charter, Chapter 2, Article 6.

49 See Peter Willetts, "The Cardoso Report on the UN and Civil Society: Functionalism, Global Corporatism, or Global Democracy?," *Global Governance* 12, no. 3 (2006): 305–24; and Teri L. Caraway, "The Political Economy of Feminization: From 'Cheap Labor' to Gendered Discourses of Work," *Politics & Gender* 1, no. 3 (2005): 399–429.

50 United Nations, "Consultative Status with ECOSOC," accessed April 13, 2012, http://www.un.org/esa/coordination/ngo/about.htm.

51 See the DESA website for more details; United Nations, "NGO Branch, De-

partment of Economic and Social Affairs," accessed March 7, 2012, http://csonet.org/.

52 As stated on the website, "applications received on 2 June will be taken up in the following year." See United Nations, "How to Apply for Consultative Status," accessed March 7, 2012, http://csonet.org/?menu=83.

53 Ibid.

54 NGOs with roster status are not required to submit reports.

55 All interviewees have been given pseudonyms.

56 NGOs representatives who were denied admission planned to submit a letter of complaint to the OHCHR. Unable to obtain admission myself, I heard via an activist listserv about other activists who also could not attend. The idea had been proposed on this listserv to generate a letter to the Office of the High Commissioner to express outrage about being denied admission. It is unclear if the letter was every officially submitted.

57 Keck and Sikkink, *Activist Beyond Borders*, 207.

58 See Jennifer Bickham Mendez, "Creating Alternatives from a Gender Perspective Transnational Organizing for Maquila Workers' Rights in Central America," in *Women's Activism and Globalization: Linking Local Struggles and Transnational Politics*, ed. Nancy A. Naples and Manisha Desai (New York: Routledge, 2002).

59 For a lengthier discussion about the NGO-industrial complex, see INCITE! Women of Color Against Violence, ed., *The Revolution Will Not Be Funded: Beyond the Non-Profit Industrial Complex* (Cambridge, MA: South End Press, 2007).

60 'Bety' Cariño gave a powerful speech in February 2010 in Dublin, Ireland, where she was honored as a human rights defender. For access to her speech and information about her assassination, please see http://www.frontlinedefenders.org/node/2478 (accessed October 5, 2014).

61 This is not a call to romanticize or homogenize "the South" but rather to heighten our consciousness about the disproportionate privileging of US approaches and understandings of human rights (and other fields).

62 Mark Goodale and Sally Engle Merry, eds., *The Practice of Human Rights: Tracking Law between the Global and the Local* (New York: Cambridge University Press, 2007).

63 Susanne Zwingel writes about three "constellations of norm translation" as it pertains to the Convention to Eliminate All Forms of Discrimination Against Women: "global discourse translation, impact translation and distorted translation"; see Zwingel, "How Do Norms Travel?" and "Translating International Women's Rights."

64 Mignolo, "Who Speaks for the 'Human' in Human Rights?," 21.

65 Santos, "Toward a Multicultural Conception," 47.

66 Brems, "Protecting the Human Rights of Women"; Shannon Speed and Jane F. Collier, "Limiting Indigenous Autonomy in Chiapas, Mexico: The

State Government's Use of Human Rights," *Human Rights Quarterly* 22, no. 4 (2000): 877–905; Richard A. Wilson, ed., *Human Rights, Culture, and Context: Anthropological Perspectives* (London: Pluto Press, 1997). See also Santos, "Toward a Multicultural Conception."

67 For a list of situations and cases that have been brought before the International Criminal Court's jurisdiction, refer to the website of the International Criminal Court, available at http://www.icc-cpi.int/en_menus/ icc/situations%20and%20cases/Pages/situations%20and%20cases.aspx (accessed October 15, 2014).

68 Overall, it would be difficult to prosecute a US official, though I do not want to suggest it would be impossible, given that the majority of Latin Americans thought former president Augusto Pinochet would never be held accountable for the atrocities he committed in Chile in the 1970s and 1980s during his dictatorship.

69 United Nations, Office of the High Commissioner for Human Rights, "Human Rights Treaty Bodies: Monitoring the Core International Human Rights Treaties," accessed March 18, 2012, http://www2.ohchr.org/english/ bodies/treaty/index.htm.

70 The UN General Assembly approved CERD in 1965 via UN General Assembly resolution 2106A (XX) for country ratification. It went into effect in 1966.

71 Many governments ratified the treaties with reservations, which address potential conflicts between international and domestic law; a government may insert a reservation as a way of limiting its legal obligations to the treaty's objectives.

72 ICERD, signed and ratified by the United States in 1994, is one of the few human rights treaties that the United States has ratified; the Women's Convention has remained stalled in the US Senate Committee on Foreign Relations since 1979, when President Jimmy Carter signed the treaty to begin the ratification process at the congressional level.

English scholar Jodi Melamed offers a genealogy that is particularly useful for understanding the political interests of the United States in the mid-1960s, when ICERD was signed, and then in the mid-1990s, when it was ratified. She states, "White supremacy gradually became residual after World War II [and] was replaced by a formally antiracist, liberal-capitalist modernity whose driving force has been a series of successive official or state-recognized U.S. antiracisms"; Jodi Melamed, *Represent and Destroy: Rationalizing Violence in the New Racial Capitalism* (Minneapolis: University of Minnesota Press, 2011), 1. Melamed identifies three key periods in this succession: 1940 to the 1960s ("racial liberalism"), the 1980s to the 1990s ("liberal multiculturalism"), and the 2000s ("neoliberal multiculturalism"), which would mean that the US government signed ICERD in the "racial liberalism" period and ratified it in the "liberal multiculturalism" period. During the racial liberalism period, the United States was at a crossroads, especially as its ability to solve its race problem with African Americans

became linked to its "capacity to lead a new world postcolonial order"; ibid.,
9. Signing ICERD could arguably have been part of this strategy, especially
as the Soviet Union applied "pressures [that] required the United States to
develop a framework for race matters that portrayed race as a contradiction to modernity rather than one of its structuring conditions," and thus
"not constitutive of liberal freedoms but in contradiction to them"; ibid.;
see also Anderson, *Eyes Off the Prize*. In the neoliberal multiculturalism
period, when the US government finally ratified ICERD, "global capitalism
had fully developed the features of a neoliberal economy," and "neoliberal
policy" had become "the key to a postracist world of freedom and opportunity"; Melamed, *Represent and Destroy*, 39 and 42.

   Melamed's analysis reinforces Santos's contention that, in the postwar
period, "human rights policies, by and large, have been at the service of
the economic and geopolitical interests of the hegemonic capitalist states"
(Santos, "Toward a Multicultural Conception," 45). The political interest of
governments, such as the US government's decision to sign ICERD in the
1960s and then ratify it in the 1990s, was about constraining racial meanings within discursive frameworks in the interest of global position, global
markets, and a capitalist agenda; Melamed, *Represent and Destroy*, 18–26.

73 United Nations, Office of the High Commissioner for Human Rights,
    "What Are Human Rights?," accessed October 20, 2014, http://www.ohchr
    .org/EN/Issues/Pages/WhatareHumanRights.aspx.

74 United Nations, Office of the High Commissioner for Human Rights,
    "What We Do," accessed October 20, 2014, http://www.ohchr.org/EN/
    AboutUs/Pages/WhatWeDo.aspx.

75 Mignolo, "Who Speaks for the 'Human' in Human Rights?"

76 Ibid.

77 Governments wanted to undermine and limit the rights of indigenous
    peoples by ensuring they were not considered separate nations. Including
    an "s" in "peoples" indicates that each indigenous group can constitute a
    separate nation. Excluding the "s," or eliminating the significance of the
    plural form, limits their sovereignty rights. Interview with author, Febru-
    ary 6, 2004, Oakland.

78 Arturo Escobar, "Latin America at a Crossroads," *Cultural Studies* 24, no. 1
    (2010): 4.

79 Mario Blaser, "Ontology and Indigeneity: On the Political Ontology of Het-
    erogeneous Assemblages," *Cultural Geographies* 21, no. 1 (Jan. 2014): 49–58;
    Escobar, "Latin America at a Crossroads," 39.

80 Mignolo, "Who Speaks for the 'Human' in Human Rights?," 22, 21, and 11.

81 Ibid., 11.

82 Marisol de la Cadena, "Indigenous Cosmopolitics in the Andes: Conceptual
    Reflections beyond 'Politics.'" *Cultural Anthropology* 25, no. 2 (2010): 334–70.

83 Maria Lugones, "Toward a Decolonial Feminism," *Hypatia* 25, no. 4 (2010):
    754.

84 Rosa-Linda Fregoso, "For a Pluriversal Declaration of Human Rights," *American Quarterly* 66, no. 3 (2014): 583–608.

85 Speed and Collier, "Limiting Indigenous Autonomy," 879. See also Wilson, *Human Rights*.

86 Speed and Collier, "Limiting Indigenous Autonomy," 878.

87 Ibid.

88 Wilson, *Human Rights*, 5.

89 William Armaline and Davita Silfen Glasberg, "What Will States Really Do for Us? The Human Rights Enterprise and Pressure from Below," *Societies without Borders* 4 (2010); William Armaline, Davita Silfen Glasberg, and Bandana Purkayastha, eds., *Human Rights in Our Own Backyard: Injustice and Resistance in the United States* (Philadelphia: University of Pennsylvania Press, 2012); and Micheline Ishay, *The History of Human Rights: From Ancient Times to the Globalization Era* (Berkeley: University of California Press, 2008).

90 Armaline et al., *Human Rights*, 17.

91 Ibid. Also see William Armaline, Davita Silfen Glasberg, and Bandana Purkayastha, *The Human Rights Enterprise: The State, Resistance, Human Rights* (London: Polity Press, 2014).

92 Quoted in Speed and Collier, "Limiting Indigenous Autonomy," 879. This quote is from an earlier version of "Toward a Multicultural Conception of Human Rights" by Boaventura de Sousa Santos that was published in a working paper series on political economy and legal change for the University of Wisconsin in 1996.

93 "United Nations Declaration on the Rights of Indigenous Peoples," accessed December 18, 2013, http://www.ohchr.org/en/Issues/IPeoples/Pages/Declaration.aspx. It merits mention that the creation of prior UN documents has never involved nongovernmental delegates—except for the creation of the UN Declaration on the Rights of Indigenous Peoples. Here, indigenous peoples were asked to be involved in the writing and in the debates. But indigenous peoples from the global North were disproportionately represented. Indigenous rights advocate and teacher Russel Lawrence Barsh states that only twelve indigenous groups have ECOSOC accreditation, and ten of those groups came from the global North, even though the majority of indigenous peoples live in South America. See Russel Lawrence Barsh, "Indigenous Peoples and the UN Commission on Human Rights: A Case of the Immovable Object and the Irresistible Force," *Human Rights Quarterly* 18, no. 4 (1996): 782–813.

94 United Nations, Committee on the Elimination of Racial Discrimination, "Summary Record of the 1166th Meeting," Forty-Ninth Session, August 14, 1996, doc. no. CERD/C/SR.1166, accessed June 13, 2015, http://tbinternet.ohchr.org/_layouts/treatybodyexternal/Download.aspx?symbolno=CERD%2fC%2fSR.1166&Lang=en.

95 Falcón, "Invoking Human Rights."

96 Ibid.

97 Barsh, "Indigenous Peoples," 801.

98 Ibid.

99 The more forceful language initially proposed that linked land and indigenous autonomy had to be removed because land translates into economic wealth. See Eve Tuck and K. Wayne Yang, "Decolonization Is Not a Metaphor," *Decolonization: Indigeneity, Education, & Society* 1, no. 1 (2013): 1–40; Charmaine White Face and Zumila Wobaga, *Indigenous Nations' Rights in the Balance: An Analysis of the Declaration on the Rights of Indigenous Peoples* (St. Paul, MN: Living Justice Press, 2013).

100 Face and Wobaga, *Indigenous Nations' Rights*; Elvira Pulitano, ed., *Indigenous Rights in the Age of the UN Declaration* (Cambridge: Cambridge University Press, 2012).

101 Barsh, "Indigenous Peoples," 783.

102 See also Douglas Sanders, "Developing a Modern International Law on the Rights of Indigenous Peoples," December 1994, accessed December 18, 2013, http://www.anthrobase.com/Browse/home/hst/cache/Developing.doc.htm.

103 Kabeer, *Inclusive Citizenship*, xii.

104 Dianne Otto, "Nongovernmental Organizations in the United Nations System: The Emerging Role of International Civil Society," *Human Rights Quarterly* 18, no. 1 (1996): 107–41; and Welch Jr., *NGOs and Human Rights*.

105 Speed and Collier, "Limiting Indigenous Autonomy," 879.

106 Ibid., 878–79.

107 Falcón, "Invoking Human Rights."

3. A GENEALOGY OF WORLD CONFERENCES AGAINST RACISM

Epigraph: Phone interview with author, June 24, 2003.

1 Resolutions are also voted on within General Assembly committees. The Third Committee of the General Assembly approved this resolution with a vote of 69 in favor and 17 against, with 29 abstentions. For further information on the positions of the United States within this committee, refer to "World Conference to Combat Racism to be Convened in Geneva, August 1978," *United Nations Chronicle*, New York, January 1978, 72 and 106.

2 "World Conference to Combat Racism to be Convened in Geneva, August 1978," 72.

3 Associated Press, "Fourteen Western Nations Walked Out," August 25, 1978. The GA eventually overturned this resolution in 1991. For more information, see Gil Troy, *Moynihan's Moment: America's Fight Against Zionism as Racism* (New York: Oxford University Press, USA, 2012); and Abdeen Jabara, "Zionism: Racism or Liberation?" 1976, accessed March 2, 2014, http://www.al-moharer.net/falasteen_docs/abdeen_jabara.htm. A reprint of Jabara's piece appeared in May 2008 at the website of the Committee

for Open Discussion of Zionism at http://codzorg.net/2008/05/26/717/ (accessed March 2, 2014); and a *Democracy Now!* interview about him being spied on by the National Security Agency can be accessed at http://www .democracynow.org/2013/10/17/arab_american_attorney_abdeen_jabara_i (accessed March 2, 2014).

4   The actions of the state of Israel vis-à-vis Palestine and the racialist nature of Zionism persisted as an issue of contention in 2001.

5   Associated Press, "Fourteen Western Nations Walked Out."

6   Specifically, the ambassador cited two paragraphs that dealt with Israeli and South African "cooperation" in the "nuclear field" as problematic and was against governments that supported "firm action against apartheid." Associated Press, "Fourteen Western Nations Walked Out."

7   To ensure the conference's success, preparation occurred on many levels, ranging from appointing the primary UN organizers of the conference to forming committees with equal regional representation to draft the official conference documents. For the 1978 WCAR, C. V. Narasimhan of India, the UN under-secretary-general for Inter-Agency Affairs and Coordination, received an appointment to be secretary-general of the conference, and Mooki V. Molepo of Lesotho was designated conference president. Ten vice presidents were appointed, one of which was a representative from Canada (R. H. Jay), and another a representative from Peru (A. A. Schreiber). No women were elected as representatives on conference committees. Two separate committees formed to draft the official conference documents— one to draft the declaration, and the other the POA. As decided at the conference, the draft declaration and the POA would be adopted as a whole document rather than as separate ones. The final conference documents were approved by a vote of 88 in favor and 4 against (Austria, Finland, Sweden, and Switzerland), with 2 abstentions (Malawi and San Marino). "World Racism Conference Calls for Action Against Multinationals," *United Nations Chronicle*, New York, October 1978, 52.

8   Ibid., 53.

9   Ibid., 52.

10   Each conference releases an official report. The NGO statement is part of the annex of the official conference report.

11   "Conference Against Racism: Preparations," *United Nations Chronicle*, New York, May 1983, 52.

12   "Racism," *United Nations Chronicle*, New York, October 1983, 44.

13   I was unable to locate the voting tally in the conference record.

14   "Main Focus: Women, Human Rights, Refugees," *United Nations Chronicle*, New York, January 1983, 58.

15   The Budgetary Committee disagreed with an earlier recommendation of the Third Committee that an exception be made to General Assembly Resolution 2609 (1969). This resolution "stipulated that a government issuing an invitation to host a UN conference should defray the actual additional

costs directly or indirectly involved in convening the meeting away from the established U.N. location." The Third Committee proposed that half of the additional costs involved by holding conference in Manila be paid by the UN regular budget.

16 Interview with author, January 16, 2004, San Francisco.

17 See Jonah's report on conference preparation at "Second World Conference to Combat Racism and Racial Discrimination: Provisional Draft Rules of Procedure," UN document E/AC.68/1982/L.3.

18 United Nations, "Building the Consensus Against Racism," DPI/809/12594, May 1984, 2.

19 A twenty-three-member subcommittee formed to begin preparations for the conference. In its first session (PrepCom), held March 15–26, 1982, in New York City, the subcommittee decided on the rules of procedure for the conference. In this meeting, they proposed to establish two main drafting committees, recommended the establishment of national committees in Member States to publicize the conference, and raised the importance of documenting the UN antiracism activities. Discussions and debate regarding the draft POA occurred at the second PrepCom, held in New York City March 21–25, 1983. The Secretariat was asked to prepare a list of UN resolutions and decisions that contributed to the struggle against racism, racial discrimination, and apartheid. See "Conference Against Racism: Preparations," *United Nations Chronicle*, New York, May 1983.

20 United Nations, "Report of the Second World Conference to Combat Racism and Racial Discrimination," Geneva, August 1–12, 1983, doc. no. A/CONF.119/26, 52–54.

21 See "Conference Against Racism: Preparations," 52.

22 United Nations, "Report of the Second World Conference," 21.

23 Ibid., 23–24.

24 The United Nations adopted the International Convention on the Protection of the Rights of All Migrant Workers and Members of their Families in 1990.

25 CERD had problems with Member States not submitting a declaration in support of CERD Article 14. Therefore, the POA for the second Decade urged Member States to submit a Declaration, in support of CERD Article 14, regarding the competence of CERD.

26 United Nations, "Report of the Second World Conference," 28.

27 Ibid.

28 Ibid.

29 Ibid., 17.

30 Against: Australia, Belgium, Canada, Denmark, France, Federal Republic of Germany, Iceland, Ireland, Italy, Luxemburg, Netherlands, New Zealand, Norway, Switzerland, and the United Kingdom. Abstaining: Austria, Barbados, Botswana, Chile, Costa Rica, Ecuador, Finland, Greece, Haiti, Japan, Lesotho, Peru, Portugal, Spain, Sweden, and Uruguay.

31 Against: Australia, Belgium, Canada, Denmark, Finland, France, Federal Republic of Germany, Iceland, Ireland, Italy, Luxemburg, Netherlands, New Zealand, Norway, Sweden, Switzerland, and the United Kingdom. Abstaining: Austria, Barbados, Chile, Costa Rica, Ecuador, Greece, Haiti, Japan, Lesotho, Peru, Portugal, Saint Lucia, Sweden, and Uruguay.

32 A roll-call vote, which has to be requested by a participating Member State, was not taken on the entire Declaration; therefore, the governments that voted against the Declaration are unknown.

33 United Nations, "Building the Consensus Against Racism," 4. See also "Racism" in *United Nations Chronicle*, New York, October 1983.

34 United Nations, "Building the Consensus Against Racism," 3.

35 Two world conferences on women had already taken place, in 1975 in Mexico City, and in 1980 in Copenhagen.

36 The governments of Mexico and Peru did not submit reservations. See United Nations, "Report of the Second World Conference," 98.

37 Ibid., 98.

38 Dr. Nkosazana Dlamini Zuma, the South African foreign minister and a trained medical doctor, received her appointment as president of the conference, and Mary Robinson, the high commissioner for human rights at the time, received her appointment as the conference's secretary-general.

39 The United Nations has organized states into five regional groups for the purposes of ensuring even geographical representation. The formation of various WCAR committees relied on these regional groupings, which are the African Group, the Asian-Pacific Group, the Eastern European Group, the Latin American and Caribbean Group, and WEOG. The United States is not considered an official member of any of these regional groups. The United States retains WEOG voting privileges and attends WEOG meetings with observer status. See "United Nations Regional Groups of Member States," accessed March 2, 2014, http://www.un.org/depts/DGACM/RegionalGroups.shtml.

40 I was unable to determine why Wareham had been selected to testify at this hearing.

41 The December 12th Movement International Secretariat, named after a 1987 protest in Newburgh, New York, against policy brutality, is an African American NGO fighting against racism. This group, which has consultative status, organizes hearings on human rights abuses in the United States (criminal justice, death penalty) and has worked within the UN since the late 1980s. See http://www.millionsforreparations.com/background.html and http://www.rastafarispeaks.com/cgi-bin/forum/archive1/config.pl?noframes;read=54079 (accessed October 22, 2005).

42 United States Congress, House of Representatives, Committee on International Relations, "A Discussion on the U.N. World Conference Against Racism: Hearing before the Subcommittee on International Operations and Human Rights of the Committee on International Relations," ser.

no. 107–36, Washington, DC: US Government Printing Office, 2001, 98. The entire hearing is available at http://www.house.gov/international_ relations/107/74408.pdf (accessed October 22, 2005).

43 US Congress, "Discussion on the U.N. World Conference," 98.

44 Interview with author, April 27, 2004, Mexico City.

45 The following quote appeared on a Canadian organization's website, http:// www.ceris.metropolis.net/ (accessed May 3, 2010) about the WCAR themes with regard to the word "compensatory": "The Western Europe and Others Group (WEOG) did not agree to this word. At the suggestion of Pakistan, it was 'bracketed' in order for the UN to get agreement on the rest." The site has been updated and the quoted material removed. The meaning of "compensatory" never reached consensus in the preparatory period. "The World Conference against Racism, Racial Discrimination, Xenophobia, and Related Intolerance: Basic Information," accessed March 5, 2014, http:// www.un.org/WCAR/e-kit/backgrounder1.htm.

46 Interview with author, June 19, 2003, Washington, DC.

47 For example, the Indian government, with the support of other governments, argued at the 2001 WCAR that the issues raised by Dalits were not about race, because some Dalits are light-skinned, and some upper castes are dark-skinned. Dalits are people who have been historically disadvantaged and represent the lowest rung in the caste system in India. Known as the "untouchables," the Dalit community countered this argument by stating that the definition in ICERD covered their experiences. The Indian government, however, continued to argue that issue of caste/Dalits is a national issue, and compared itself to Israel as being singled out and the target of unfair attacks.

48 I was never able to locate a bus to take me to a session off-site, so for those first couple of days I shared a cab to attend nearby sessions. By the end of the third day, I was attending only sessions or plenaries that were on-site or within walking distance of Cricket Stadium because sessions off-site would be canceled without notice, causing me to waste many hours searching for another cab to return to Cricket Stadium.

49 Interview with author, June 24, 2003, Brooklyn.

50 In interviews I discussed the caucus work rather than the commission work.

51 I do not discuss the Israeli government walkout in this book.

52 Interview with author, January 21, 2004, San Francisco.

53 Interviewee requested anonymity. Interview conducted in 2003 in the United States.

54 A list of the members of the US NGO Coordinating Committee can be found at http://www.ipunlimited.org/WCAR/Coordinating_Committee/ coordinating_committee.html (accessed March 9, 2014).

55 Interview with author, January 21, 2004, San Francisco.

56 According to my interviewee, the US delegation did address the "Indig-

enous Caucus before they walked out to announce [their plans]." She believed this occurred because one of the members of the Caucus had established a relationship with a US government delegate. Interview with author, May 26, 2003, New York City.

57 Interview with author, May 28, 2003, Brooklyn.

58 Based on the typology of intersectionality discussed in the introduction, a combination of group-centered and process-centered approaches prevails in UN discourse about the gender dimensions of racism.

59 "NGO Declaration and Programme of Action for the World Conference against Racism, Racial Discrimination, Xenophobia, and Related Intolerance," Durban, South Africa, August 27–September 1, 2001, para. 119, p. 19, accessed April 11, 2012, http://academic.udayton.edu/race/06hrights/WCAR2001/NGOFORUM/Globalization.htm.

60 Ibid., para. 63, p. 10.

61 Ibid., para. 83, p. 13.

62 Ibid., para. 121, p. 20.

63 World Conference against Racism, Racial Discrimination, Xenophobia, and Related Intolerance, "Durban Declaration and Programme of Action," paragraph 11. To read the DDPA in its entirety, please go to www.un.org/WCAR/durban.pdf (accessed April 11, 2012).

64 Other topics discussed in the Declaration were a women's right to religious expression (Article 71); gender, women, and migration (Articles 28, 30(h), 31, 36, 97, 138, and 186 of the POA); violence against women (Articles 18, 30(h), 36, 54(a) and (b), and 62 of the POA); and education and gender equality (Articles 10, 52, 56, 136, 137, 175, and 212 of the POA).

65 Refer to Article 30 of the Declaration, and Articles 38, 63, 64, 69, 78(m), 88, 138, 174, 175, 186, and 201 of the POA.

66 See also Sylvanna M. Falcón, "Rape as a Weapon of War: Advancing Human Rights for Women at the US-Mexico Border Region," *Social Justice* 28, no. 2 (2001): 31–50.

67 Chan-Tiberghien, "Gender-Skepticism or Gender Boom? Poststructural Feminists, Transnational Feminisms and the World Conference Against Racism," *International Feminist Journal of Politics* 6, no. 3 (2004): 462.

68 See Annelise Riles, "[Deadlines]: Removing the Brackets on Politics in Bureaucratic and Anthropological Analysis," in *Documents: Artifacts of Modern Knowledge*, edited by Annelise Riles (Ann Arbor: University of Michigan Press, 2006).

69 Chan-Tiberghien, "Gender-Skepticism or Gender Boom?"

70 "Durban Declaration and Programme of Action," 61n1.

71 See Maylei Blackwell and Nadine Naber, "Intersectionality in an Era of Globalization: The Implications of the UN World Conference Against Racism for Transnational Feminist Practices," *Meridians: feminism, race, transnationalism* 2, no. 2 (2002): 237–48.

72 Interview with author, September 25, 2003, Lima.

73 Mary Robinson, phone interview with author, June 24, 2003. Some Durban activists felt the Israeli-Palestinian issue could have been handled better because it did not emerge out of nowhere. For instance, a US interviewee with extensive experience lobbying at the UN said, "the kinds of intransigence around Israeli-Palestinian issues . . . that could have been anticipated and it could have been brokered." Interview with author, June 24, 2003, Brooklyn.

74 Interview with author, June 19, 2003, Washington, DC.

75 Mary Robinson, *A Voice for Human Rights*, ed. Kevin Boyle (Philadelphia: University of Pennsylvania Press, 2007), 25.

76 Schecther, *United Nations-sponsored World Conferences.*

77 As is customary at the UN, the General Assembly approved a follow-up conference in 2006 for this purpose via resolution (A/RES/61/149).

78 United Nations, "Durban Review Conference: Background," accessed March 2, 2014, http://www.un.org/en/durbanreview2009/background.shtml.

79 Naomi Klein, "Minority Death Match: Jews, Blacks, and the 'Post-racial Presidency,'" *Harper's Magazine*, September 2009, 54; see also Dimitrina Petrova, "'Smoke and Mirrors': The Durban Review Conference and Human Rights Politics at the United Nations," *Human Rights Law Review* 10, no. 1 (2010): 129–50.

80 UN protocol dictates that heads of state are always given priority for speaking at the UN. Ahmadinejad would not have been the first speaker if another head of state had been present.

81 Several of my interviewees, specifically those from the United States, received their funding to attend the 2001 WCAR and the NGO Forum from the Ford Foundation. All of these organizations had their funding cut upon their return from South Africa, and many organizations went into substantial debt as a result.

82 In 2004, in response to "heightened concerns among the public and policymakers about violence, terrorism, and bigotry and the possible misuse of philanthropic money for these purposes," the Ford Foundation board revamped its contractual language; the agreement states that grantees will not "promote or engage in violence, terrorism, bigotry or the destruction of any state." Ford Foundation, memorandum to Ford Foundation Grantees, January 8, 2004, accessed March 1, 2012, http://www.fordfound .org/pdfs/about/ff_grantee_memo.pdf. If any project *appears* to violate the agreement in any way, the board reviews the project. For example, outraged by the Ford Foundation's financial support of a proposed meeting to debate academic boycotts by the American Association of University Professors (AAUP) in 2006, Steinberg sent the foundation a letter demanding an explanation for its support and an evaluation of whether the support violated the guidelines. The controversy persuaded the AAUP, which does not support academic boycotts, to cancel the event. See Gerald M. Steinberg, "Letter to President of the Ford Foundation on the Academic Boycott

and Post-Durban Guidelines," NGO Monitor, January 27, 2006, accessed April 27, 2010, http://www.ngo-monitor.org/article/letter_to_president_ of_ford_foundation_on_the_academic_boycott_and_post_durban_ guidelines.

83 NGO Monitor, "Ford Foundation NGO Funding Update—Implementation of Post-Durban Guidelines Is Slow and Lacks Transparency," April 28, 2005, accessed April 27, 2010, http://www.ngo-monitor.org/article/ford_founda tion_ngo_funding_update_implementation_of_post_durban_guidelines_ is_slow_and_lacks_transparency.

84 This exchange comes from my field notes during the NGO meeting with High Commissioner Pillay.

85 United Nations, Office of the High Commissioner for Human Rights, "High Commissioner for Human Rights Shocked by U.S. Withdrawal from Review Conference and Urges States to Focus on Racism not Politics," April 2009, accessed January 13, 2014, http://www.ohchr.org/EN/NewsEvents/Pages/ HCshockedByUSWithdrawalReviewConferenceRacism.aspx. Mary Robinson had made a similar point several years ago during our interview. Both women faced and endured similar criticisms for their roles in these antiracism conferences.

86 "High Commissioner Shocked."

87 United Nations, Office of the High Commissioner for Human Rights, "Opening Remarks by the High Commissioner for Human Rights, Navi Pillay, at the Closing Press Conference of the Durban Review Conference," April 29, 2009, accessed January 13, 2014, http://www.ohchr.org/EN/ NewsEvents/Pages/DisplayNews.aspx?NewsID=8511&LangID=E.

88 Ibid.

89 Ibid. Pillay singled out Iran as "part of the consensus" that adopted the outcome document, which included a condemnation of anti-Semitism.

90 Ibid.

91 United Nations Human Rights, "Outcome Document of the Durban Review Conference, 2009," accessed March 1, 2012, http://www.un.org/ durbanreview2009/pdf/Durban_Review_outcome_document_En.pdf.

92 Bonnie Erbe, "Barack Obama's Appointment of Susan Rice as U.N. Ambassador," CBS News, February 11, 2009, accessed March 14, 2012, http://www .cbsnews.com/2100–501445_162–4648152.html.

93 Klein, "Minority Death Match."

94 Stephen Schlesinger, "Obama Gets Good Grades at the United Nations," *Huffington Post*, November 3, 2009, accessed March 14, 2012, http:// www.huffingtonpost.com/stephen-schlesinger/obama-gets-good-grades- at_b_344206.html.

95 Mary Robinson, *Voice for Human Rights*, 25.

96 Ibid., 26.

Epigraph: Phone interview with author, June 24, 2003.

1 Interview with author, March 9, 2004, Toronto.

2 Henry, *Long Overdue*, 8.

3 Alvarez, "Translating the Global: Effects of Transnational Organizing on Local Feminist Discourses and Practices in Latin America," *Meridians: feminism, race, transnationalism* 1, no. 1 (2000): 34.

4 Crenshaw, "Mapping the Margins"; Collins, *Black Feminist Thought*; Lisa A. Crooms, "Indivisible Rights and Intersectional Identities, or, What Do Women's Human Rights Have to Do with the Race Convention?" *Howard Law Journal* 40, no. 3 (1997): 619–40; McCall, "Complexity of Intersectionality"; Nira Yuval-Davis, "Intersectionality and Feminist Politics," *European Journal of Women's Studies* 13, no. 3 (2006): 193–209; and Maylei Blackwell and Nadine Naber, "Intersectionality in an Era of Globalization: The Implications of the UN World Conference Against Racism for Transnational Feminist Practices," *Meridians: feminism, race, transnationalism* 2, no. 2 (2002): 237–48.

5 Collins, *Black Feminist Thought*.

6 Deborah K. King, "Multiple Jeopardy, Multiple Consciousness: The Context of a Black Feminist Ideology," *Signs: Journal of Women in Culture and Society* 14, no. 1 (1988): 42–72.

7 Anastasia Vakulenko, "'Islamic Headscarves' and the European Convention on Human Rights: An Intersectional Perspective," *Social and Legal Studies* 16, no. 2 (2007): 185; Susan Stranford Friedman, "Beyond White and Other: Relationality and Narratives of Race in Feminist Discourse," *Signs: Journal of Women in Culture and Society* 21, no. 1 (1995): 17.

8 Friedman, "Beyond White and Other," 17.

9 Stasiulis, "Relational Positionalities of Nationalisms," 194.

10 Chan-Tiberghien, "Gender-Skepticism or Gender Boom?," 460, 477.

11 See Mallika Dutt, "Some Reflections on United States Women of Color and the United Nations Fourth World Conference on Women and NGO Forum in Beijing, China," in *Global Feminisms since 1945: Rewriting Histories*, ed. Bonnie G. Smith (New York: Routledge, 2000), 305–13.

12 Tram Nguyen, "North-South Differences Challenge Women at the UN," *Colorlines Magazine*, October 21, 2001, 25.

13 Escobar, "Latin America at a Crossroads," 43.

14 Phone interview with author, May 24, 2005.

15 Vaughn, "Afro-Mexico."

16 Paulo Drinot, *The Allure of Labor: Workers, Race, and the Making of the Peruvian State* (Durham, NC: Duke University Press, 2011).

17 *El Comercio*, "Jorge Benavides defendió el regreso a la TV de la Paisana Jacinta y del Negro Mama," *El Comercio*, March 25, 2010, accessed March 10, 2012, http://elcomercio.pe/espectaculos/451838/noticia-jorge-benavides-defendio-regreso-tv-paisana-jacinta-negro-mama.

18 CERD identified the Canadian multiculturalism policies to be a model for other nations. See "Concluding Observations of the Committee on the Elimination of Racial Discrimination: Canada," in *Report of the Committee on the Elimination of Racial Discrimination*, November 1, 2002, doc. no. A/57/18, para. 320: "The Committee notes the central importance and significance of the Multiculturalism Act and the relevant policy developed by the State party, which includes measures to protect and promote cultural diversity."

19 See Juliet Hooker, *Race and the Politics of Solidarity* (New York: Oxford University Press, 2009).

20 Phone interview with author, July 23, 2004.

21 Ibid.

22 Ibid.

23 Interviews with author, March and April 2004, Toronto.

24 Ibid.

25 Ibid.

26 Canadian interviewees told me that they were eligible to apply for up to $7,500 of travel funds for attending the 2001 WCAR.

27 Interview with author, January 13, 2004, Oakland.

28 During an NGO session about youth at the NGO Forum Against Racism, translators never arrived at the session. A couple of US African American youth who were on the panel asked how many people in the audience spoke English. When over half of the participants raised their hand, they concluded that the session should "just be in English then." The tent full of people began to boo and hiss. The US panelists had, inadvertently perhaps, revealed their lack of knowledge about how the prevalence of the English language—a symbol of US cultural hegemony—is received globally, and they likely did not anticipate that speaking in English would be perceived as being hostile toward multilingualism. In fact, this assumption of the primacy of English left a number of participants increasingly frustrated as conference organizers were forced to cut translation services due to limited funding.

29 Crooms, "To Establish My Legitimate Name," 253.

30 MADRE, "Mission/Vision," accessed March 28, 2012, http://www.madre .org.

31 Interview with author, January 13, 2004, Oakland.

32 See Academia Mexicana de Derechos Humanos, *Foro Regional de México y Centroamerica Sobre Racismo Discriminacion e Intolerancia* (Mexico City: Academia Mexicana de Derechos Humanos, 2001).

33 Foro de las Américas, "Declaration of the Satellite Meeting on Racism, Discrimination, and Intolerance of Sexual Diversity," pamphlet, March 13, 2001, distributed Foro de las Américas, Quito, Ecuador. I received a copy of the pamphlet from an interviewee.

34 Interview with author, April 27, 2004, Mexico, City. Other interviews I

conducted in Lima with a lesbian feminist group corroborated this Mexican interviewee's understanding of the Durban conference as a major success for lesbians, not in terms of concrete results from the official conference documents but of the process of preparing, organizing, and mobilizing for the conference specifically with regard to intersectionality.

35   Foro de las Américas, "Plan de Acción: Foro de las Américas por la Diversidad y la Pluridad," accessed March 12, 2012, http://movimientos.org/dhplural/foro-racismo/plan_final1.phtml.

36   Interview with author, September 21, 2003, Lima.

37   "Declaration of Afrodescendent Women of the Americas to the Forum of the Americas for Diversity and Pluralism," in *Race, Ethnicity, Gender, and Human Rights in the Americas: A New Paradigm for Activism*, ed. Celina Romany (Washington, DC: The Race, Ethnicity, and Gender Justice Project in the Americas, American University, Washington College of Law, 2001), 302–5.

38   Interview with author, September 11, 2011, Lima.

39   See Tanya Maria Golash-Boza, *Yo Soy Negro: Blackness in Peru* (Gainesville: University Press of Florida, 2011).

40   Interview with author, September 11, 2011, Lima.

41   Interview with author, September 21, 2003, Lima.

42   To read the full Women's Caucus statement, please go to http://www.hurights.or.jp/wcar/E/gendercomstmt.htm (accessed April 12, 2012).

43   The statement, titled "The Prevention of Racism: Challenges in the Age of Globalization, Indigenous Women's statement for the WCAR," was available at the MADRE (http://www.madre.org) but has been removed. The statement was endorsed by the University of the Autonomous Regions of the Caribbean Coast of Nicaragua (URACCAN), Chirapaq, the Plural National Indigenous Assembly for Autonomy (ANIPA), the Rigoberta Menchú Tum Foundation, the International Indigenous Women's Forum (FIMI), MADRE, and the Indigenous Initiative for Peace.

44   See Amílcar Antonio Barreto, *Vieques, the Navy, and Puerto Rican Politics* (Gainesville: University Press of Florida, 2002); and Katherine T. McCaffrey, *Military Power and Popular Protest: The U.S. Navy in Vieques, Puerto Rico* (New Brunswick, NJ: Rutgers University Press, 2002).

45   Interview with author, January 21, 2004, San Francisco.

46   To learn more about Center for Women's Global Leadership, go to "About CWGL: History and Current Work" at http://www.cwgl.rutgers.edu/about-110 (accessed June 13, 2015).

47   Interview with author, June 10, 2003, New Brunswick, New Jersey. The Center for Women's Global Leadership published a book and produced a video about the hearing; see Rita Raj, Charlotte Bunch, and Elmira Nazombe, eds., *Women at the Intersection: Indivisible Rights, Identities, and Oppressions* (New Brunswick, NJ: Center for Women's Global Leadership, 2002).

48 Maria Toj Mendoza, "Guatemala: Genocide and Ethnocide of Indigenous People," in *Women at the Intersection: Indivisible Rights, Identities, and Oppressions*, ed. Rita Raj, Charlotte Bunch, and Elmira Nazombe (New Brunswick, NJ: Center for Women's Global Leadership, 2002), 70–73. The book contains all of the testimonies given at the CWGL hearing in Durban; I was in attendance and can attest to the emotional intensity of the hearing.

49 Douglas Farah, "Papers Show U.S. Role in Guatemalan Abuses, *Washington Post*, March 11, 1999, A26.

5. INTERSECTIONALITY AS THE NEW UNIVERSALISM

Epigraph: United Nations General Assembly, "World Conference against Racism, Racial Discrimination, Xenophobia, and Related Intolerance, Preparatory Committee, Third Session," Geneva, July 30 –August 10, 2001, doc. A/CONF.189/PC.3/5, report submitted by UN special rapporteur Radhika Coomarawamy, July 27, 2001, paragraph 21, page 8.

1 Ann Marie Clark, Elisabeth J. Friedman, and Kathryn Hochstetler, "The Sovereign Limits of Global Civil Society: A Comparison of NGO Participation in UN World Conferences on the Environment, Human Rights, and Women," *World Politics* 51, no. 1 (1998): 1–35; Keck and Sikkink, *Activist Beyond Borders*; Naples and Desai, *Women's Activism and Globalization*.

2 Robinson, *Voice for Human Rights*, 25.

3 United Nations, Committee on the Elimination of Racial Discrimination, "General Recommendation 25: Gender Related Dimensions of Racial Discrimination," Fifty-sixth Session, 2000. The text of General Recommendation 25 is on the United Nations website, accessed March 18, 2012, http://www.unhchr.ch/tbs/doc.nsf/%28Symbol%29/76a293e49a88bd23802568bd0 0538d83?Opendocument.

4 An ongoing debate regarding the meaning of the term "NGO" and whether or not NGOs are truly representative of global civil society is a topic I do not fully explore in this book. The critiques regarding the legitimacy of NGOs are, I believe, fair, but they can also be a tactic to discredit some of the political work of progressive and activist NGOs. See Kenneth Anderson and David Rieff, "Global Civil Society: A Skeptical View," in *Global Civil Society 2004/5*, ed. Mary H. Kaldor, Helmut K. Anheier, and Marlies Glasius (Thousand Oaks, CA: Sage Publications, 2004), 26–39.

5 Bennis, *Challenging Empire*.

6 Basu, "Globalization of the Local," 70.

7 At the same time, the language of transnationalism has significant limitations: it can obscure the role of state power and appear to trump domestic-based movements. As sociologist Nancy Naples argues, "The terms *global, transnational, international*, and 'the' grassroots remain hotly contested among postcolonial, Third World, and international feminist scholars," with additional terms such as "*Third World* and *postcolonial*" also being "con-

tested constructs." Yet "feminist scholars interested in analyzing women's agency in a globalizing context . . . prefer the term *transnational* to other conceptualizations like *international women's movement* or *global feminism*." See Naples, "Changing the Terms," 5.

8   Niamh Reilly, "Cosmopolitan Feminism and Human Rights," *Hypatia* 22, no. 4 (2007): 180–98.

9   Ibid.

10 The George W. Bush administration's appointment in 2005 of John Bolton, a neoconservative and vocal anti-UN critic, as ambassador to the UN symbolized how much the US government's position toward the UN deteriorated in the aftermath of the Durban conference and September 11.

11 Immanuel Wallerstein, *World-Systems Analysis: An Introduction* (Durham, NC: Duke University Press, 2004), 87.

12 In October 2004 a group of sixty women from the United States and abroad convened in New York City to discuss the democratization of the UN. Regarded as a success by one of the principal conference organizers, women at this particular conference criticized both the US role in undermining the UN and the undemocratic model that is the foundation of the Security Council. My interviewees expressed the same criticisms.

13 Interview with author, June 23, 2003, New York City.

14 Interview with author, June 10, 2003, New Brunswick.

15 Interview with author, June 16, 2003, New York City.

16 Interview with author, June 10, 2003, New Brunswick.

17 Interview with author, September 24, 2003, Lima.

18 Interview with author, April 27, 2004, Mexico City.

19 Interview with author, May 17, 2004, Mexico City.

20 Interview with author, January 21, 2004, San Francisco.

21 Interview with author, September 21, 2003, Lima. This interview was done with a Canadian national living in Peru at the time of the interview.

22 Interview with author, September 24, 2003, Lima.

23 Interview with author, June 30, 2003, New York City.

24 Interview with author, January 13, 2004, Oakland.

25 Interview with author, June 19, 2003, Washington, DC.

26 Interview with author, June 4, 2003, New York City.

27 Interview with author, April 28, 2004, Mexico City.

28 Interview with author, September 28, 2003, Lima.

29 Interview with author, May 28, 2003, Brooklyn.

30 Interview with author, June 4, 2003, New York City.

31 Interview with author, April 2, 2004, Toronto.

32 Henry, *Long Overdue*, 8.

33 Interview with author, September 11, 2003, Lima.

34 Interview with author, April 2, 2004, Toronto.

35 Enloe, *Bananas, Beaches, and Bases*, 196.

BIBLIOGRAPHY

Academia Mexicana de Derechos Humanos. *Foro Regional de México y Centroamerica Sobre Racismo Discriminacion e Intolerancia*. Mexico City: Academia Mexicana de Derechos Humanos, 2001.

Alcoff, Linda Martín. "The Problem of Speaking for Others." Accessed December 18, 2013. http://www.alcoff.com/content/speaothers.html.

Alcoff, Linda, and Elizabeth Potter, eds. *Feminist Epistemologies*. New York: Routledge, 1992.

Aldridge III, Daniel W. "Black Powerlessness in a Liberal Era: The NAACP, Anti-Colonialism, and the United Nations Organization, 1942–1945." In *Imperialism on Trial: International Oversight of Colonial Rule in Historical Perspective*, edited by R. M. Douglas, Michael D. Callahan, and Elizabeth Bishop, 85–110. Oxford: Lexington Books, 2006.

"Alert/Press Release: Peru/Peruvian Government Sanctions TV Station $27,000 for Racist Programming." Accessed September 17, 2013. http://afrolatinoproject.org/2013/08/28/alert-press-release-peru-peruvian-government-sanctions-tv-station-27000-for-racist-programming/.

Alexander, Jacqui M., and Chandra Talpade Mohanty, eds. *Feminist Genealogies, Colonial Legacies, Democratic Futures*. New York: Routledge, 1997.

Alexander, Michelle. *The New Jim Crow: Mass Incarceration in the Age of Colorblindness*. New York City: The New Press, 2012.

Alvarez, Sonia E. "Advocating Feminism: The Latin American Feminist NGO Boom." *International Feminist Journal of Politics* 1, no. 2 (1999): 181–209.

———. "Translating the Global: Effects of Transnational Organizing on Local Feminist Discourses and Practices in Latin America." *Meridians: feminism, race, transnationalism* 1, no. 1 (2000): 29–67.

Anderson, Carol. *Eyes Off the Prize: The United Nations and the African American Struggle for Human Rights, 1944–1955*. New York: Cambridge University Press, 2003.

Anderson, Kenneth, and David Rieff. "Global Civil Society: A Skeptical View." In *Global Civil Society 2004/5*, edited by Mary H. Kaldor, Helmut K. Anheier, and Marlies Glasius, 26–39. Thousand Oaks, CA: Sage Publications, 2004.

Anghie, Anthony. *Imperialism, Sovereignty, and the Making of International Law*. Cambridge: Cambridge University Press, 2007.

Anstee, Margaret Joan. *Learn to Type: A Woman at the United Nations*. West Sussex, UK: Wiley, 2003.

Anzaldúa, Gloria. *Borderlands / La Frontera: The New Mestiza*. 2nd ed. San Francisco: Aunt Lute Books, 1999.

Armaline, William, and Davita Silfen Glasberg. "What Will States Really Do for Us? The Human Rights Enterprise and Pressure from Below." *Societies without Borders* 4 (2010): 430–51.

Armaline, William, Davita Silfen Glasberg, and Bandana Purkayastha, eds. *Human Rights in Our Own Backyard: Injustice and Resistance in the United States*. Philadelphia: University of Pennsylvania Press, 2012.

———. *The Human Rights Enterprise: Political Sociology, State Power, and Social Movements*. London: Polity Press, 2014.

Associated Press. "Fourteen Western Nations Walked Out of a U.N. Conference." August 25, 1978.

Bacchetta, Paola, Tina Campt, Inderpal Grewal, Caren Kaplan, Minoo Moallem, and Jennifer Terry. "Transnational Feminist Practices against War." *Meridians: feminism, race, transnationalism* 2, No. 2 (2002): 302–8.

Barreto, Amílcar Antonio. *Vieques, the Navy, and Puerto Rican Politics*. Gainesville: University Press of Florida, 2002.

Barsh, Russel Lawrence. "Indigenous Peoples and the UN Commission on Human Rights: A Case of the Immovable Object and the Irresistible Force." *Human Rights Quarterly* 18, no. 4 (1996): 782–813.

Basu, Amrita. "Globalization of the Local/Localization of the Global: Mapping Transnational Women's Movements." *Meridians: feminism, race, transnationalism* 1, no. 1 (2000): 68–84.

———, ed. *Women's Movements in the Global Era: The Power of Local Feminisms*. Boulder, CO: Westview Press, 2010.

BBC News. "Peru Apologises for Abuse of African-Origin Citizens." BBC News, November 29, 2009. Accessed March 9, 2014. http://news.bbc.co.uk/2/hi/8384853.stm.

Bello, Walden. "As Obama Arrives in London for G20, Tens of Thousands Gather to Protest in the Streets." Democracy Now!, April 1, 2009. Accessed April 14, 2010. http://www.democracynow.org/2009/4/1/as_obama_arrives_in_london_for.

Bennis, Phyllis. *Calling the Shots: How Washington Dominates Today's U.N.* New York: Olive Branch Press, 1996.

———. *Challenging Empire: How People, Governments, and the U.N. Defy U.S. Power*. New York: Olive Branch Press, 2005.

Blackwell, Maylei, and Nadine Naber. "Intersectionality in an Era of Globalization: The Implications of the UN World Conference Against Racism for Transnational Feminist Practices." *Meridians: feminism, race, transnationalism* 2, no. 2 (2002): 237–48.

Blaser, Mario. "Ontology and Indigeneity: On the Political Ontology of Heterogeneous Assemblages." *Cultural Geographies* 21, no. 1 (Jan. 2014): 49–58.

Blum, Yehuda Z. "Proposals for UN Security Council Reform." *American Journal of International Law* 99, no. 3 (2005): 632–49.

Bordieu, Pierre. "The Forms of Capital." In *Handbook of Theory and Research for the Sociology of Education*, edited by John G. Richardson, translated by Richard Nice, 241–58. New York: Greenwood Press, 1986.

Bose, Christine E. "Intersectionality and Global Gender Inequality." *Gender & Society* 26, no. 1 (2012): 67–72.

Brems, Eva. "Protecting the Human Rights of Women." In *International Human Rights in the Twenty-first Century*, edited by G. Lyons and J. Mayall, 100–37. Lanham, MD: Rowman & Littlefield, 2003.

Brown, Wendy. "'The Most We Can Hope For . . .': Human Rights and the Politics of Fatalism." *South Atlantic Quarterly* 103, no. 2/3 (2004): 451–63.

Bunch, Charlotte, and Susana Fried. "Beijing '95: Moving Women's Human Rights from Margin to Center." *Signs: Journal of Women in Culture and Society* 22, no. 1 (1996): 200–204.

Bunch, Charlotte, and Niamh Reilly. *Demanding Accountability: The Global Campaign and Vienna Tribunal for Women's Human Rights*. East Brunswick, NJ: Center for Women's Global Leadership, Rutgers University, 1994.

Callaway, Barbara, and Lucy Creevey. *Women, Religion, and Politics in West Africa: The Heritage of Islam*. Boulder, CO: Lynne Rienner Publishers, 1994.

Caraway, Teri L. "The Political Economy of Feminization: From 'Cheap Labor' to Gendered Discourses of Work." *Politics & Gender* 1, no. 3 (2005): 399–429.

Carozza, Paolo G. "From Conquest to Constitutions: Retrieving a Latin American Tradition of the Idea of Human Rights." *Human Rights Quarterly* 25 (2003): 281–313.

Carruyo, Light. *Producing Knowledge, Protecting Forests: Rural Encounters with Gender, Ecotourism, and International Aid in the Dominican Republic*. University Park: Penn State University Press, 2008.

Center for Reproductive Rights. "UN Committee Finds US Is Falling Short in Tackling Racism in Reproductive Health Care." Press release, March 7, 2008. Accessed March 11, 2012. http://reproductiverights.org/en/press-room/un-committee-finds-us-is-falling-short-in-tackling-racism-in-reproductive-health-care.

Center for Women's Global Leadership. "About CWGL: History and Current Work." Accessed June 13, 2015. http://www.cwgl.rutgers.edu/about-110.

Chan-Tiberghien, Jennifer. "Gender-Skepticism or Gender Boom? Poststructural Feminists, Transnational Feminisms and the World Conference Against Racism." *International Feminist Journal of Politics* 6, no. 3 (2004): 454–84.

Choo, Hae Yeon, and Myra Marx Ferree. "Practicing Intersectionality in Sociological Research: A Critical Analysis of Inclusions, Interactions, and Institutions in the Study of Inequalities." *Sociological Theory* 28, no. 2 (2010): 129–49.

Chow, Esther Ngan-Ling. "Making Waves, Moving Mountains: Reflections on

Beijing '95 and Beyond." *Signs: Journal of Women in Culture and Society* 22, no. 1 (1996): 185–92.

Chowdhury, Elora. "Locating Global Feminisms Elsewhere: Braiding US Women of Color and Transnational Feminisms." *Cultural Dynamics* 21, no. 1 (2009): 51–78.

Clark, Ann Marie, Elisabeth J. Friedman, and Kathryn Hochstetler. "The Sovereign Limits of Global Civil Society: A Comparison of NGO Participation in UN World Conferences on the Environment, Human Rights, and Women." *World Politics* 51, no. 1 (1998): 1–35.

Collins, Dana, Sylvanna Falcón, Sharmila Lodhia, and Molly Talcott. "New Directions in Feminism and Human Rights: An Introduction." *International Feminist Journal of Politics* 12, no. 3–4 (2010): 304.

Collins, Patricia Hill. *Black Feminist Thought: Knowledge, Consciousness, and the Politics of Empowerment.* 2nd ed. New York: Routledge, 2000.

Collyns, Dan. "Peru's Minorities Battle Racism." BBC News, June 13, 2013. Accessed March 9, 2014. http://www.bbc.co.uk/news/10205171.

Connell, Thomas. *America's Japanese Hostages: The World War II Plan for a Japanese-Free Latin America.* Westport, CT: Greenwood Publishing Group, 2002.

Conway, Janet. "Geographies of Transnational Feminisms: The Politics of Place and Scale in the World March of Women." *Social Politics: International Studies in Gender, State, and Society* 15, no. 2 (2008): 207–31.

Crenshaw, Kimberlé Williams. "Gender-Related Aspects of Race Discrimination." Paper presented at the Expert Seminar Group Meeting on Gender and Racial Discrimination, Zagreb, Croatia, November 21–24, 2000.

———. "Mapping the Margins: Intersectionality, Identity Politics, and Violence against Women of Color." In *The Public Nature of Private Violence: The Discovery of Domestic Abuse*, edited by Martha Albertson Fineman and Roxanne Mykitiuk, 93–120. New York: Routledge, 1994.

Crooke, John R. "U.S. Views on UN Reform, Security Council Expansion." *American Journal of International Law* 99, no. 4 (2005): 906–8.

Crooms, Lisa A. "Indivisible Rights and Intersectional Identities, or, What Do Women's Human Rights Have to Do with the Race Convention?" *Howard Law Journal* 40, no. 3 (1997): 619–40.

———. "'To Establish My Legitimate Name Inside the Consciousness of Strangers': Critical Race Praxis, Progressive Women-of-Color Theorizing, and Human Rights." *Howard Law Journal* 46 (2003): 229–68.

Davis, Kathy. "Intersectionality as Buzzword: A Sociology of Science Perspective on What Makes a Feminist Theory Successful." *Feminist Theory* 9, no. 1 (2008): 67–85.

de la Cadena, Marisol. "Indigenous Cosmopolitics in the Andes: Conceptual Reflections beyond 'Politics.'" *Cultural Anthropology* 25, no. 2 (2010): 334–70.

Desai, Ashwin. *We Are the Poors: Community Struggles in Post-Apartheid South Africa.* New York: Monthly Review Press, 2002.

Desai, Manisha. "The Possibilities and Perils for Scholar-Activists and Activist-

Scholars: Reflections on the Feminist Dialogues." In *Insurgent Encounters: Transnational Activism, Ethnography, and the Political*, edited by Jeffrey S. Juris and Alex Khasnabish, 89–107. Durham, NC: Duke University Press, 2013.

———. "Transnationalism: The Face of Feminist Politics Post-Beijing." *International Social Science Journal* 57, no. 2 (2005): 319–30.

d'Escoto, Miguel. "The United Nations Is Beyond Reform . . . It Has to Be Reinvented." Interview with the former UN General Assembly president. Democracy Now!, April 26, 2010. Accessed May 26, 2010. http://www.democracynow.org/2010/4/26/the_united_nations_is_beyond_reformit.

Douglas, R. M., Michael P. Callahan, and Elizabeth Bishop, eds. *Imperialism on Trial*. Lanham, MD: Lexington Books, 2006.

Drinot, Paulo. *The Allure of Labor: Workers, Race, and the Making of the Peruvian State*. Durham, NC: Duke University Press, 2011.

Du Bois, W. E. B. "The Negro and Imperialism." In *W. E. B. Du Bois on Asia: Crossing the World Color Line*, edited by Bill V. Mullen and Cathryn Watson, 37–47. Mississippi: University Press of Mississippi, 2005.

DuBois, Ellen, and Lauren Derby. "The Strange Case of Minerva Bernardino: Pan American and United Nations Women's Right Activist." *Women's Studies International Forum* 32 (2009): 43–50.

Dutt, Mallika. "Reclaiming a Human Rights Culture: Feminism of Difference and Alliance." In *Talking Visions: Multicultural Feminism in a Transnational Age*, edited by Ella Shohat, 225–46. Cambridge, MA: The MIT Press, 1998.

———. "Some Reflections on United States Women of Color and the United Nations Fourth World Conference on Women and NGO Forum in Beijing, China." In *Global Feminisms since 1945: Rewriting Histories*, edited by Bonnie G. Smith, 305–13. New York: Routledge, 2000.

El Comercio. "Jorge Benavides defendió el regreso a la TV de la Paisana Jacinta y del Negro Mama." *El Comercio*, March 25, 2010. Accessed March 12, 2012. http://elcomercio.pe/espectaculos/451838/noticia-jorge-benavides-defendio-regreso-tv-paisana-jacinta-negro-mama.

Enloe, Cynthia. *Bananas, Beaches, and Bases: Making Feminist Sense of International Politics*. 2nd ed. Berkeley: University of California Press, 2000.

Erbe, Bonnie. "Barack Obama's Appointment of Susan Rice as U.N. Ambassador." CBS News, February 11, 2009. Accessed March 14, 2012. http://www.cbsnews.com/2100-501445_162-4648152.html.

Escárcega, Sylvia. "The Global Indigenous Movement and Paradigm Wars: International Activism, Network Building, and Transformative Politics." In *Insurgent Encounters: Transnational Activism, Ethnography, and the Political*, edited by Jeffrey S. Juris and Alex Khasnabish, 129–50. Durham, NC: Duke University Press, 2013.

Escobar, Arturo. "Latin America at a Crossroads." *Cultural Studies* 24, no. 1 (2010): 1–65.

Face, Charmaine White, and Zumila Wobaga. *Indigenous Nations' Rights in the*

Balance: An Analysis of the Declaration on the Rights of Indigenous Peoples. St. Paul, MN: Living Justice Press, 2013.

Falcón, Sylvanna M. "Invoking Human Rights and Transnational Activism in Racial Justice Struggles at Home: US Antiracist Activists and the UN Committee to Eliminate Racial Discrimination." *Societies without Borders* 4 (2009): 295–316.

———. "Mestiza Double Consciousness: The Voices of Afro-Peruvian Women on Gendered Racism." *Gender & Society* 22, no. 5 (2008): 660–80.

———. "Rape as a Weapon of War: Advancing Human Rights for Women at the U.S.-Mexico Border Region." *Social Justice* 28, no. 2 (2001): 31–50.

———. "Transnational Feminism and Contextualized Intersectionality at the 2001 World Conference Against Racism." *Journal of Women's History* 24, no. 4 (2012): 99–120.

Falcón, Sylvanna M., and Jennifer Nash. "Shifting Analytics and Linking Theories: A Conversation about the 'Meaning-making' of Intersectionality and Transnational Feminism." *Women's Studies International Forum* 50 (2015): 1–10. Accessed March 3, 2015. doi:10.1016/j.wsif.2015.02.010.

Farah, Douglas. "Papers Show U.S. Role in Guatemalan Abuses." *Washington Post*, March 11, 1999, A26.

Feminist Majority Foundation. "Campaign for Afghan Women and Girls." Accessed September 16, 2013. http://www.feminist.org/afghan/aboutcampaign.asp.

Fernandes, Leela. *Transnational Feminism in the United States*. New York: New York University Press, 2013.

Foran, John, and Richard Widick. "Breaking Barriers to Climate Justice." *Contexts* 12, no. 2 (Spring 2013): 34–39.

Ford Foundation. "Memorandum to Ford Foundation Grantees." January 8, 2004. Accessed March 1, 2012. http://www.fordfound.org/pdfs/about/ff_grantee_memo.pdf.

Foro de las Américas. "Declaration of the Satellite Meeting on Racism, Discrimination, and Intolerance of Sexual Diversity." Pamphlet, March 13, 2001. Distributed by Foro de las Américas, Quito, Ecuador.

———. "Plan de Acción: Foro de las Américas por la Diversidad y la Pluridad." Accessed June 13, 2015. http://www.corteidh.or.cr/tablas/20259.pdf.

Fregoso, Rosa-Linda. "For a Pluriversal Declaration of Human Rights." *American Quarterly* 66, no. 3 (2014): 583–608.

Friedman, Susan Stranford. "Beyond White and Other: Relationality and Narratives of Race in Feminist Discourse." *Signs: Journal of Women in Culture and Society* 21, no. 1 (1995): 1–49.

Galeano, Eduardo. *Open Veins of Latin America: Five Centuries of the Pillage of a Continent*. 25th anniversary ed. New York: Monthly Review Press, 1997.

Gallagher, Julie A. "The National Council of Negro Women, Human Rights, and the Cold War." In *Breaking the Wave: Women, Their Organizations, and Feminism, 1945–1985*, edited by Kathleen A. Laughlin and Jacqueline L. Castledine, 80–98. New York: Routledge, 2011.

Gates, Henry Louis. "Blacks in Latin America." Accessed December 17, 2013. http://www.pbs.org/wnet/black-in-latin-america/featured/full-episode-mexico-peru/227/.

General Federation of Women's Clubs. "GFWC International Past Presidents: 1890–2014." Accessed June 13, 2015. http://www.gfwc.org/who-we-are/history-and-mission/gfwc-international-past-presidents/.

———. "Logos, Emblems, Icons." Accessed June 13, 2015. http://www.gfwc.org/membership/gfwc-resources/logos-emblems-icons/.

Gildersleeve, Virginia Crocheron. *Many a Good Crusade: Memoirs of Virginia Crocheron Gildersleeve.* New York: The Macmillan Company, 1955.

Glendon, Mary Ann. "The Forgotten Crucible: The Latin American Influence on the Universal Human Rights Idea." *Harvard Human Rights Journal* 16 (2003): 27–39.

Golash-Boza, Tanya Maria. *Yo Soy Negro: Blackness in Peru.* Gainesville: University Press of Florida, 2011.

Goodale, Mark, and Sally Engle Merry, eds. *The Practice of Human Rights: Tracking Law between the Global and the Local.* New York: Cambridge University Press, 2007.

Grewal, Inderpal, and Caren Kaplan. *Scattered Hegemonies: Postmodernity and Transnational Feminist Practices.* Minneapolis: University of Minnesota Press, 1994.

Hahner, June E. "The Beginnings of the Women's Suffrage Movement in Brazil." *Signs: Journal of Women in Culture and Society* 5, no. 1 (1979): 200–204.

Henry, Charles P. *Long Overdue: The Politics of Racial Reparations.* New York: New York University, 2009.

Hooker, Juliet. *Race and the Politics of Solidarity.* New York: Oxford University Press, 2009.

INCITE! Women of Color Against Violence. "INCITE! Analysis." Accessed December 17, 2013. http://www.incite-national.org/page/analysis.

———. "Posters." Accessed September 16, 2013. http://www.incite-national.org/page/posters.

———, ed. *The Revolution Will Not Be Funded: Beyond the Non-Profit Industrial Complex.* Cambridge, MA: South End Press, 2007.

Inter-Agency Network on Women and Gender Equality. "Bangladesh Court Combats Sexual Harassment." Accessed March 12, 2012. http://www.unifem.org/cedaw30/success_stories/#bangladesh (site discontinued).

International Possibilities Limited. "U.S. NGO Coordinating Committee." Accessed March 8, 2014. http://www.ipunlimited.org/WCAR/Coordinating_Committee/coordinating_committee.html.

Ishay, Micheline. *The History of Human Rights: From Ancient Times to the Globalization Era.* Berkeley: University of California Press, 2008.

Jabara, Abdeen. "Zionism: Racism or Liberation?" 1976. Accessed March 2, 2014. http://www.al-moharer.net/falasteen_docs/abdeen_jabara.htm.

Jones, Nikki. *Between Good and Ghetto: African American Girls and Inner-City Violence.* New Jersey: Rutgers University Press, 2009.

Kabeer, Naila, ed. *Inclusive Citizenship: Meanings and Expressions.* London: Zed Books, 2005.

Kaplan, Caren, Norma Alarcón, and Minoo Moallem, eds. *Between Woman and Nation: Nationalisms, Transnational Feminisms, and the State.* Durham, NC: Duke University Press, 1999.

Keck, Margaret E., and Kathryn Sikkink. *Activist Beyond Borders: Advocacy Networks in International Politics.* Ithaca, NY: Cornell University Press, 1998.

King, Deborah K. "Multiple Jeopardy, Multiple Consciousness: The Context of a Black Feminist Ideology." *Signs: Journal of Women in Culture and Society* 14, no. 1 (1988): 42–72.

Klein, Naomi. "Minority Death Match: Jews, Blacks, and the 'Post-racial' Presidency." *Harper's Magazine,* September 2009. Accessed March 9, 2014. http://harpers.org/archive/2009/09/minority-death-match/.

Kumar, Radha. *A History of Doing.* New Delhi: Zubaan Books, 1990.

Lantos, Tom. "The Durban Debacle: An Insider's View of the UN World Conference Against Racism." *Fletcher Forum of World Affairs* 26, no. 1 (Winter/Spring 2002): 31–52.

Levi, Robin, and Eve McCabe. "Rights and Reform: The Impact of Structural Adjustment and Welfare Reform." San Francisco: Women's Institute for Leadership Development (WILD) for Human Rights, 2001.

Lugones, Maria. "Toward a Decolonial Feminism." *Hypatia* 25, no. 4 (2010): 742–59.

MADRE. "Mission/Vision." Accessed March 28, 2012. http://www.madre.org.

Mary McLeod Bethune Papers. Bethune Foundation Collection. Part 1: Writings, Diaries, Scrapbooks, Biographical Materials, and Files on the National Youth Administration and Women's Organizations, 1918–1955. Stanford, CA: Hoover Institute, Stanford University.

May, Vivian M. "'Speaking into the Void'? Intersectionality Critiques and Epistemic Backlash." *Hypatia* 18, no. 1 (2014): 94–112.

McCaffrey, Katherine T. *Military Power and Popular Protest: The U.S. Navy in Vieques, Puerto Rico.* New Brunswick, NJ: Rutgers University Press, 2002.

McCall, Leslie. "The Complexity of Intersectionality." *Signs: Journal of Women in Culture and Society* 30, no. 3 (2005): 1771–800.

Melamed, Jodi. *Represent and Destroy: Rationalizing Violence in the New Racial Capitalism.* Minneapolis: University of Minnesota Press, 2011.

Mendez, Jennifer Bickham. "Creating Alternatives from a Gender Perspective Transnational Organizing for Maquila Workers' Rights in Central America." In *Women's Activism and Globalization: Linking Local Struggles and Transnational Politics,* edited by Nancy A. Naples and Manisha Desai, 121–41. New York: Routledge, 2002.

Mendoza, Maria Toj. "Guatemala: Genocide and Ethnocide of Indigenous People." In *Women at the Intersection: Indivisible Rights, Identities, and Op-*

pressions, edited by Rita Raj, Charlotte Bunch, and Elmira Nazombe, 70–73. New Brunswick, NJ: Center for Women's Global Leadership, 2002.

Meridians. "Ama Ata Aidoo, Edna Acosta-Belén, Amrita Basu, Maryse Condé, Nell Painter, and Nawal El Saadawi Speak on Feminism, Race, and Transnationalism." *Meridians: feminism, race, transnationalism* 1, no. 1 (2000): 1–28.

Meyer, Anges E. "Frank, Fearless, and Internationally Experienced: Dean Gildersleeve Popular Choice." *Washington Post*, March 11, 1945.

Mignolo, Walter D. "Citizenship, Knowledge, and the Limits of Humanity." *American Literary History* 18, no. 2 (2006): 312–31.

———. "Who Speaks for the 'Human' in Human Rights?" *Hispanic Issues On Line* 5, no. 1 (2009): 7–24.

Moghadam, Valentine M. *Globalizing Women: Transnational Feminist Networks*. Baltimore: The John Hopkins University Press, 2005.

Mohanty, Chandra Talpade. *Feminism without Borders: Decolonizing Theory, Practicing Solidarity*. Durham, NC: Duke University Press, 2003.

Mohanty, Chandra Talpade, Ann Russo, and Lourdes Torres, eds. *Third World Women and the Politics of Feminism*. Bloomington: Indiana University Press, 1991.

Morphet, Sally. "Multilateralism and the Non-Aligned Movement: What Is the Global South Doing and Where Is It Going?" *Global Governance* 10, no. 4 (2004): 517–37.

Morrell, Gordon W. "A Higher Stage of Imperialism? The Big Three, the UN Trusteeship Council, and the Early Cold War." In *Imperialism on Trial: International Oversight of Colonial Rule in Historical Perspective*, edited by Michael D. Callahan, R. M. Douglas, and Elizabeth Bishop, 111–37. Oxford: Lexington Books, 2006.

Nakano Glenn, Evelyn. *Unequal Freedom: How Race and Gender Shaped American Citizenship and Labor*. Cambridge, MA: Harvard University Press, 2002.

Naples, Nancy A. "Changing the Terms: Community Activism, Globalization, and the Dilemmas of Transnational Feminist Praxis." In *Women's Activism and Globalization: Linking Local Struggles and Transnational Politics*, edited by Nancy A. and Manisha Desai Naples, 3–14. New York: Routledge, 2002.

Naples, Nancy A., and Manisha Desai, eds. *Women's Activism and Globalization: Linking Local Struggles and Transnational Politics*. New York: Routledge, 2002.

Nash, Jennifer C. "Re-Thinking Intersectionality." *Feminist Review* 89 (2008): 1–15.

"NGO Declaration and Programme of Action for the World Conference against Racism, Racial Discrimination, Xenophobia, and Related Intolerance," Durban, South Africa, August 27–September 1, 2001. Accessed April 11, 2012. http://academic.udayton.edu/race/06hrights/WCAR2001/NGOFORUM/ Globalization.htm.

NGO Monitor. "Ford Foundation NGO Funding Update—Implementation of Post-Durban Guidelines Is Slow and Lacks Transparency." April 28, 2005. Accessed April 27, 2010. http://www.ngo-monitor.org/article/ford_

foundation_ngo_funding_update_implementation_of_post_durban_
guidelines_is_slow_and_lacks_transparency.

Nguyen, Tram. "North-South Differences Challenge Women at the UN." *Colorlines Magazine*, October 21, 2001, p. 25.

Organization of American States. "Brief History of the Commission." Accessed
March 12, 2012. http://www.oas.org/en/cim/history.asp.

Otto, Dianne. "Nongovernmental Organizations in the United Nations System:
The Emerging Role of International Civil Society." *Human Rights Quarterly*
18, no. 1 (1996): 107–41.

Petrova, Dimitrina. "'Smoke and Mirrors': The Durban Review Conference and
Human Rights Politics at the United Nations." *Human Rights Law Review* 10,
no. 1 (2010): 129–50.

Pew Research Center's Global Attitudes Project. "Americans and Euro-
peans Differ Widely on Foreign Policy Issues." April 17, 2002. Accessed August 12, 2014. http://www.pewglobal.org/2002/04/17/
americans-and-europeans-differ-widely-on-foreign-policy-issues/.

Philipose, Elizabeth. "Decolonizing the Racial Grammar of International Law."
In *Feminism and War: Confronting U.S. Imperialism*, edited by Robin L. Riley,
Chandra Talpade Mohanty, and Minnie Bruce Pratt, 103–16. London: Zed
Books, 2008.

Prashad, Vijay. *The Darker Nations: A People's History of the Third World*. New
York: New Press, 2007.

Pulitano, Elvira, ed. *Indigenous Rights in the Age of the UN Declaration*. Cambridge: Cambridge University Press, 2012.

Purkayastha, Bandana. "Intersectionality in a Transnational World." *Gender &
Society* 26, no. 1 (2012): 55–66.

Purkayastha, Bandana, Anjana Narayan, and Sudipto Banerjee. "Constructing
Virtual, Transnational Identities on the Web: The Case of Hindu Student
Groups in the US and UK." *Journal of Intercultural Studies* 32 (2011): 495–517.

Quijano, Anibal. "Coloniality of Power, Eurocentrism, and Latin America."
Nepantia: Views from South 1, no. 3 (2000): 533–80.

Raj, Rita, Charlotte Bunch, and Elmira Nazombe, eds. *Women at the Intersection:
Indivisible Rights, Identities, and Oppressions*. New Brunswick, NJ: Center for
Women's Global Leadership, 2002.

Reilly, Niamh. "Cosmopolitan Feminism and Human Rights." *Hypatia* 22, no. 4
(2007): 180–98.

Riles, Annelise. *Documents: Artifacts of Modern Knowledge*. Ann Arbor: University of Michigan Press, 2006.

Robins, Dorothy B. *Experiment in Democracy: The Story of U.S. Citizen Organizations in Forging the Charter of the United Nations*. New York: Parkside Press,
1971.

Robinson, Mary. *A Voice for Human Rights*. Edited by Kevin Boyle. Philadelphia:
University of Pennsylvania Press, 2007.

Romany, Celina, ed. *Race, Ethnicity, Gender, and Human Rights in the Americas:*

A New Paradigm for Activism. Washington, DC: The Race, Ethnicity, and Gender Justice Project in the Americas, American University, Washington College of Law, 2001.

Sanders, Douglas. "Developing a Modern International Law on the Rights of Indigenous Peoples." December 1994. Accessed December 18, 2013. http://www.anthrobase.com/Browse/home/hst/cache/Developing.doc.htm.

Santos, Boaventura de Sousa. "Toward a Multicultural Conception of Human Rights." In *Moral Imperialism: A Critical Anthology*, edited by Berta Hernández-Truyol, 39–60. New York: New York University Press, 2002.

Schecther, Michael G., ed. *United Nations-sponsored World Conferences: Focus on Impact and Follow-up*. Tokyo: United Nations University Press, 2001.

———. *United Nations Global Conferences*. London: Routledge, 2005.

Schlesinger, Stephen. *Act of Creation: The Founding of the United Nations*. Boulder: Westview Press, 2003.

———. "Obama Gets Good Grades at the United Nations." *Huffington Post*, November 3, 2009. Accessed March 14, 2012. http://www.huffingtonpost.com/stephen-schlesinger/obama-gets-good-grades-at_b_344206.html.

Shohat, Ella. "Introduction." In *Talking Visions: Multicultural Feminism in a Transnational Age*, edited by Ella Shohat, 1–64. Cambridge, MA: MIT Press, 1998.

Sklair, Leslie. *Globalization: Capitalism and Its Alternatives*. New York: Oxford University Press, 2002.

Smith, Andrea. "Human Rights and Social-Justice Organizing in the United States." *Radical History Review*, no. 101 (2008): 211–19.

Somers, Margaret. "Rights, Relationality, and Membership: Rethinking the Making and Meaning of Citizenship." In *Public Rights, Public Rules: Constituting Citizens in the World Polity and National Policy*, edited by Connie L. McNeely, 153–206. New York: Routledge, 1998.

Soto, Sandra. "Where in the Transnational World Are U.S. Women of Color?" In *Women's Studies for the Future: Foundations, Interrogations, Politics*, edited by Agatha Meryl Beins and Elizabeth Lapovsky Kennedy, 111–24. New Brunswick, NJ: Rutgers University Press, 2005.

Speed, Shannon, and Jane F. Collier. "Limiting Indigenous Autonomy in Chiapas, Mexico: The State Government's Use of Human Rights." *Human Rights Quarterly* 22, no. 4 (2000): 877–905.

Stasiulis, Daiva K. "Relational Positionalities of Nationalisms, Racisms, and Feminisms." In *Between Woman and Nation: Nationalisms, Transnational Feminisms, and the State*, edited by C. Kaplan, Norma Alarcón, and Minoo Moallem, 182–218. Durham, NC: Duke University Press, 1999.

Steinberg, Gerald M. "Letter to President of the Ford Foundation on the Academic Boycott and Post-Durban Guidelines." NGO Monitor, January 27, 2006. Accessed April 27, 2010. http://www.ngo-monitor.org/article/letter_to_president_of_ford_foundation_on_the_academic_boycott_and_post_durban_guidelines.

Suchland, Jennifer. "Is Postsocialism Transnational?" *Signs: Journal of Women in Culture and Society* 36, no. 4 (2011): 837–62.

Sue, Christina A., and Tanya Golash-Boza. "More Than 'A Hidden Race': The Complexities of Blackness in Mexico and Peru." *Latin American and Caribbean Ethnic Studies* 8, no. 1 (2013): 1–7.

Thayer, Millie. *Making Transnational Feminism: Rural Women, NGO Activists, and Northern Donors in Brazil.* New York: Routledge, 2009.

Troy, Gil. *Moynihan's Moment: America's Fight against Zionism as Racism.* New York: Oxford University Press, 2012.

Tuck, Eve, and K. Wayne Yang. 2012. "Decolonization Is Not a Metaphor." *Decolonization: Indigeneity, Education & Society* 1, no. 1 (2012): 1–40.

United Nations. "Building the Consensus against Racism." DPI/809/12594. May 1984.

———. "Charter of the United Nations." Accessed September 25, 2011. http://www.un.org/en/documents/charter/.

———. "Commission on the Status of Women Founding Resolution." ECOSOC Resolution 11 (II), June 21, 1946. *United Nations Journal of the Economic and Social Council* 29 (July 13, 1946). Accessed September 25, 2011. http://www.un.org/womenwatch/daw/csw/pdf/CSW_founding_resolution_1946.pdf.

———. "Durban Review Conference: Background." Accessed June 13, 2015. http://www.un.org/en/durbanreview2009/background.shtml.

———. "How to Apply for Consultative Status." Accessed March 7, 2012. http://csonet.org/?menu=83.

———. "NGO Branch, Department of Economic and Social Affairs." Accessed March 7, 2012. http://csonet.org/.

———. "Report of the Second World Conference to Combat Racism and Racial Discrimination." Geneva, August 1–12, 1983. Doc. no. A/CONF.119/26.

———. "Report of the Special Rapporteur on Violence Against Women, Its Causes and Consequences, Rashida Manjoo." May 2, 2011. Doc. no. A/HRC/17/26. Accessed June 13, 2015. http://daccess-dds-ny.un.org/doc/UNDOC/GEN/G11/130/22/PDF/G1113022.pdf?OpenElement.

———. "Report of the World Conference against Racism, Racial Discrimination, Xenophobia, and Related Intolerance." 2001. Doc. no. A/CONF.189/12.

———. "Second World Conference to Combat Racism and Racial Discrimination: Provisional Draft Rules of Procedure." New York, March 5, 1982. Doc. no. E/AC.68/1982/L.3.

———. "Secretary-General Says Non-Aligned Movement's Mission More Relevant Than Ever in Light of Growing Gulf Between Rich and Poor Countries." Press release. New York: United Nations Department of Information, 2006.

———. "United Nations Declaration on the Rights of Indigenous Peoples." Accessed December 18, 2013. http://www.ohchr.org/en/Issues/IPeoples/Pages/Declaration.aspx.

———. "World Conference against Racism, Racial Discrimination, Xenophobia, and Related Intolerance, Durban Declaration and Program of Action." Accessed April 11, 2012. www.un.org/WCAR/durban.pdf.

United Nations Chronicle. "Conference Against Racism: Preparations." New York, May 1983, 52–54.

———. "Main Focus: Women, Human Rights, Refugees." New York, January1983, 58.

———. "Racism." New York, October 1983, 41–56.

———. "World Conference to Combat Racism to be Convened in Geneva, August 1978." New York, January 1978, 71–72, 106.

———. "World Racism Conference Calls for Action against Multinationals." New York, October 1978, 52–54.

United Nations Committee on the Elimination of Discrimination against Women. "General Recommendation No. 3: Education and Public Information Campaigns." Sixth session, 1987. Accessed March 18, 2012. http://www .un.org/womenwatch/daw/cedaw/recommendations/recomm.htm.

———. "General Recommendation No. 18: Disabled Women." Tenth session, 1991. Accessed March 18, 2012. http://www.un.org/womenwatch/daw/ cedaw/recommendations/recomm.htm.

———. "General Recommendation No. 19: Violence against Women." Eleventh session, 1992. Accessed March 18, 2012. http://www.un.org/womenwatch/ daw/cedaw/recommendations/recomm.htm.

———. "General Recommendation No. 25: Temporary Special Measures." Thirtieth session, 2004. Accessed March 18, 2012. http://www.un.org/women watch/daw/cedaw/recommendations/recomm.htm.

———. "Report of the Committee on the Elimination of Discrimination against Women." Forty-second session, General Assembly, 1987. Doc. no. A/42/38. Accessed June 13, 2015. http://tbinternet.ohchr.org/_layouts/ treatybodyexternal/Download.aspx?symbolno=A%2f42%2f38&Lang=en.

———. "Report of the Committee on the Elimination of Discrimination against Women." Forty-ninth session, General Assembly, 1994. Doc. no. A/49/38 (SUPP). Accessed June 13, 2015. http://tbinternet.ohchr.org/_layouts/ treatybodyexternal/Download.aspx?symbolno=A%2f49%2f38%28SUPP%29& Lang=en.

United Nations Committee on the Elimination of Racial Discrimination. "Consideration of Reports Submitted by States Parties under Article 9 of the Convention: Concluding Observations of the Committee on the Elimination of Racial Discrimination." May 8, 2008. Doc. no. CERD/C/USA/CO/6. Accessed June 13, 2015. http://tbinternet.ohchr.org/_layouts/treatybodyexternal/Download.aspx?symbolno=CERD%2fC%2fUSA%2fCO%2f6&Lang=en.

———. "General Guidelines on Form and Content of the Parties under Article 9, Paragraph 1, Reports to Be Submitted to the Convention." July 23, 1993. Doc. no. CERD/C70/REV.3.

———. "General Recommendation No. 15: On Article 4 of the Convention." Forty-second session, 1993. Doc. no. A/48/18. Accessed June 13, 2015.

http://tbinternet.ohchr.org/_layouts/treatybodyexternal/Download.aspx?s
ymbolno=INT%2fCERD%2fGEC%2f7487&Lang=en.

———. "General Recommendation No. 25: Gender Related Dimensions of
Racial Discrimination." Fifty-sixth session, 2000. Accessed June 13, 2015.
http://tbinternet.ohchr.org/_layouts/treatybodyexternal/Download.aspx?s
ymbolno=INT%2fCERD%2fGEC%2f7497&Lang=en.

———. "General Recommendation No. 27: Discrimination against Roma." Fifty-
seventh session, 2000. Accessed June 13, 2015. http://tbinternet.ohchr.
org/_layouts/treatybodyexternal/Download.aspx?symbolno=INT%2fCERD
%2fGEC%2f7499&Lang=en.

———. "General Recommendation No. 34, adopted by the Committee: Racial
Discrimination against People of African Descent." Seventy-ninth session,
2011. Doc. no. CERD/C/GC/34. Accessed June 13, 2015. http://tbinternet.
ohchr.org/_layouts/treatybodyexternal/Download.aspx?symbolno=CERD%
2fC%2fGC%2f34&Lang=en.

———. "Report of the Committee on Elimination of Racial Discrimination." September 15, 1993. Doc. no. A/48/18 (SUPP). Accessed June 13,
2015. http://daccess-dds-ny.un.org/doc/UNDOC/GEN/N94/032/66/PDF/
N9403266.pdf?OpenElement.

———. "Report of the Committee on the Elimination of Racial Discrimination."
Forty-ninth session, General Assembly, 1994. Doc. no. A/49/18 (SUPP).
Accessed June 13, 2015. http://daccess-dds-ny.un.org/doc/UNDOC/GEN/
N95/003/37/PDF/N9500337.pdf?OpenElement.

———. "Report of the Committee on the Elimination of Racial Discrimina-
tion." Fiftieth session, General Assembly, 1995. Doc. no. A/50/18 (SUPP).
Accessed June 13, 2015. http://daccess-dds-ny.un.org/doc/UNDOC/GEN/
N96/010/80/PDF/N9601080.pdf?OpenElement.

———. "Report of the Committee on the Elimination of Racial Discrimination."
Fifty-first session, General Assembly, 1996. Doc. no. A/51/18. Accessed June
13, 2015. http://daccess-dds-ny.un.org/doc/UNDOC/GEN/N96/257/38/PDF/
N9625738.pdf?OpenElement.

———. "Report of the Committee on the Elimination of Racial Discrimination."
Fifty-fourth session, General Assembly, 1999. Doc. no. A/54/18 (SUPP).
Accessed June 13, 2015. http://daccess-dds-ny.un.org/doc/UNDOC/GEN/
N99/280/37/PDF/N9928037.pdf?OpenElement.

———. "Report of the Committee on the Elimination of Racial Discrimina-
tion." Fifty-fifth session, General Assembly, 2000. Doc. no. A/55/18 (SUPP).
Accessed June 13, 2015. http://daccess-dds-ny.un.org/doc/UNDOC/GEN/
N00/694/61/PDF/N0069461.pdf?OpenElement.

———. "Report of the Committee on the Elimination of Racial Discrimination."
Fifty-seventh session, General Assembly, 2002. Doc. no. A/57/18 (SUPP).
Accessed June 13, 2015. http://daccess-dds-ny.un.org/doc/UNDOC/GEN/
N02/643/57/PDF/N0264357.pdf?OpenElement.

———. "Summary Record of the 1166th Meeting." Forty-ninth session, 1996.

Doc. no. CERD/C/SR.1166. Accessed June 13, 2015. http://tbinternet.ohchr. org/_layouts/treatybodyexternal/Download.aspx?symbolno=CERD%2fC%2 fSR.1166&Lang=en.

United Nations Conference on International Organization. "Amendments to the Dumbarton Oaks Proposals Presented by the Delegation of Mexico." May 5, 1945. Doc. 2, G/7 (c) (1). In *Documents of the United Nations Conference on International Organization, San Francisco, 1945.* Vol. 2, *General.* London: United Nations Information Organizations, 1945.

———. "Amendments to the Dumbarton Oaks Proposals Submitted by the Delegations of Brazil, the Dominican Republic, and the United States of Mexico." May 5, 1945. Doc. no. 2 G/25. In *Documents of the United Nations Conference on International Organization, San Francisco, 1945.* Vol. 2, *General.* London: United Nations Information Organizations, 1945.

———. "Analysis of Papers Presented by Australia, China, France, United Kingdom, and United States." May 11, 1945. Doc. no. 230, II/4/5. In *Documents of the United Nations Conference on International Organization, San Francisco, 1945.* Vol. 40, *Commission 2—General Assembly.* London: United Nations Information Organizations, 1945.

———. "Documentation for Meetings of Committee I/1." May 11, 1945. Doc. no. 215 I/1/10. In *Documents of the United Nations Conference on International Organization, San Francisco, 1945.* Vol. 10, *Commission 2—General Assembly.* London: United Nations Information Organizations, 1945.

———. "Invitation of the United States of America to the Conference." April 26, 1945. Doc. no. 3, G/2. In *Documents of the United Nations Conference on International Organization, San Francisco, 1945.* Vol. 1, *General.* London: United Nations Information Organizations, 1945.

———. "Proposed New Part (C) to Be Added to Working Paper Submitted by the Delegation of Australia." May 25, 1945. Doc. no. 575, II/4/12 (a). In *Documents of the United Nations Conference on International Organization, San Francisco, 1945.* Vol. 10, *Commission 2—General Assembly.* London: United Nations Information Organizations, 1945.

———. "Report of the Rapporteur (General) of Committee I/2 on Chapter IV." May 21, 1945. Doc. no. 464 I/2/28. In *Documents of the United Nations Conference on International Organization, San Francisco, 1945.* Vol. 10, Commission 2—*General Assembly.* London: United Nations Information Organizations, 1945.

———. "Section B of Chapter on Dependent Territories and Arrangements for International Trusteeship." June 17, 1945. Doc. no. 1044 II/4/37 (2). In *Documents of the United Nations Conference on International Organization, San Francisco, 1945.* Vol. 10, *Commission 2—General Assembly.* London: United Nations Information Organizations, 1945.

———. "Statement by Mr. John Sofianopoulos, Chairman of Technical Committee III/1 on the Structures and Procedures of the Security Council." June 8, 1945. Doc. no. 852 III/1/27. In *Documents of the United Nations Conference on*

International Organization, San Francisco, 1945. Vol. 11, *Commission 3—Security Council.* London: United Nations Information Organizations, 1945.

———. "Summary Report of Fourth Meeting of Commission III/3." May 11, 1945. Doc. no. 231 III/3/9. In *Documents of the United Nations Conference on International Organization, San Francisco, 1945.* Vol. 12, *Commission 3—Security Council.* London: United Nations Information Organizations, 1945.

———. "Summary Report of Seventh Meeting of Committee III/1." May 16, 1945. Doc. no. 338, III/1/14, 290–91. In Documents of the United Nations Conference on International Organization, San Francisco, 1945. Vol. 11, *Security Council.* London: United Nations Information Organizations, 1945.

———. "Summary Report of the Eleventh Meeting of Committee III/1." May 21, 1945. Doc. no. 486, III/I/24, May 22, 1945. In *Documents of the United Nations Conference on International Organization, San Francisco, 1945.* Vol. 11, *Commission 3—Security Council.* London: United Nations Information Organizations, 1945.

———. "Summary Report of Eighteenth Meeting of Committee III/I." June 12, 1945. Doc. no. 936, III/1/45. In *Documents of the United Nations Conference on International Organization, San Francisco, 1945.* Vol. 11, *Commission 3—Security Council.* London: United Nations Information Organizations, 1945.

———. "Summary Report of Nineteenth Meeting of Committee III/I." June 13, 1945. Doc. no. 956, III/1/47. In *Documents of the United Nations Conference on International Organization, San Francisco, 1945.* Vol. 11, *Commission 3—Security Council.* London: United Nations Information Organizations, 1945.

———. "Summary Report of Twentieth Meeting of Committee II/3." June 7, 1945. Doc. no. 833 II/3/57. In *Documents of the United Nations Conference on International Organization, San Francisco, 1945.* Vol. 8, *Commission 2—General Assembly.* London: United Nations Information Organizations, 1945.

———. "Verbatim Minutes of Third Meeting of Commission 2." June 21, 1945. Doc. no. 1144, II/16. In *Documents of the United Nations Conference on International Organization, San Francisco, 1945.* Vol. 8, *Commission II—General Assembly.* London: United Nations Information Organizations, 1945.

———. "Verbatim Minutes of Fourth Meeting of Commission 3." June 22, 1945. Doc. no. 1149 III/11. In *Documents of the United Nations Conference on International Organization, San Francisco, 1945.* Vol. 11, *Security Council.* London: United Nations Information Organizations, 1945.

———. "Verbatim Minutes of Opening Session." April 25, 1945. Doc. no. 8 G/5. In *Documents of the United Nations Conference on International Organization, San Francisco, 1945.* Vol. 1, *General.* London: United Nations Information Organizations, 1945.

The United Nations Conference on International Organization Journal, no. 42. June 12, 1945.

United Nations Department for General Assembly and Conference Management. "United Nations Regional Groups of Member States." Accessed March 2, 2014. http://www.un.org/depts/DGACM/RegionalGroups.shtml.

United Nations Department of Economic and Social Affairs. "NGOs in Consultative Status, by Region (2007 & 1996)." Accessed April 13, 2012. http://esa .un.org/coordination/ngo/new/index.asp?page=pie2007.

United Nations Department of Economic and Social Affairs, Division for the Advancement of Women. "Convention on the Elimination of All Forms of Discrimination against Women." Accessed December 21, 2011. http://www .un.org/womenwatch/daw/cedaw.

United Nations Economic and Social Council. "About ECOSOC." Accessed March 7, 2012. http://www.un.org/en/ecosoc/.

———. "Consultative Status with ECOSOC." Accessed April 13, 2012. http:// www.un.org/esa/coordination/ngo/about.htm.

———. "List of Non-Governmental Organizations in Consultative Status with the Economic and Social Council as of 1 September 2011." Accessed March 18, 2012. http://csonet.org/content/documents/E2011INF4.pdf.

United Nations General Assembly. "Declaration on Apartheid and Its Destructive Consequences in Southern Africa." December 14, 1989. Doc. no. A/ RES/S-16/1. Accessed March 18, 2012. http://daccess-dds-ny.un.org/doc/ RESOLUTION/GEN/NR0/210/34/IMG/NR021034.pdf?OpenElement.

———. "Resolution 2873: Activities of Foreign Economic. . . ." Twenty-sixth session, December 20, 1971. Accessed March 8, 2012. http://www.un.org/ documents/resga.htm.

———. "Resolution 3151: Policies of Apartheid of the Government of South Africa." Twenty-eighth session, December 14, 1973, 30. Accessed March 8, 2012. http://www.un.org/documents/resga.htm.

———. "Resolution 3519: Women's Participation in the Strengthening of International Peace and Security and in the Struggle against Colonialism, Racism, Racial Discrimination, Foreign Aggression and Occupation and Forms of Foreign Domination." Thirtieth session, December 15, 1975. Accessed March 8, 2012. http://www.un.org/documents/resga.htm.

———. "Resolution 32/142: Women's Participation in the Strengthening of International Peace and Security and in the Struggle against Colonialism, Racism, Racial Discrimination, Foreign Aggression and Occupation and Forms of Foreign Domination." Thirty-second session, December 16, 1977. Accessed March 8, 2012. http://www.un.org/documents/resga.htm.

———. "Resolution 34/161: Women Refugees." Thirty-fourth session, December 17, 1979. Accessed March 8, 2012. http://www.un.org/documents/ resga.htm.

———. "Resolution 37/1: Appeal for Clemency in Favour of South African Freedom Fighters." Thirty-seventh session, December 7, 1982. Accessed March 8, 2012. http://www.un.org/documents/resga.htm.

———. "Resolution 37/68: Further Appeal for Clemency in Favour of South African Freedom Fighters." Thirty-seventh session, December 7, 1982. Accessed March 8, 2012. http://www.un.org/documents/resga.htm.

———. "Resolution 38/11: Proposed New Racial Constitution of South Africa."

Thirty-eighth session, November 15, 1983. Accessed March 8, 2012. http://
www.un.org/documents/resga.htm.

———. "Resolution 39/124: Participation of Women in Promoting International
Peace and Co-operation." Thirty-ninth session, December 14, 1984. Accessed
June 13, 2015. http://www.un.org/en/ga/search/view_doc.asp?symbol=A/
RES/39/124.

———. "Resolution 45/176: Policies of Apartheid of the Government of South
Africa." Forty-fifth session, December 19, 1990. Accessed March 8, 2012.
http://www.un.org/documents/resga.htm.

———. "Resolution 46/79: Policies of Apartheid of the Government of South
Africa." Forty-sixth session, December 13, 1991. Accessed March 8, 2012.
http://www.un.org/documents/resga.htm.

———. "Resolution 47/77: Second Decade to Combat Racism and Racial Discrimination." Forty-seventh session, December 16, 1992. Accessed March 8,
2012. http://www.un.org/documents/resga.htm.

———. "Resolution 47/96: Violence against Migrant Women Workers." Forty-
seventh session, December 16, 1992. Accessed March 8, 2012. http://www
.un.org/documents/resga.htm.

———. "Resolution 53/132: Third Decade to Combat Racism and Racial Discrimination and the Convening of the World Conference against Racism, Racial
Discrimination, Xenophobia and Related Intolerance." Fifty-third session,
February 23, 1989. Accessed March 8, 2012. http://www.un.org/documents/
resga.htm.

———. "World Conference against Racism, Racial Discrimination, Xenophobia,
and Related Intolerance, Preparatory Committee, Third Session," Geneva,
July 30–August 10, 2001. Doc. No. A/CONF.189/PC.3/5. Report submitted
by UN Special Rapporteur Radhika Coomarawamy, July 27, 2001.

United Nations Office of the High Commissioner for Human Rights. "Annual
Appeal 2000: Overview of Activities and Financial Requirements." Accessed September 20, 2013. http://www.ohchr.org/Documents/AboutUs/
annualappeal0.pdf.

———. "Annual Report 2001: Implementation of Activities and Use of
Funds, 2002." Accessed September 20, 2013. http://www.refworld.org/
docid/47fdfbod0.html.

———. "High Commissioner for Human Rights Shocked by U.S. Withdrawal
from Review Conference and Urges States to Focus on Racism not Politics."
April 2009. Accessed June 13, 2015. http://www.ohchr.org/EN/NewsEvents/
Pages/HCshockedByUSWithdrawalReviewConferenceRacism.aspx.

———. "Human Rights Treaty Bodies: Monitoring the Core International
Human Rights Treaties." Accessed March 18, 2012. http://www2.ohchr.org/
english/bodies/treaty/index.htm.

———. "International Convention on the Elimination of All Forms of Racial Discrimination." Accessed June 13, 2015. http://www.ohchr.org/EN/
ProfessionalInterest/Pages/CERD.aspx.

———. "Opening Remarks by the High Commissioner for Human Rights, Navi Pillay, at the Closing Press Conference of the Durban Review Conference." April 29, 2009. Accessed January 13, 2014. http://www.ohchr.org/EN/NewsEvents/Pages/DisplayNews.aspx?NewsID=8511&LangID=E.

———. "Outcome Document of the Durban Review Conference, 2009." Accessed June 13, 2015. http://www.ohchr.org/Documents/Press/Durban_Review_Conference_outcome_document.pdf

———. "What Are Human Rights?" Accessed October 20, 2014. http://www.ohchr.org/EN/Issues/Pages/WhatareHumanRights.aspx.

———. "What We Do." Accessed October 20, 2014. http://www.ohchr.org/EN/AboutUs/Pages/WhatWeDo.aspx.

United Nations Women. "Commission on the Status of Women." Accessed June 13, 2015. http://www.unwomen.org/en/csw.

United States Congress, House of Representatives, Committee on International Relations. "A Discussion on the UN World Conference against Racism: Hearing before the Subcommittee on International Operations and Human Rights of the Committee on International Relations." Ser. no. 107–36.Washington, DC: US Government Printing Office, 2001.

United Women's Conference. *Women's Share in Implementing the Peace*. San Francisco: Executive Committee of the United Women's Conference, 1945.

Vakulenko, Anastasia. "'Islamic Headscarves' and the European Convention on Human Rights: An Intersectional Perspective." *Social and Legal Studies* 16, no. 2 (2007): 183–99.

Vaughn, Bobby. "Afro-Mexico: Blacks, Indígenas, Politics, and the Greater Diaspora." In *Neither Enemies nor Friends: Latinos, Blacks, and Afro-Latinos*, edited by Anani Dzidzienyo and Suzanne Oboler, 117–36. New York: Palgrave MacMillan, 2005.

Wallerstein, Immanuel. *World-Systems Analysis: An Introduction*. Durham, NC: Duke University Press, 2004.

Weber, Max. *The Methodology of the Social Sciences*. Edited by Edward Shils and Henry Finch. New York: Free Press, 1949.

Welch, Claude E., Jr., ed. *NGOs and Human Rights: Promise and Performance*. Philadelphia: University of Pennsylvania Press, 2000.

Whitworth, Sandra. *Feminism and International Relations: Towards a Political Economy of Gender in Multilateral Institutions*. New York: MacMillan Press, 1994.

Willetts, Peter. "The Cardoso Report on the UN and Civil Society: Functionalism, Global Corporatism, or Global Democracy?," *Global Governance* 12, no. 3 (2006): 305–24.

Wilson, Richard A., ed. *Human Rights, Culture, and Context: Anthropological Perspectives*. London: Pluto Press, 1997.

Worsnip, Patrick. "U.N. Launches Talks to Expand Security Council." Reuters News Service, February 19, 2009. Accessed September 25, 2011. http://www.reuters.com/article/2009/02/19/us-un-council-idUSTRE51I71V20090219.

Yuval-Davis, Nira. *Gender and Nation*. London: SAGE Publications, 1997.

———. "Intersectionality and Feminist Politics." *European Journal of Women's Studies* 13, no. 3 (2006): 193–209.

Zinn, Maxine Baca, Pierrette Hondagneu-Sotelo, and Michael A. Messner, eds. *Gender through the Prism of Difference*. 3rd ed. New York City: Oxford University Press, 2005.

Zwingel, Susanne. "How Do Norms Travel? Theorizing International Women's Rights in Transnational Perspective." In *International Studies Quarterly* 56, no. 1 (2012): 115–29.

———. "Translating International Women's Rights: CEDAW in Context." Accessed March 2, 2014. http://graduateinstitute.ch/files/live/sites/iheid/files/sites/genre/shared/conference_october_2010/Susanne%20Zwingel.pdf.

INDEX

Page numbers in italics refer to figures or tables.

A

Aboriginal activism. *See* indigenous peoples
Academia Mexicana de Derechos Humanos, 139
accreditation, UN, 67, 75–81, *76*, *78*, 198n93
Afghanistan, US military intervention in, 7–8
African descendants: black Canadians, 136; blackness in Peru vs. US, 143–44; Durban Declaration statements on, 116; erasure of, in Mexico and Peru, 181n80; human rights and, 87
African National Congress (ANC), 74, 103–4
African PrepCom (2001), 109
Ahmadinejad, Mahmoud, 121, 205n80
Akina wa Mama Africa, 146
Alarcón, Norma, 180n57
Allende, Salvador, 182n81
American Association of University Professors (AAUP), 205n82
American Association of University Women (AAUW), 53
Americas PrepCom, Santiago (2001), 85–86, 109–10, 111, 134–35, 140
Amnesty International, 67, 144
Anderson, Carol, 186n58

Annan, Kofi, 74, 81, 159
antiracism agenda. *See* racism, UN agenda against
Anzaldúa, Gloria, 16
apartheid: 1983 POA on, 107; "Declaration on Apartheid and Its Destructive Consequences in Southern Africa" (1989), 72; GA resolutions on, 70–73; Nongovernmental Organizations Sub-Committee on Decolonization, Racial Discrimination, and Apartheid, 102; Special Committee on Apartheid, 72; UN focus on, 5
Applied Research Center, 146
Arab governments and delegations, 186n47
Armaline, William, 89
Asian descendants, 116
Asian-Pacific PrepCom (2001), 109
Australian delegations, 38

B

Barsh, Russel Lawrence, 198n93
Basu, Amrita, 155
Bello, Walden, 67
Bernardino, Minerva, 47–48, 51–52, 57, 58, 59
Bethune, Mary McLeod, 46, 50, 53
black Canadians, 136
blackness in Peru vs. US, 143–44
Bolton, John, 211n10
Bose, Christine, 17

Bourdieu, Pierre, 66
boycotts of conferences: Durban Review Conference (2009), 121–22, 125; Geneva (1978), 100. *See also* walkouts
Brazilian delegations, 39–40, 51–52
Bunche, Ralph, 37
Bush, George W., 125, 211n10

C

Canada: 1983 POA, opposition to, 108; Aboriginal women activism, 133–35; Americas PrepCom (2001) and, 109–10; Durban WCAR, role in, 21–22; on first UN Decade to Combat Racism and Racial Discrimination, 100; intersectional subjectivities and, 157; multiculturalism discourse and policy, 130, 133, 208n18; travel funds for Durban, 208n26; youth activism and black Canadians, 135–37
capital (economic, social, and cultural): NGO accreditation and, 79; South Africa and, 194n43; UN citizenship and access to, 64, 66–69
Cariño Trujillo, Alberta Beatríz "Bety," 82, 87, 195n60
Carrillo, Monica, 23
Castro, Fidel, 11–12
CEDAW. *See* Committee on the Elimination of Discrimination against Women
CEDAW treaty (Women's Convention), 84, 196n72
Center for Women's Global Leadership (CWGL), 147–49
CERD. *See* Committee to Eliminate Racial Discrimination
Chan-Tiberghien, Jennifer, 117–18, 129
Charry Samper, Hector, 103, 104
Chile, 85–86

Chirapaq, 209n43
Choo, Hae Yeon, 16–17, 180n53
Chowdhury, Elora, 12–13
Christianity, role of, 36, 54
citizenship, UN: access, influence, and practice of, 95–97; access to economic, social, and cultural capital and, 64, 66–69; accreditation process for NGOs, 75–81, 76, 78; GA resolutions and patterns of cooperation among global South members, 69–75; new social actors and, 153; NGOs and, 89; number of Member States, 63; rights of members, 63–64, 65; as social practice, 66; vertical and horizontal relationships and, 66
Clinton, Hillary, 9
Collier, Jane, 65, 88
Collins, Patricia Hill, 16, 179n42
Colombian delegations, 40–41
coloniality: decolonization of human rights, 86–87; Mignolo on, 34; UNCIO and coloniality of power, 34, 39–40, 45, 61; UNCIO debate on Trusteeship Council and, 42–47
Commission on the Status of Women, 12–13, 52, 101–2
Committee on the Elimination of Discrimination against Women (CEDAW), 12–13
Committee to Eliminate Racial Discrimination (CERD): adoption of, 84, 196n70; Article 14, Member States not declaring support for, 201n25; on Canadian multiculturalism, 208n18; documents released from, 26; General Recommendations, 90, 91–92; intersectionality and, 90–93; US review, 92–93
"compensatory" as controversial term at Durban, 110–11, 203n45

Durban Review Conference (DRC; Geneva, 2009), 99, 119–25

E

Economic and Social Council (ECO-SOC): accreditation by, 75–80; Commission on the Status of Women and, 52; policy recommendations, 75, 194n46; role of, 75–76; vertical relationships and, 66

economic capital, 64, 67

ECOSOC. *See* Economic and Social Council

English language and US cultural hegemony, 208n28

Enloe, Cynthia, 35, 47, 129, 164

Escobar, Arturo, 86, 130

F

feminism: global sisterhood narrative, 13; phases of global feminism, 155; political economy of feminisms at UN, 13; racial fault lines at UN level, 8; universal woman image and, 12–13. *See also* transnational feminism

Feminist Majority Foundation, 7–8

Fernandes, Leela, 191n11

Ferree, Myra Marx, 16–17, 180n53

First World as term, 27

Ford Foundation, 121–22, 205nn81–82

Forde, Francis M., 38, 39, 40, 188n85

Foro de las Américas (Quito, Ecuador, 2001), 140–44

France, 184n31, 185n43

Fraser, Peter, 45

Fregoso, Rosa-Linda, 87

G

GA resolutions. *See* resolutions, GA

gay and lesbian groups, 139–40, 141–43

gender: CERD, intersectionality, and movement beyond gender neutrality, 90–93; Durban Declaration statements and "gender compromise," 117–18; as intersectionality, at Durban, 129; racialized violence, gender's role in understanding of, 148–49; UN Charter, gender equality language in, 51, 60; universal woman image, 12–13. *See also* intersectionality; paternalism; patriarchy

general consultative status, 76–77, 78–79

General Federation of Women's Clubs (GFWC), 53, 189n99

Gildersleeve, Virginia: Spurgeon and, 188n87; Trusteeship Council and, 187n66; UNCIO and, 37, 39, 41, 43, 47, 48–50; at UWC, 52, 56–58

Glasberg, Davita, 89

Global Tribunal on Violations of Women's Rights, 10

globalization, 116–17, 145–46

God, references to, 36

"great powers," 32–33, 37–42, 184n31

Grewal, Inderpal, 21

group-centered intersectionality, 16, 204n58

H

hegemonies, scattered, 21

Henry, Charles, 127, 163

Hiroshima and Nagasaki, atomic bombing of, 182n2

human rights: CERD and movement beyond gender neutrality, 90–93; constellations model (overview), 64–65, 82–83; counterpublic approaches constellation, 85–88; Declaration on the Rights of Indigenous Peoples and, 93–95; decolonization of, 86–87; dominant

Stasiulis, Daiva K., 19
Steinberg, Gerald M., 121, 205n82
Stettinius, Edward R., Jr., 36, 187n66
structural adjustment policies, 179n42
Suchland, Jennifer, 27
system-centered intersectionality,
    16–17

T

"The Prevention of Racism: Chal-
    lenges in the Age of Globalization,
    Indigenous Women's statement
    for the WCAR" (MADRE), 209n43
Third World, 27, 28. *See also* South,
    global
transnational feminism: as antisub-
    ordination logic, 155–56; "interna-
    tional is personal" paradigm and,
    164; new universality of cosmo-
    politanism and, 156; theoretical
    logics of intersectionality and,
    14–15; theory, 18–21
"Transnational Feminist Practices
    Against War," 8
transnationalism: intersectionality
    and, 17; limitations of language
    of, 210n7; UN as international
    space vs., 20; world conferences
    and transnationalization, 20
Trujillo, Rafael, 59
Truman, Harry, 36
Trusteeship Council, 42–47, 187n60

U

UN agenda on women, 6, 8, 14, 154–55
UN Charter: as deeply contested
    document, 37; gender equality lan-
    guage in, 51, 60; Latin American
    proposed amendments regarding
    women, 48–52, 49; ratification of,
    33, 37. *See also* UN Conference on
    International Organization

UN citizenship. *See* citizenship, UN
UN Conference on International
    Organization, San Francisco, 1945
    (UNCIO): about, 32–34; dynamics
    of gender and race, 60–62; four
    chairs of, 36; geopolitical context
    and model of power, 34–37; se-
    curity council structure and veto
    power, debate on, 38–42; Trustee-
    ship Council debate and main-
    tenance of colonial rule, 42–47;
    United Women's Conference and,
    52–60; women's representation
    and participation, debate on,
    47–52
UN Decade for Women, 73
UN Decade to Combat Racism and
    Racial Discrimination, 73, 100,
    102, 106
UN General Assembly (GA): apart-
    heid focus of, 5; Dumbarton Oaks
    amendment on, 186n54; Security
    Council and, 39; UN citizenship
    and, 63, 76
UN General Assembly resolutions. *See*
    resolutions, GA
UN Security Council structure nego-
    tiations, 38–42
United Nations (UN): alternate
    names proposed for, 41; as collec-
    tive vs. superstructure, 158; five
    regional groups of, 202n39; as
    gendered and racialized institu-
    tion, 60–62; as international vs.
    transnational space, 20; moral
    crisis and continuing importance
    of, 158–63; new social actors as
    essential counterpublics in, 152;
    number of Member States, 63;
    structural limitations of engaging,
    159; US relationship with, under
    Obama, 124–25; website welcome
    message, 165. *See also specific
    conferences*

DECOLONIZING FEMINISMS
Piya Chatterjee, Series Editor

Humanizing the Sacred: Sisters in Islam and the Struggle for Gender Justice in Malaysia, by Azza Basarudin

Power Interrupted: Antiracist and Feminist Activism inside the United Nations, by Sylvanna M. Falcón